RAGGED WAR

RAGGED WAR

The Story of Unconventional and Counter-Revolutionary Warfare

LEROY THOMPSON

ARMS AND
ARMOUR

Arms and Armour Press
A Cassell Imprint
Villiers House, 41-47 Strand, London WC2N 5JE.

Distributed in the USA by Sterling Publishing
Co. Inc., 387 Park Avenue South, New York, NY
10016-8810.

Distributed in Australia by Capricorn Link
(Australia) Pty. Ltd, 2/13 Carrington Road, Cas-
tle Hill, NSW 2154..

British Library Cataloguing-in-Publication Data:
a catalogue record for this book is available
from the British Library

ISBN 1-85409-057-7

Designed and edited by DAG Publications Ltd.
Designed by David Gibbons; edited by Philip
Jarrett; indexed by Jonathan Falconer; printed
and bound in Great Britain,
Hartnolls Limited, Bodmin, Cornwall

Contents

CHAPTER I

Origins and Theories of Guerrilla Warfare

There is a tendency to think that guerrilla warfare is a twentieth-century invention. Admittedly the post-World War Two era has seen this style of warfare raised to its highest level, but guerrilla warfare has been practised by irregulars perhaps as long as one group of men has attempted to kill another. Those practising guerrilla warfare in the past may not have known what it was they were doing, but their tactics, and frequently their strategies, were often the same as those used by guerrilla forces which have stalled mighty armies in jungles or mountains.

Among the first great practitioners of the 'indirect approach', a basic tenet of guerrilla warfare, were the Scythians, who practised their hit and run tactics successfully against Darius the Great and his Persians, then Alexander the Great, and finally the Romans. Alexander, master tactician that he was, had some success in countering the Scythians by using light infantry, and even today this tactic remains one of the best. Hannibal encountered guerrillas in crossing the Alps. No doubt they were the ancestors of today's Swiss, who would still make formidable guerrillas in their Alpine fastness. It was Rome, however, the ultimate military system of antiquity, which ran up against guerrillas most frequently.

In Spain, Africa and Asia, Rome's legions spent much of their time in combat engaged in what we would call counter-insurgency warfare. Perhaps it was in Gaul that the Romans encountered the best guerrillas, who used their local knowledge and mobility to inflict defeats on the Romans. The fact that the Gauls were at times led by some of Rome's best generals, who had become disaffected, certainly did not hurt their cause.

In China during antiquity appeared the first great theorist of unconventional/irregular warfare, Sun Tzu, whose *Art of War* remains a classic today. Stressing the indirect approach in political, strategic, and tactical operations, Sun Tzu felt that all warfare was based on deception. This ancient Chinese sage of warfare also established the precepts of using conventional and unconventional forces to complement each other; the conventional to attack the front, the unconventional to attack the flanks. Many of the later Eastern nomads who would threaten the West used hit-and-run tactics which would have been approved by Sun Tzu, but more to the point, Mao, the wellspring of modern guerrilla warfare strategy and tactics, was a student of Sun Tzu's writings.

The professional soldiers of the Eastern Roman Empire constantly found themselves waging war against irregulars, and as a result became the foremost practitioners of counter-guerrilla warfare in the classical world. Combining frontier fortresses for area control with local militias and highly mobile reserves, the Byzantines made the maximum use of their resources to counter their enemies. Unlike many modern powers who have failed to realize the importance of political action as well as military action in countering irregulars, the Byzantines also used deception and disinformation to sow discord and foment conflict between their various barbarian enemies. The Emperor Leo's tactical manual stressed the methods for drawing irregulars into ambushes, but also pointed out that the tactics must be suited to the enemy, and suggested other techniques against other opponents.

The Middle Ages saw many successful irregulars in addition to those faced by the Byzantines, including the Vikings, Mongols, Saracens, and many others. Astute as ever, the Byzantines actively recruited Vikings for the Imperial bodyguard – the Varangians - and thus turned potential enemies into loyal defenders. The Mongols, perhaps better than any force before the invention of motorized transport, used mobility and the ability to cover great distances rapidly to exploit the strategy of indirect approach to conquer much of Asia. When the Mongols attempted to invade Vietnam in the 13th century, however, they encountered guerrillas themselves, ably commanded by Marshal Dao, who used many of the techniques that the Viet Minh and Viet Cong would use centuries later against the French and the Americans.

In Europe, Bertrand du Guesclin used guerrilla tactics to regain, finally, the territory in France which the English had held for centuries. The English also faced guerrillas in Ireland and Wales as the locals resorted to hit-and-run tactics.

In the Renaissance warfare became more formalized, but the Cossacks and Tartars continued to use irregular tactics in Eastern Europe. Frederick the Great had problems, too, with Serb and Hungarian irregulars. As European colonists spread across the globe they encountered irregulars of various types. In North America, both the French and British found the American indian a formidable guerrilla warrior. American colonists adopted many of the same tactics they had learned fighting the Indians and turned them first against the French, in the case of Rogers' Rangers, and then later against the British in the American War of National Liberation, as one military historian has termed the Revolutionary War. Francis Marion, the 'Swamp Fox', in particular, used guerrilla tactics against the British in the southern colonies.

During the Napoleonic Wars, Arthur Wellesley, later to become the Duke of Wellington, proved a skilled practitioner of irregular warfare, having learned the effectiveness of such tactics while attempting to counter them in India. Wellesley put the lessons he had learned to good use in his Peninsular Campaign, when they proved particularly effective at striking the French lines of communication. Napoleon faced guerrilla warfare again in Russia, where partisan bands sprang up along his retreat route, while the Russian Army's professional irregulars, the Cossacks, harried the retreating French forces. During the retreat from Russia the French lost about half a million men, a substantial portion to the guerrillas.

Among the great nineteenth-century military theorists, Karl von Clausewitz discussed partisan operations only in passing, but Baron de Jomini went into some detail about irregular operations in what he called 'national wars'. Jomini, who had seen guerrilla warfare at first hand while serving in the Napoleonic Wars, seemed to have a better grasp of the concept than Clausewitz.

The French had to face irregulars once again when they invaded Algeria in the 1830s. Not until the arrival of Gen Bugeaud in 1836 did the French really begin to develop a counter-guerrilla strategy, however. Bugeaud used light 'flying columns' to harry the mobile enemy. The British had to learn the same lessons themselves in their colonial campaigns in Africa and Asia.

During the American Civil War, the Confederates, outnumbered and undersupplied, used guerrilla warfare most effectively. In fact, Mosby's Partisan Rangers carried out a classic guerrilla campaign in support of conventional forces. While fighting the same war, the Union had to wage another counter-guerrilla compaign to the west against the plains indians. Once the Civil War was won, the Union was able to concentrate some of the effective cavalry forces it had developed against the Confederates in the west, thus providing a highly mobile force to counter the indians. Food denial, by killing off the Buffalo, however, proved the most effective counter-guerrilla tactic against the American indian.

In the Philippines and Cuba, the Spanish had been involved in counter-insurgency operations throughout much of the latter half of the nineteenth century. General Weyler had some success against the insurgents in Cuba through the use of draconian tactics, but the Spanish-American War began before the insurgency had been completely controlled. In the Philippines, the insurgents initially wanted American assistance, but once the Americans had taken the Philippines they had to fight their own counter-insurgency war. Atrocities committed by the guerrillas caused the American troops to reply in kind, thus setting the stage for bitter fighting. Making use of the rough terrain of much of the Philippines, the guerrillas harried US supply lines. Under Arthur MacArthur, Gen Douglas MacArthur's father, effective counter-guerrilla measures were finally implemented. The Philippine Scouts were formed as a light infantry force with local knowledge to hunt down the guerrillas. A combination of Scouts and Americans also waged an effective pseudo-guerrilla operation of the type which would later prove so effective in Kenya and Rhodesia to infiltrate a guerrilla camp and capture Don Emilio Aquinaldo, the guerrilla leader. These tactics were soon combined with population and food control, as well as land redistribution, to bring most parts of the Philippines under government control.

As the twentieth century loomed on the horizon, the potential for successful guerrilla warfare grew, along with the burgeoning technology of the age. Armies were becoming ever more dependent on their supply lines, which allowed the guerrilla much broader scope for his operations. The year 1896 saw the publication of the first work devoted to guerrilla warfare, Charles Callwell's *Small Wars – Their Principles and Practice*. Callwell analysed guerrilla warfare and the way to counter it. He saw three types of 'small wars': 1. campaigns of conquest or annexation, 2. campaigns to suppress insurrection or lawlessness, and 3. campaigns to avenge a wrong or overthrow a despised enemy. Astutely, he stressed that an army facing small wars must be versatile, as each campaign would differ from the others. Perhaps most importantly, *Small Wars* showed how effective guerrilla warfare could be, and attempted to formulate a counter-strategy.

Shortly after the publication of Callwell's landmark work, the Boers in South Africa demonstrated just how effective guerrilla tactics could be against a major power. Drawing upon limited manpower, but manpower skilled with weapons and with excellent knowledge of the land for which they fought, the Boers very effectively harassed the extended British lines of communication. Kitchener implemented land and resource control in an attempt to isolate the Boers. Blockhouses were built along the lines of communication, and much of the Boer population was incarcerated in concentration camps. However, the lack of forethought about these camps and their atrocious conditions led to a large number of civilian deaths, and allowed the Boers a propaganda victory against the British.

Another important individual in the history of counter-guerrilla warfare was the French Gen Lyautey, who, during the early part of the twentieth century, developed his famous 'oil slick' strategy for pacifying Algeria. Lyautey believed that, from certain controlled areas, French influence could slowly spread throughout the country, like an oil slick. Although this strategy proved only marginally effective if at all, the French were to continue to use it in colonial or counter-insurgency campaigns for the next half-century.

The First World War did not offer wide scope for guerrilla warfare, though the German Von Lettow-Vorbeck effectively used irregular tactics to tie down large numbers of British and colonial troops in East Africa. On the British side, T. E. Lawrence worked with Arabian irregulars against the Turks. In the midst of the First World War, too, the British had to quell the Irish Easter Rebellion in 1916. This rebellion, which had received some assistance from the Germans, who hoped to create dissension in the British rear, contained elements of guerrilla warfare and of terrorism. The early stages of the Russian Revolution also contained some elements of guerrilla warfare, but, of course, the real importance of the Russian Revolution would come with the establishment of the Comintern, which would support revolution and insurgencies throughout the world.

During the period after the First World War, Mao Tse-tung, perhaps the most important theorist of guerrilla war, realized the need for a political base before the Chinese Revolution could succeed. The fact that the Chinese Nationalist government was so corrupt and inept could only help the revolution. Mao concluded that, to set up a successful guerrilla movement/underground government it was necessary to have five major components:

1. mass support
2. party organization
3. military organization
4. favourable terrain
5. economic strength.

After Mao had prematurely attempted a revolution among the workers in China's cities, his belief that revolutions must have their primary base in the countryside was reinforced. In re-establishing the revolution's strength, Mao and other Communist revolutionaries undertook the Long March to reach more rugged terrain. Of the 130,000 who started, only 30,000 completed the march. Those who survived were not only toughened for the struggle ahead, but established a mythic basis to inspire support.

In 1937 Mao wrote his classic work *Guerrilla Warfare*, establishing the precepts upon which the Chinese Communist Revolution and most successful guerrilla wars for the next half-century would be based. Most important was the realization of the three basic steps in a successful guerrilla war:

1. organization, consolidation, and preservation of isolated bases. During this stage agitators could be trained.
2. sabotage and terrorism, along with political indoctrination of the population
3. when the force was strong enough, an orthodox military campaign could be launched.

Mao emphasised that different areas of a country could be in different stages of the revolution simultaneously. He also emphasised the fact that military and political objectives must complement each other.

The corruption of the Chinese Nationalists made the task of winning over the population much simpler for the Chinese Communists, but Mao still formulated logical rules for dealing with the population.

1. All actions are subject to command
2. Do not steal from the people
3. Be neither selfish nor unjust
    He amplified these three basic tenets as follows:
1. Replace the doors when you leave the house (guests in Chinese homes often slept on the doors)
2. Roll up the bedding on which you've slept
3. Be courteous
4. Be honest in your transactions
5. Return what you borrow
6. Replace what you break
7. Do not bathe in the presence of women
8. Do not without authority search the pocketbooks of those you arrest.

Commanders were reminded to propagandize at every opportunity. As a result, those captured were well treated and often deserted the enemy and joined the cause. According to Mao guerrillas should be lightly equipped, with surprise and deception among their most important weapons. The guerrilla mission was to exterminate small forces, weaken larger forces, attack lines of communication, establish bases for operations in the enemy rear, force the enemy to disperse his strength, and co-ordinate with regular forces. Very importantly, guerrillas were to attempt to hold territory until the very last stages of the campaign. Mao's theories of guerrilla warfare were, of course, validated in 1949, when the Chinese Communists successfully drove Nationalist forces from mainland China.

Between the First and Second World Wars other insurgencies raged with greater or lesser intensity. In the Sahara, the Spanish and then the French faced a rebellion in the Rif. The Spanish Foreign Legion received its baptism of fire in this counter-insurgency campaign, as did Legion officer Francisco Franco. The Rif rebellion was aided by outside interests who hoped to gain lucrative access to the Rif's mineral wealth. Initially the guerrillas achieved successes against Spanish outposts, but the Rif rebels never progressed beyond the initial stages of guerrilla warfare to move into a successful conventional campaign. As a result, Spanish and French forces isolated the Rif using blockhouses, mines, and light infantry, and this allowed them to exercise both area and food control.

While the British used the RAF for counter-insurgency duties on the Northwest Frontier of India, the United States sent in the Marines. In Santa Domingo the USMC developed a four-step programme which would remain the heart of United States counter-insurgency doctrine for the next half-century:

1. Organize a native constabulary
2. Use cordon and search tactics to round up potential guerrillas
3. Use amnesties to bring guerrillas over to the government side
4. Form teams of former guerrillas to harry their ex-comrades.

In Nicaragua the Marines encountered a similar insurgency, though the popularity of Sandino, the guerrilla leader, combined with the fact that the guerrillas operated well in the rough terrain of Nicaragua, made this a harder insurgency to defeat. Once again, however, the Marines trained local counter-insurgency forces, which eventually tracked and killed Sandino, though his ghost would haunt the USA much later in the form of the Sandinista guerrillas who eventually conquered Nicaragua.

The Second World War saw the formalization of certain basics of guerrilla warfare when the British SOE and American OSS were formed to aid guerrillas behind the German and Japanese lines. After the German invasion of the Soviet Union, Stalin, too, called for guerrilla war against the Germans, resulting in successful partisan activities in the Soviet Union and elsewhere. Perhaps the most successful guerrilla campaign, though, was fought in Yugoslavia, where mountains gave Tito and his Partisans the perfect operational base. France,

Italy, Burma and the Philippines also saw successful operations. In each case, terrain conducive to guerrilla warfare was important in the success or failure of such operations. The Chindits and Merrill's Marauders were not guerrillas in the strictest terms, though they operated behind Japanese lines, harrying the enemy's rear in a manner that guerrillas might be expected to adopt.

Perhaps most important in the development of guerrilla warfare was the fact that many of the post-war insurgencies were really continuations of insurgencies started against the Germans, Italians or Japanese during the war. In Asia, especially, nationalist groups who had seen the British, French, Dutch or Americans driven from their countries by the Japanese were not willing to accept a return to colonial business as usual. Intensive guerrilla warfare was often the result, in many cases using arms supplied by the United States or other Allied powers during the war. Mao's ascension to power in China also gave Asian Communist guerrillas someone to attempt to emulate and a powerful ally.

CHAPTER II

The End of Empire

THE FRENCH EXPERIENCE IN INDOCHINA AND ALGERIA

The pre-war colonial powers faced an extreme uphill struggle in attempting to re-establish their control over former colonies during the decade after World War Two. This was especially true in Asia, since the Japanese, no matter how distasteful they had proved to the local population, had shown that the colonial overlords – especially the French and British, but also the Americans and Dutch – could be defeated. Throughout many countries occupied by the Axis, the most effective guerrillas had been Communists who had kept their weapons and viewed the struggle against Japan, Germany or Italy as a preliminary to the anti-colonial campaign to follow. This meant, too, that many of the post-war guerrilla movements would be based upon experienced cadre armed with modern weapons, often supplied by the very powers they would be fighting. The successful precepts of guerrilla warfare developed by Mao also gave 'national liberation movements' a blueprint for defeating an established government.

When France began to reoccupy Indochina at the end of World War Two, even re-establishing the government became a struggle, because the nationalists, largely composed of Communists but certainly not entirely Communist, had quickly moved to fill the vacuum left by the Japanese with their own government. As a result the French faced a Viet Minh government in being, even though it was not a particularly strong government at this point.

The Indochinese Communist movement, known as the Viet Minh, was extremely effectively led politically by Ho Chi Minh and militarily by Vo Nguyen Giap. This movement had received extensive support from the OSS during the war, as they were the only ones really fighting against the Japanese. American agents, too, had been extremely impressed with Ho Chi Minh, who they believed was truly much more of a Nationalist than a Communist. Ho had even patterned much of his political philosophy after American precepts of freedom; however, once the United States chose to support France's re-colonization of Indochina, Ho was forced to take a much more Marxist position in order to gain the support of the Soviet Union and China. Throughout the decades immediately after World War Two, the Soviet Union and China would support Communist guerrillas as widely as possible, to drain American and Allied resources in the struggle against these movements. An additional advantage to the Communist cause was that, in may cases, the US ended up backing totalitarian anti-Communist regimes, regimes which were distasteful to the American people, and even more distasteful to those who had to live under them. As a result, a large reservoir of resentment against the US built up throughout much of Asia and the Middle East.

In Indochina the Communists, having learned from Mao, retreated from the cities as French troops moved back in and established their power base in the countryside. Consequently, France soon controlled the cities, built strong points throughout the country and protected the lines of communication, but most of the rest of the country truly belonged to the Viet Minh. France also used the 'quadrillage' tactic to break the country into squares and clear them. The long-standing 'oil slick' method was used as well, in an attempt to spread French influence back through the country.

In March 1946 France had recognized an independent Vietnam, but only as a state within the Indochinese Federation of the French Union. By 1947 the Viet Minh were strong enough to besiege Hue for several weeks. That same year Ho offered a political solution, but the French were not interested in a settlement which recognized the Viet Minh. Ho and Giap therefore began waging a classic guerrilla war of the type foreseen by Mao. Drawing on the nationalism throughout the country, the Viet Minh emphasized that the French were attempting to reimpose the hated colonial rule.

Ho developed his own rules for the Viet Minh. These were similar to Mao's precepts, but Ho adapted them specifically for the Indochina situation.

Six 'Forbiddances' to Bureaucrats and Soldiers:
1. Do not commit actions likely to damage the land, crops, houses, or belongings of the people
2. Do not insist on borrowing or buying what the people are not willing to lend or sell
3. Do not bring living hens into mountain people's homes
4. Do not break your word
5. Do not give offence to people's faith or customs
6. Do not speak to the people in such a way as to indicate that you hold them in contempt

Six 'Permissibles':
1. Help the people in their daily work
2. Whenever possible, buy commodities for those who live far from markets
3. Tell the people interesting stories about the resistance without betraying secrets
4. Teach the people the basics of reading, writing and hygiene
5. Study the customs of the area and create an atmosphere of sympathy with the people
6. Show the people that you are correct, diligent, and disciplined.

The Viet Minh also carefully organized each area politically, and by 1948 they were well into the first phase of a classic guerrilla war, and had moved into the second phase in the northern part of Vietnam. French heavy-handedness in attempting to re-establish colonial rule certainly did not hurt the Viet Minh cause, either.

In 1950 both the Soviet Union and the new Chinese Communist state recognized the Viet Minh, thus giving the guerrilla movement both credibility and material support. Direct support from China, just to the north, allowed the Viet Minh to receive the heavier weapons necessary to move into the third stage of guerrilla warfare, full military conflict, though they would continue to use guerrilla tactics as well. In late 1949 and early 1950 the Viet Minh launched a major offensive against the Black River outposts of the French. By early 1950 these outposts had been overrun and the Viet Minh had successfully separated the Red River Delta and the Thai Hills.

In February 1950 Giap began the mobile-warfare (third) phase along the northern border with China, to clear the French and allow free movement of personnel and supplies back and forth. By late 1950 he had been almost entirely successful, despite the French attempt to use their highly mobile airborne forces as fire brigades.

France was facing various other difficulties, too. The US was France's primary supporter, both financially and politically, in the struggle for Indochina, yet many Americans considered this a colonial campaign and opposed their country's involvement. Increasingly, too, the French were finding their outposts isolated and their control over routes of communication tenuous. Mobile Groups were formed to fight their way through to isolated outposts, but these groups suffered heavy casualties in the process and were frequently used only to withdraw survivors. More and more the French were in a reactive mode and, thus, were losing. They did take some positive steps, but for the most part the French command did not seem to understand guerrilla war. This was ironic, as France itself had used guerrilla tactics against the occupying Germans only a few years before. On the plus side, the Groupements de Commandos Mixtes Aeroportes (GCMA), for example, functioned much as the US Special Forces would later, training local tribesmen as counter-guerrilla warriors. The GCMA effort was never great enough, however, to have more than a local impact on the war. An interesting sidelight on the GCMA is that US Special Forces personnel allegedly encountered surviving GCMA members with their tribesmen a decade after the French had pulled out of Vietnam. Another attempt at implementing counter-insurgency tactics was the formation of the Groupes Administratifs Mobiles Operationnels (GAMO), which were civil affairs units attempting to implement a 'hearts and minds' campaign. As with GCMA, however, the GAMO were too little, too late.

The French kept hoping to lure the Viet Minh into a decisive set-piece battle, something their commanders understood but normally a futile tactic against guerrilla fighters. If Giap accepted full-scale battle, it would be because he knew he could win. The French also tried to raise a viable Vietnamese army, a step that was necessary but was only carried out halfheartedly. French officers, for the most part, still viewed the Vietnamese as colonial troops of the French Army.

As the French will to pursue a victory in Indochina declined at home, Communist successes in Korea helped inspire Giap to plan an attack on Vinh Yen in January 1951, as a prelude to attacking Hanoi itself. No longer were the Viet Minh a lightly armed guerrilla army. They now had artillery captured from the nationalist Chinese and supplied by their supporters to the north. As it transpired, the French repulsed the attack on Vinh Yen, but it was a close-run thing, saved by the use of American-supplied napalm. The Viet Minh had unsuccessfully employed human wave attacks during this offensive, indicating Giap's growing confidence in his manpower reserves. Even after being repulsed Giap continued to attack to the south and south-east, but in June, after suffering heavy casualties, the Viet Minh pulled back. Though his strength was growing, this defeat persuaded Giap to wait longer before moving into the third phase of his guerrilla war. Instead, he would employ the classic guerrilla tactic of thrusting where the French were weak, towards the Thai Hills and Laos.

De Lattre, the new French commander, did not really understand counter-insurgency warfare, and tried to seal off the Red River Delta with 1,200 forts and blockhouses - the 'De Lattre Line'. The French were still exercising the 'Maginot Line' mentality the Germans had proved invalid in 1940. Although the De Lattre Line and other static defensive positions tied down 70 per cent of De Lattre's 500,000 men, he did retain eight para battalions and seven mobile groups as his striking forces. To keep the important waterways open for supply, the French also used riverine forces known as *Dinaussauts*. During this period US diplomatic support was sometimes luke warm, but De Lattre's obvious anti-communism helped retain US backing.

Still based on land warfare in Europe, De Lattre's tactics were designed to lure Giap into a 'meat grinder' set-piece battle. Giap, however, was too astute a guerrilla warrior to fall for this ploy. Therefore, when De Lattre sent troops to occupy the town of Hoa-Binh, hoping to draw Giap, the guerrilla leader let the French occupy their objective and then attacked their supply lines. By January 1952 De Lattre, sick and dying, had been replaced by Gen Salan, who pulled out of Hoa-Binh, suffering heavy casualties from the harassing Viet Minh in the process.

The situation continued to deteriorate, and by March 1952 the French were having to use their Mobile Groups behind their own lines to keep the roads open. After building his strength and using traditional guerrilla tactics through early 1952, in the fall Giap decided to strike in force towards Laos. As Giap struck across the north-east, Salan responded with a plan to establish air-supplied strongpoints, known as Bases Aero-Terrestre. Their function was to maintain a French presence, draw a Viet Minh attack, and assist the GCMA working with local tribesmen.

Salan also planned to launch an attack on Giap's supply bases at Yen Bai and Phu Doan using 30,000 troops, the most ever committed to an operation in Vietnam. Giap, however, was not really very dependent on these supply centres, coolies being surprisingly versatile. He detached two divisions to fight a delaying action, and continued to push towards Laos. When Salan began pulling back in November, the Viet Minh harassed the retreating French, inflicting heavy casualties in the process.

By now the French had realized that it was absolutely essential to form a viable Vietnamese Army. Unfortunately, sufficient colonialism remained to ensure that few Vietnamese became officers or NCOs, and these units were still led by Frenchmen. As a result, the Vietnamese Army itself became a political liability rather than a success.

The De Lattre Line was proving increasingly ineffective, and by the spring of 1953 Giap had control of much of central Vietnam, though the French maintained outposts at Hue, Da Nang, and Nha Trang. At the beginning of the rainy season in 1953, Giap pulled back most of his forces from Laos, though cadres remained to work with the Pathet Lao.

Salan's lack of success resulted in his replacement by another very traditional general, Henri Navarre, whose experience had been as an armour officer with some intelligence assignments. The British, one of France's primary allies, using their own experience in Palestine and Malaya, had advised the French that political reform was absolutely critical to winning a counter-insurgency war, but still the French did not act. In fact, Navarre himself had concluded that the best France could hope for was a draw, especially when his government told him that he would receive no additional troops. As a result, although he had twice the number of troops that the Viet Minh had available, Salan was normally outmanned because a large number of his men were tied to static defensive positions. To his credit, Navarre did realize that aggressive patrolling and reconnaissance were necessary, but he just did not have the manpower to carry out enough patrols.

To make the French situation worse, the Korean ceasefire in July 1953 freed the Chinese to give even more material support to the Viet Minh. The US, in fact, was even afraid that China might choose to invade Vietnam. It should be borne in mind, too, that at this time the US overestimated the strategic importance of Vietnam, adhering to the 'domino theory' which held that all of Southeast Asia would fall if Vietnam fell.

Giap continued to probe for French vulnerability throughout 1953 while building his strength, especially in artillery. In November 1953 Navarre established additional fortified airheads in the north, the largest at Dien Bien Phu. Giap responded by deferring his planned invasion of Laos, and began concentrating forces around Dien Bien Phu. Still thinking as a conventional warrior, Navarre saw this as his chance to defeat the Viet Minh decisively. However, he still regarded the Viet Minh as incapable of striking decisively at a modern army. Beginning on 13 March 1954, Giap proved him wrong. The French were caught completely by surprise by the intensity of the Viet Minh artillery barrage. They had not considered the Viet Minh's ability to dismantle their artillery and transport it through jungles and over mountains, then reassemble it on the heights commanding Dien Bien Phu. Showing their strength elsewhere, the Viet Minh also stepped up attacks on French airfields and logistical centres, thus inhibiting their opponent's ability to provide air support or air supply to the besieged fortress.

So critical did the situation at Dien Bien Phu become that the US considered launching carrier air strikes in support, quite possibly using nuclear weapons, but the US Congress did not approve the proposal. As a result, the fortress of Dien Bien Phu fell on 8 May 1954, to be quickly followed by the fall of the French and Vietnamese governments. Forced to bargain from a position of weakness, the French granted concessions to the Communists which, in effect, divided the country at the 17th Parallel pending the results of a national election. Although theoretically the Viet Minh withdrew their forces from the south, many cadre were left to continue the fight. Another result of the partition of Vietnam was the formation of SEATO to prevent a Communist takeover of the remainder of Southeast Asia. The many unresolved remnants of the Indochina War, however, would continue to haunt the US for the next quarter of a century.

The French defeat can be attributed to various factors. By tying too many troops to static defensive duties, the French lost mobility and the initiative in fighting the Viet Minh. Owing to the lack of a really effective campaign to deal with political issues, too, the French ceded to the Viet Minh the political as well as military initiative. With the massive resources of China available to the North, the Communists had a safe haven from which they could draw supplies and to which they could send troops for training. China's propinquity should never be underestimated as a factor in the French defeat. Furthermore, the fact that France was a colonial power trying to re-establish colonial rule eroded support from the US, its most powerful ally. Even more importantly, the French public lost the will to make the sacrifices necessary to achieve victory in Indochina, even if the generals had grasped the concepts of fighting a counter-insurgency war.

Indochina's drain on French resources, manpower and collective will struck the French colonial empire an even more decisive blow in the North African colony of Algeria, which considered itself a part of metropolitan France. The problems in Algeria were very typical of those of other residual colonies which began to assert their nationalism after the Second World War. Land ownership and government control in Algeria were centered almost entirely among European colonists and a small Moslem élite. The country, in fact, was run in a very feudal manner reminiscent of Europe hundreds of years before. France's defeat at the beginning of World War Two, the collaboration of the Petain government, and the return of Arab veterans of the Indochina War, many of whom had been indoctrinated in Viet Minh prison camps, were all fuel for nationalistic sentiments which had been simmering since just after World War One.

On VE Day, 8 May 1945, Moslem riots in Algeria led to the death of approximately 100 Europeans. In retaliation, European 'militias' killed over 20,000 Moslems. The year 1947 did see minor reforms in the government of Algeria, but Europeans, who amounted to less than ten per cent of the population, retained most of the power. As a result, Algerian veterans of World War Two formed the Organisation Secrete (OS) under Ahmed Ben Bella, a self-educated student of guerrilla warfare, especially the theories and operations of Mao and Tito. The OS did not really begin operations until 1949, when it robbed the Oran post office, and this proved a failure, as Ben Bella and many others were captured soon after. Key lieutenants fled to Cairo where, in 1952, Ben Bella joined them after escaping from prison. While Ben Bella and some senior lieutenants remained in Cairo to raise money and support, other members of the OS returned to Algeria and began training guerrillas.

Although the French government had been attempting some reforms in Algeria, the colons (as the colonists were known) had short-circuited them whenever possible. No one realized the depth of the nationalistic feeling among the Algerians. In late 1954, on the heels of France's defeat at Dien Bien Phu, the OS began operations. On 1 November 30 targets were hit by the guerrillas, mostly gendarmerie posts in the Aures Mountains. Pamphlets were also distributed announcing that the Front de Liberation Nationale (FLN) would be willing to negotiate independence, and guaranteeing European rights and close contacts with France in the process. In response, the French dispatched a mechanized column towards the area and sent three para battalions from France as reinforcements. In the wake of these initial operations, draconian measures adopted by the police drove many moderates towards the FLN. The guerrillas began intimidating moderates as well, forcing them to join the revolution or at least pay it lip service.

The rebellion spread, and by April 1955 the French government had declared a limited emergency. Once again the colons frustrated any attempts at reform. On the military side, the Sections Administratives Specialisées (SAS) were formed to bring military administrators closer to the local population. However, even the best of these administrators were fighting an uphill battle, as indiscriminate arrests by the police and army often negated any gains they had made. External support for the guerrillas was growing as well, as the Arab League became very vocal in the United Nations and elsewhere.

Perhaps at this stage political concessions could have undermined the insurgency, but French political weakness was manifest, as only officials who were unacceptable to the colons were appointed. The French military command had adopted a hard-line approach, too, based on a counter-revolutionary strategy developed in the wake of Indochina. Unfortunately, the generals seemed to have learned some of the tactical lessons of that conflict but virtually none of the political ones. The French Army viewed counter-insurgency as a fight to the death against Communism, but did not address the political aspirations of the local population in order to understand the appeal of Communism.

Tunisia and Morocco had always been more independent than Algeria, and in 1956 France granted these two countries their independence. As a result, the FLN not only took heart from the independence of these two neighbours, but also gained allies, and thus safe havens, on Algeria's borders.

At this point the ALN, the military arm of the FLN, could field 8,500 guerrillas backed by 21,000 auxiliaries. By late 1956 they faced 400,000 French soldiers. Things were not all rosy within the FLN/ALN, however, as disagreements within the ranks combined with poor communication between the leadership in Cairo and the fighters in the field eroded operational efficiency. Although these problems hurt the guerrilla cause, they were not fatal, as the French really failed to exploit the problems.

The next major assault by the FLN was in the cities, where they began a terror campaign, in part to draw harsh reprisals and force more of the population to take sides. The January 1957 Battle of Algiers was particularly bloody. Under paratroop leader Jacques Massu the Military Special Police, the Detachments Operationales de Protection, were formed. These units, as well as others, used informants in the Casbah to find terrorists, though the reliability of the informants was often open to severe question. The 'ilot' system was also implemented, in which family and block leaders were appointed to be responsible for their area. Fear and violence became a primary weapon for the paras, and the use of torture became widely accepted as a means of obtaining information. Admittedly, the harsh tactics worked in Algiers, as by October 1957 the FLN was broken. Many uncommitted members of the population felt such revulsion at French tactics, however, that their sympathies were now with the FLN, which through abdication had assumed the moral high ground. Moreover, while the French were occupied with Algiers, the FLN had organized the countryside.

French tactics in the countryside also remained reminiscent of those in Indochina. The same 'quadrillage' system of dividing the country was used in conjunction with sweeps - the 'ratissage' or the 'bouclage' - by the paras and the Foreign Legion. Once again, though, too many troops were tied to static garrisons. The large number of conscripts now committed to the war limited the Army's effectiveness as well. Other problems at this point included the ready sanctuaries just across the border, a source of constant political strife between France, Morocco and Tunisia, and the endemic use of torture by the French which, as it became known, turned opinion at home and around the world against the French security forces.

Still enamoured of the Magniot Line, the French attempted to stop infiltration into Algeria with the Maurice Line, an interlocking mesh of radar, searchlights, artillery, electric fences and patrols. Although the Maurice Line did curtail infiltration, it certainly did not stop it. In September 1957 the French issued a declaration of the right of pursuit into Tunisia, a policy predestined to create diplomatic problems even though it was militarily sound as it limited the FLN/ALN's safe havens. Another programme which was tactically sound but proved disastrous in implementation was the forced relocation programme for those living along the borders. As a result of poor planning, many of those relocated died, thereby creating a propaganda victory for the FLN and driving more into the insurgent camp. Attempts were made by the SAS and other psy-war troops to convert those relocated to the French cause, but they were so obviously more concerned with getting information about the FLN than with winning hearts and minds that they were remarkably unsuccessful.

In the spring of 1958 European colonists rioted in Algiers, contributing to the fall of the French government. The new leader of France was Charles De Gaulle, who immediately began taking steps to bring the military under control by ordering officers in Algeria to desist from becoming involved in colonist political activity. He also expressed a willingness to negotiate with the FLN. Among other concessions, he offered an amnesty.

The ALN had grown overconfident and had begun launching battalion-sized attacks as a prelude to the third phase of guerrilla warfare. It was not, however, ready to take on a NATO army in the field and was suffering heavy casualties. Many of these resulted from the very effective French use of Commandos de Chasse, light infantry units of 60 to 100 men able to carry out long-range patrols into rebel territory to seek and destroy guerrilla bands. Helicopters were used to bring in paras or Foreign Legionnaires to exploit contacts with guerrillas. These same tactics would prove quite successful in guerrilla wars for the next quarter of a century, whether in Vietnam, Rhodesia or Afghanistan.

French successes in the countryside drove the FLN to renew its campaign of urban terrorism, but the FLN's most effective weapon at this point was time. In September 1959 De Gaulle offered Algeria self-determination. Algeria simmered and in January 1960 the colons took to the streets, backed by many French soldiers, but troops loyal to De Gaulle fired on the French colonists. In January 1961 a referendum in France showed widespread support for De Gaulle's policies. In response the Organisation de l'Armée Secrète (OAS) was formed to bring the conflict to France itself, with bombings and assassination attempts against the president.

In conjunction with the terror campaign in France, some military leaders launched a 'putsch' in Algeria, but too many units remained loyal to De Gaulle and the 'Colonels' Revolt', as it was also called, failed. In the process, France's most decorated military unit, the 1st Foreign Legion Parachute Regiment, was disbanded for its participation. Algeria's fate had been decided. In the spring of 1962 the OAS collapsed, and in the following July Algeria became independent.

In Algeria, France failed to apply lessons which should have been learnt in Indochina, in particular the need to understand the political aspirations of the mass of the population. Too many officers viewed themselves as crusaders against Communism and therefore failed to realize that nationalism was at the root of the insurgency. Once again, too, France relied too heavily on static installations and conscript troops assigned static duties. The élite light-infantry units such as the paras and Foreign Legion, and especially the Commandos de Chasse, proved highly effective. The use of helicopter-borne quick reaction forces also proved an important innovation in carrying out counter-guerrilla operations. The French Army in Algeria, especially the professional units, became too politicized and involved in helping the local colonists maintain the status quo. As a result, troops were blinded to many of the basic tenets of winning a guerrilla war, especially the importance of broad-based support of the population. The use of torture and other unsavoury tactics only alienated the population from the French even more. Perhaps Algeria offers more lessons than most in how *not* to fight a counter-guerrilia war.

THE BRITISH LEARNING EXPERIENCE THROUGHOUT THE FORMER COLONIES

In the first two decades after the Second World War, the cliché 'the sun never sets on the British Empire' could well have been rephrased as 'the sun never sets on insurgencies in the British Empire', because the British had to deal with more than half a dozen guerrilla wars.

The first, a classic no-win situation, was in Palestine, where the British had had a mandate since immediately after World War One. The Zionist movement had started at the end of the nineteenth century and had grown in intensity over the next 50 years as events showed the desperate need for a Jewish homeland. The Balfour Declaration during World War One had pledged the United Kingdom's support for a Jewish homeland. This support continued during the early post-World War One era as the British under the mandate encouraged Jewish immigration. As the Jews bought land from absentee owners, however, the Arabs who were dispossessed became embittered. This bitterness was enhanced in 1929, when the Mufti of Jerusalem incited attacks against the Jews in Palestine.

The British, growing worried about offending the Arabs, tried to take a middle ground in the conflict, but in doing so satisfied no one. By 1935 nearly 500,000 Jews were in Palestine, making them a presence to be reckoned with, but in 1936 an Arab rebellion which would rage until 1938 broke out. Many British officers were openly supportive of the Arabs and their attacks against the Jews, but Orde Wingate, later to win fame with the Chindits, organized 'Special Night Squads' of Jewish raiders to harass the Arabs. Finally, in 1939, to appease the Arabs, Jewish land purchases were inhibited and immigration was severely limited. This, of course, doomed many Jews wishing to flee Europe to death in concentration camps in the next few years.

Because of the need to defeat the greater evil, Adolph Hitler and Nazism, most Zionists remained moderate and continued to support Great Britain in the war. In fact, from the Haganah, the Jewish self-defence force, shock units known as the 'Palmach' were formed for fighting in Syria. During the war 32,000 Palestinian Jews served in the British Army. However, not all Jews were willing to remain moderate in the face of overt British support for the Arabs. In 1925 some Zionists had formed a Revisionist Party, which wanted to take Palestine by force. In 1935 this group split from the Zionist Movement, and in 1937 formed the Irgun under Daniel Raziel, a student of military history.

The Irgun began by smuggling Jewish refugees into Palestine, but, after Arab attacks on Jews in 1939, Raziel's fighters responded with a terrorist campaign against Arabs, then against the British in retaliation for torturing Irgun members. In 1940 Raziel was willing to lay off the British, but an even more militant member of the Irgun, Abraham Stern, broke away to continue a terrorist campaign against the British 'occupation forces'. Officially known as the Fighters for the Freedom of Israel (FFI), this group was more widely known as the 'Stern Gang'. Stern himself was killed in 1941 and replaced by David Friedman-Yellin, and in 1943 Menachem Begin became the new commander of the Irgun. During the war the Stern Gang killed Jewish, Arab and British policemen. Beginning in 1944, frustrated by British unwillingness to allow immigration and by other matters, the Irgun renounced its truce and formed an alliance with the Stern Gang, though they still refused to attack the British Army as long as it was fighting Hitler.

January 1944 saw bomb attacks on immigration department offices, income tax offices, and police CID headquarters throughout Palestine. Many moderate Jews were murdered, also, as the Stern Gang sent a message that 'collaboration' with the British would not be tolerated. The Irgun strategy was a classic guerrilla one, too; they wanted to destroy British prestige. Perhaps one of the strongest weapons in the Irgun arsenal was the fact that the world, and particularly the very vocal American Jews, would be watching Palestine.

It seemed that the more militant groups had destroyed their own credibility when the Stern Gang assassinated Lord Mayne, the Minister of State, in Cairo. Jews and Gentiles alike were horrified. The Zionist leaders even ordered the Haganah and the Palmach to act against the Irgun and Stern Gang in conjunction with the British. Now that they were co-operating, though, the Jewish Agency expected some reciprocity from the British, and in May 1945 requested increased immigration quotas, especially for survivors of the Holocaust. British intransigence on this issue not only caused the Haganah to start smuggling refugees, but also led to the rapprochement between the Irgun, Stern Gang and Haganah.

On 31 October 1945 the Palmach, Irgun and Stern Gang carried out widespread attacks on railways, ships and the oil refineries at Haifa. As bitterness grew between Jews and British soldiers the intensity of the raids against British sites also increased. In December 1945, for example, the Irgun raided two police headquarters and an arms dump, killing nine soldiers in the process. In retaliation for the latest series of raids, the British High Commissioner, Sir Alan Cunningham, implemented strict emergency laws including the death penalty for membership of a terrorist organization.

World opinion, heavily influenced by the horrors of the concentration camps, which were now being revealed in full, favoured admitting Jewish refugees, but the British refused owing to pressure from the Arabs. Counter-pressure was applied by the US, but still the British refused to relent. This led to a new wave of terrorist incidents which culminated in the bombing of 22 RAF aeroplanes in June 1946, in a raid that would have done credit to David Sterling, whose SAS had specialized in blowing up Luftwaffe aircraft in the Western Desert. The fact that some Palestinian Jews had served with the Long Range Desert Group may well have influenced this raid.

Once again the British authorities made the wrong political choice, ordering widespread arrests of Jewish Agency members and thus offering a slap in the face to moderate Jews. However, during the arrests documents were captured which showed that the Jewish Agency had been aware of Haganah involvement in terrorist operations. To destroy these documents and gain revenge for the raids, the King David Hotel, the British HQ, was bombed, killing 91 and wounding 45. The world was horrified, but rather than make useful propaganda of the incident to temper feeling against the British, the British command issued a non-fraternization order which read as though it had been dictated by Heinrich Himmler. This turned the incident into a Jewish propaganda victory, as the British authorities were now linked in many minds to the Nazis. Even those horrified by the bombings hated the British for this order.

In the face of widespread criticism abroad, in August 1946 the British launched a massive cordon and search operation in Tel Aviv, though of 800 people rounded up it was said that only two were terrorists. Finally, a new Colonial Secretary more sympathetic to the Zionist cause was appointed and many of the Jewish Agency leaders were freed. Attempts were made, too, to arrive at a compromise on immigration. As a result, the Zionist organizations and Haganah once again distanced themselves from the terrorists. Things certainly were not rosy for the security forces, however, as the Arabs continued to oppose the partition of Palestine into a Jewish state and an Arab state; America continued to pressure the British; and the Irgun and Stern Gang continued their campaign of terrorism.

To carry out an effective counter-terror/counter-insurgency campaign, the British needed good intelligence, but both Jewish and Arab segments of the population were so alienated that it was very difficult to obtain useful information. In frustration the British even tried using corporal punishment, but this stopped when the Irgun kidnapped British soldiers and lashed them in retaliation. The capital punishment order was invoked in early 1947, when a terrorist was sentenced to die. In retaliation, in March 1947 various terrorist incidents throughout Palestine resulted in 80 British soldiers being killed or wounded. The ensuing martial law proclamation alienated the population even more. Three more terrorists were hanged, and in response the Irgun kidnapped two British soldiers and hanged them. Finally, in November 1947 the British announced that they would terminate their mandate in May 1948.

The irony, of course, is that the Jewish state which was established at least partly through the efforts of terrorists, including such prominent men as Menachem Begin, has itself been waging a war for almost half a century against the same types of acts. The Irgun and other Jewish organizations were successful for a combination of reasons. The British, emerging from a long and expensive war, really did not have the will nor the capital to continue garrisoning Palestine. Hence, forcing them out at least tacitly accomplished an end desired by both sides. Moreover, the British could not win the 'public relations' battle in the face of the horrors of the Holocaust. The Jewish fighters, on the other hand, had certain advantages. Many had served with the British Army and understood its tactics. The Jewish population was united in its desire for a homeland and, hence, the Irgun et al. were addressing the people's political aspirations. The large and wealthy

Jewish population in the US offered massive financial, moral, and political support and was an ever present reminder to the British that they could not go too far without alienating their most important ally. In the end, the British just did not want to continue fighting a no-win war in Palestine, but they would prove themselves very able counter-insurgency warriors in future campaigns.

In their rich Malayan colony, the British faced another insurgency in the post-war years, one that stemmed directly from the confusion in the wake of World War Two. A combination of political confusion during the period when the British were re-establishing their authority, the memory of an Asian victory over the white colonials (even though it had been by the hated Japanese), economic hardship, and the rise of Communism in Asia contributed to the insurgency, which would rage in Malaya for more than a decade.

The Malayan Communist Party (MCP) was actually in relatively good shape at the end of World War Two, having gained experience in guerrilla warfare against the Japanese and having buried some weapons for future use. By 1947 the MCP was led by Ch'en Ping, who had worked with the Special Operations Executive (SOE) during the war and had received an OBE for his anti-Japanese activities.

The MCP sent representatives to the 'Asia Youth Conference', where, many believe, most of the insurgencies in Southeast Asia for the next two decades had their germination. Shortly thereafter Ch'en Ping began his revolution in Malaya, based on Mao's classic three-stage plan. Ch'en's first step was to reactivate many jungle-based guerrilla bands who had gone underground at the end of the war. The Malayan People's Anti-British Army numbered about 4,000, 90 per cent of which were Chinese. A substantial portion had guerrilla warfare experience against the Japanese. Realizing the importance of organization, Ch'en had them formed into eight regional regiments, each of which lived in a large camp from which raids were launched against economic and political targets. The actual fighters were supported by the Min Yuen, the communist civilian organization, which included many rubber and tin workers among its membership. Since these were the two most important industries in Malaya, these workers would be able to wreak havoc if they committed acts of sabotage. Additional cells were formed in villages bordering the jungle, where they could supply the guerrillas with food, manpower, and intelligence. Finally, in classic guerrilla fashion, there were some Min Yuen part-time guerrillas who performed sabotage, propaganda, and terror missions.

To act as 'enforcers' and carry out acts of terrorism in urban areas, groups of thugs called 'Blood and Steel Corps' functioned independently. Communists were well-organized into provincial, regional and village hierarchies.

During the initial stages of the insurgency in Malaya, strikes, bombings, assassinations, extortion, bank robberies and other acts of terrorism were carried out in the cities. In rural areas, assassinations of village officials and policemen were combined with acts of sabotage on rubber plantations and in mines. The Malayan police and the British Army reacted slowly to these initial outrages. As a result, by 1948 Ch'en Ping had stepped up his campaign. In reaction, in June 1948, the British High Commissioner, Sir Edward Gent, declared a state of emergency which included a declaration of martial law. Under the martial law regulations, all citizens under 12 years of age had to register and receive identification, habeas corpus was suspended, searches without warrants were allowed, the death penalty was instituted for possession of illegal weapons, prison sentences were imposed for aiding the Communist propaganda effort and curfews were enforced. Once these regulations were in effect, later declarations included the institution of free-fire zones allowing security forces to shoot anyone in prohibited areas. Prison sentences were also instituted for anyone supplying the guerrillas.

Although the measures implemented were draconian, they received a surprisingly strong amount of support from the population, at least partly owing to government guarantees that the harsh measures would be repealed as soon as the emergency ended. Also, the government handled the strict laws intelligently and fairly, with an appeals process and an effort to educate the population to make sure that the reason for the measures was understood.

The next step was to provide security for the population and separate the guerrillas from possible support. In addition, the mines and rubber plantations, as well as lines of communication, had to be secured. The eleven battalions of troops spread throughout Malaya soon proved too inadequate to accomplish this task. The Malayan Police were expanded five-fold to 45,000, while troop strength was raised to 40,000, including 10,000 tough and intensely loyal Gurkhas. During this expansion of the security forces, the guerrillas continued their raids. In 1948, for example, they killed 315 civilians, 89 policemen and 60 soldiers. Nevertheless, there was not a general uprising of the people in support of the guerrillas, and Ch'en Ping was forced to change his tactics.

Two-thirds of the Communist forces, now renamed the Malayan Races Liberation Army (MRLA) in an attempt to give them a broader appeal to the diverse population of the area, were pulled back into the deep jungle. The remainder operated among the rubber workers, miners and farmers near the jungle. This tactic did not, however, prove particularly successful. In 1949, therefore, the MRLA came back out of the jungle in force, killing 723 people. The following year also saw an increase in the number of terrorist incidents.

The police and military, however, remained in the reactive mode as they continued to allow Ch'en Ping the initiative. Conventional military thinking still led them to hope for a chance to destroy the guerrillas in one massive operation, and as a result excessive force was often used to destroy small bands. Battalion operations in the jungle were obviously too massive. It would be necessary to break forces down into company-, platoon- or even squad-sized units to achieve success. Smaller flexible units could operate more clandestinely and react much more quickly. The re-formed Special Air Service, originally the Malayan Scouts, proved especially adept at long-range, deep-penetration patrols to harry the terrorists in their former safe havens. Dyak trackers who knew the jungle intimately helped the SAS and other British units to track the guerrillas.

In April 1950 Sir Henry Briggs arrived as Director of Operations and introduced what would be called the Briggs Plan, which emphasized winning the support of the civil population while depriving the guerrillas of that self-same support. A key element of this plan was the resettlement of half a million people into 400 newly constructed villages. Unlike many previous resettlement plans, however, this one was well thought out. The new villages were better than those the people were leaving, and were normally sited in good farming areas. Briggs also realized that to fight a successful counter-insurgency a unified command structure was necessary, so he streamlined and centralized the command of security operations.

In the early stages of the Briggs Plan and the new deep-penetration patrols, the guerrillas still inflicted heavy losses - approximately 1,200 in 1950 and about 1,000 in 1951, the latter figure including Sir Henry Gurney, the High Commissioner, who was assassinated. In 1951 the guerrillas inflicted heavy economic losses, too, as they caused damage estimated at $27.5 million to rubber plantations, eroding public confidence as the rubber industry was getting re-established after the war.

Slowly, however, the government's counter-insurgency programme was beginning to work. By the autumn of 1951 a quarter of a million people had been resettled and the government was promoting an amnesty programme for former terrorists. Many of those who came over were formed into hunter teams and sent back into the jungle after their former comrades. By 1952 security operations were showing greater success, forcing the MRLA to break into smaller, more widely dispersed units. This eroded their former excellent command and control, and also made communication much more difficult. Furthermore, as SAS and other deep-penetration patrols supported by aerial surveillance ranged far into the jungles, Communist food-growing areas were eliminated, causing the MRLA to spend most of its time simply trying to find enough food to survive. So unappealing had the guerrilla cause become, that by 1952 it was estimated that 80 per cent of recruitment was through coercion.

The arrival of Sir Gerald Templer as the new High Commissioner and Director of Operations in 1952 marked the beginning of the final stage in the counter-insurgency war in Malaya. Templer announced that Malaya would become self-governing, thus removing the last political leverage that the insurgents had with the population. As a result, too, the population was willing to give Templer broad powers for the next two years. Although Templer took a tough stance against the guerrillas, he kept the military from interfering too heavily in people's lives, an important consideration if the support of the population is to be retained.

The emphasis on village security remained paramount, with each relocated village fortified and having its own police post to provide protection. Feeling secure, the villagers gave the government not only tacit support, but also active support by supplying intelligence about the Communists. With the population secure and the guerrillas denied their support, the security forces could now concentrate on re-exerting government control over large areas. The intelligence effort grew more productive as well, from co-operative members of the population and through Special Branch's effective use of Chinese operatives.

As well as being denied the support of the population, the guerrillas were harried through the jungles by SAS deep-penetration patrols and by native trackers. The terrorists' use of intimidation against the jungle tribesmen had also alienated this group, who were now trained as irregulars to assist the SAS, adding still another threat to guerrilla security. So effective had the government's intelligence become, that the military, police or irregulars could consistently ambush the guerrillas as they attempted to conduct operations or, more often, obtain food. The military forces now made extensive use of small units which knew their areas of operation and the local population well, and thus proved far more effective.

Between 1952 and 1954 two-thirds of the guerrilla strength was wiped out, and those remaining were cut off from the population and, consequently, from recruits and supplies. By 1955 the government felt it could end its offensive phase, though it continued to consolidate control until 1960. Ch'en Ping's final retreat with 400 hard-core followers was to the Malay-Thai border, where they continued to be a threat for many more years, though they really gained few, if any, new adherents.

Malaya is one of the classic examples of a counter-insurgency campaign which was carried out effectively, though it took a while for the government and the security forces to develop the proper combination of political and military/police tactics. Most importantly, the British colonial government realized that the political aspirations of the Malayan people were important, and that their rights as citizens had to be respected. As a result, the bulk of the population supported the government even when very harsh laws were enacted. Templer's declaration that self-government was in the offing removed any doubts about Malaya's political future. The relocation plan was important in removing guerrilla support, and unlike many such plans in the past was carried out with the welfare of the population in mind. Thus hearts and minds were won and government supporters gained.

The SAS worked well, too, with jungle tribesmen giving their support to the government cause. As the campaign progressed, the combination of popular support for the government and effective security operations denied the guerrillas food and recruits, making survival their primary objective, rather than continued attacks on government or economic targets. Security forces were used quite effectively, as well, once proper tactics were evolved. Small unit patrols helped deny the jungle to the guerrillas, while the use of the SAS, former guerrillas, and Dyak trackers denied the guerrillas their lairs, even deep in the jungle. In conjunction, the use of the Gurkhas, Royal Marine Commandos and other élite troops guaranteed that effective ambushes would await those terrorists that the SAS drove from the deep jungle. As an example for other counter-insurgenices, Malaya should best be remembered as an illustration of how political and military goals must complement each other to bring about a successful defeat of guerrilla warriors well versed in Mao's precepts.

British counter-insurgencies were not limited, however, to those against Communist guerrillas. Simultaneously with Malaya, British colonial officials also had to deal with the Mau Mau terrorist/guerrilla campaign in Kenya, The Mau Mau, however, were not Communist but tribal nationalists. Many problems, in fact, stemmed quite validly from the dissatisfaction of the Kikuyu (the pre-eminent tribe in Kenya) with British acquisition of tribal lands and the lack of understanding of tribal customs and ceremony by the colonial administrators and white farmers. Equally importantly, the British did not understand the chief system and, as a result, often selected individuals as chiefs who were quite distasteful to most Kikuyu. Many colonial administrators viewed the Africans as cheap labour and treated them as such, while even many of the most enlightened regarded them as children to be scolded or coddled.

As with most of the post-war insurgencies, the unrest had existed for decades. In Kenya, the political movement among blacks had really begun in the 1920s, based on the grievance of 'stolen lands'. Interference with Kikuyu ceremonies by missionaries of the Church of Scotland was another reason for the growing unrest. The Kikuyu Central Association (KCA) became the blanket group joined by most of those dissatisfied with white rule. Kikuyu veterans of World War Two, who had fought and seen comrades die for Great Britain, returned to Kenya far more aware of the extent of the discrimination they faced. Among the members of the KCA, Jomo Kenyatta rose to prominence after the war.

Kenyatta organized a militant offshoot of the KCA, the Kenya African Union, which had its own offshoots, the most famous of which was the Mau Mau, who by 1948 were talking of killing whites and organizing secret ceremonies involving oaths - a very serious undertaking among the Kikuyu. The Mau Mau grew in numbers over the next couple of years, but, despite some problems with the law, were really not considered a serious threat at this point.

Sir Phillip Mitchell, the British governor of Kenya, certainly did nothing to help counter growing unrest. Mitchell, an old-time 'white man's burden' type of colonial administrator, did not believe in Kenyan independence and was a staunch believer in the basic inferiority of the black African. Taking the lead from Mitchell, the Kenya Police, too, were ill equipped to deal with an insurgency.

In this atmosphere, In 1950, the KCA began recruiting heavily and setting up underground cells. Secret oaths were administered to growing numbers of Mau Mau recruits who flocked to the movement because of the wide basic appeal of the 'land and freedom' propaganda disseminated by the KCA. It should also be borne in mind that these oaths were incredibly binding in Kikuyu society. Another grievance was the lack of educational opportunity. By 1952 the Mau Mau had a quarter of a million members, though the colonial government continued to underestimate the threat. However, the Mau Mau were ready to begin their campaign, and they started to burn the huts of African officials and the fields of white farmers. More ominously, the Mau Mau oath now included the promise to kill on orders. The government continued to follow the ostrich system of counter-insurgency, refusing to admit that an insurgency was beginning.

In September 1952, however, the Mau Mau made it hard to continue to ignore them, as they murdered fourteen Africans, burned fields, and killed cattle. A new governor, Sir Evelyn Baring, had arrived in the fall. The seriousness of the situation was brought home shortly after his arrival, when the Mau Mau murdered a very senior chief. Unlike his predecessor, Baring realized the danger and declared a state of emergency. On 20 October a British battalion arrived from Egypt to give the colonial administration more military force, and the next morning the Kenya Police arrested Jomo Kenyatta and 182 followers. Using the carrot and stick, Baring also promised reforms to the African population.

The Mau Mau, however, were already entering a more aggressive stage. In October 1952 a Mau Mau gang killed a white farmer and two African servants. Through November, incidents against whites and Africans increased. The government remained on the defensive, using the military to reinforce the police. One very positive step towards countering the insurgency was taken at this stage by Baring. He brought in Sir Percy Sillitoe, an intelligence expert, to reorganize the police Special Branch. The security forces also began forming a Kikuyu Home Guard, an important first step in getting the population involved in defending themselves, especially at village level.

One of the greatest problems faced by the police and military was the very size of the threatened area, which included two large forest and mountain areas which offered numerous refuges. Since these areas bordered the African Reserve, the Mau Mau hiding therein had easy access to food, recruits, and intelligence. The primary security element remained the Kenya Police, with predominantly white officers. They were backed up by the Kenya Police Reserve, consisting mostly of white settlers who did not always worry about the niceties of the law and who thus could be a liability in dealing with the population if not carefully controlled. There were also the Tribal Police, composed of Africans and completely separate from the Kenya Police. The Tribal Police drew their authority from the District Officers and operated directly under them.

The military forces deployed suffered from various disadvantages at this time, most importantly their inability to speak Swahili. They, as well as the police, also lacked intelligence and co-ordination.

As it turned out, the arrest of Kenyatta and other leaders left lower-level radicals in charge of the Mau Mau, and thus led to more savage acts. Indirectly, however, this proved a boon to the counter-insurgency forces, as it turned many uncommitted Africans against the Mau Mau. Early in 1953 the Mau Mau resumed their offensive against whites and Africans. Support came from villagers who supplied food and moral support while attending meetings. When possible, supporters worked as servants so that they could gain intelligence and steal medicines and weapons. Terrorist assaults, especially to murder whites, were normally made at night with the help of servants of the victims.

The increase in killings caused the implementation of even more severe laws, including the death penalty for taking Mau Mau oaths. To remove the base of support upon which the Mau Mau relied, curfews were imposed, restrictions were placed on movement, identification passes were required, collective punishments were instituted against villages, counter Mau Mau oaths were administered, severe interrogations were carried out, anti-Mau Mau propaganda was disseminated, and forced labour was used to repair Mau Mau damage. Even harsher were some emergency regulations allowing security forces wide leeway. On the Kikuyu Reserve, for example, 'special areas' were designated in which anyone not immediately responding to a challenge could be shot. Other areas became free-fire areas; anyone entering them could be shot. As distrust of the African population grew among whites, many Africans were forced to relocate to the Reserve, causing substantial discontent which was played upon by the Mau Mau. Meanwhile, the Mau Mau continued to attack native compounds and police stations, the latter to gain weapons.

Mau Mau atrocities, however, undermined their guerrilla war. Not being Communist, and not being familiar with Mao's precepts, the Mau Mau did not understand that terror could be a weapon which would backfire, which it did, causing public opinion within and without Kenya to turn against the Mau Mau. As a result, the British colonial government was able to carry out very harsh actions against the Mau Mau with little criticism. At this point, too, the British began arming the Kikuyu Home Guard and recruiting from the 150,000 Asians living in the country. Another brigade was also brought from the UK, leading to the establishment of a separate military command.

To hamper Mau Mau freedom of movement, a one-mile-wide no-go zone was established between the reserve and the forest. Once the forest was effectively separated from the reserve, military forces needed to move into the forest and take control of it. However, the Mau Mau had been operating in the forest for some time, and blended into their surroundings. As a result, British troops once again had to relearn Chapman's precept that 'the jungle is neutral', or, in this case, the neutrality of the forest. By the fall of 1953 eleven battalions of troops were active in the forests, backed by aircraft which acted as spotters. Over 50,000 personnel were deployed against the Mau Mau by the end of 1953 - 10,000 troops, 15,000 police, 6,000 auxiliary police and 20,000 Home Guard. By that time 3,000 Mau Mau had been killed in the campaign and another 1,000 captured, while

150,000 Kikuyu had been arrested for activities assisting the insurgency, of which 64,000 had been tried. Despite this effort the Mau Mau still managed to kill sixteen Europeans and 600 others during 1953, but their support was beginning to erode. Communication between Mau Mau gangs was becoming increasingly difficult, and leadership was becoming fragmented.

Early in 1954 'Gen China', one of the principal Mau Mau leaders, was captured. He provided a great deal of intelligence about the Mau Mau remaining at large. The campaign in the forests had absorbed so much attention that, in Nairobi, the Mau Mau had been operating as gangsters in the criminal sense as well as in the terrorist sense. Consequently, a giant sweep by 25,000 police and soldiers was launched to clean up the capital, resulting in thousands of Mau Mau sympathizers being taken to detention camps. Not only did the Mau Mau lose their urban base, but crime within Nairobi was cut drastically. To make operations even more difficult for the Mau Mau, an even stricter identity card system was instituted in conjunction with continued resettlement. By the end of 1954 about a million people had been resettled in villages which were easier to protect.

One of the most effective methods of fighting the Mau Mau was the use of pseudo-gangs consisting of Mau Mau turncoats, loyal Africans and white leaders in black face. These pseudo-gangs could approach Mau Mau gangs and either arrest or ambush them. In addition to their successful kills and captures, the pseudos also sewed the seeds of paranoia among the Mau Mau, who now found it difficult to know who to trust.

To make the sterile zone along the edge of the Reserve even more effective, a ditch 18ft wide and 10ft deep and stretching over 50 miles was added. Perhaps most effective, though, were the strict food control measures, which included locking all cattle up after dark and allowing no food crops within three miles of the forests.

The Mau Mau still had to be cleared from the forests, however. Early in 1955 a massive sweep was attempted, but this cumbersome operation actually resulted in very few Mau Mau casualties. A new 'domination' strategy was then instituted, using small units which controlled a small area of forest. In two months in Mount Kenya forest this tactic resulted in 277 Mau Mau casualties, but as it required 100,000lb of air-dropped supplies it proved quite expensive.

The real key to the defeat of the Mau Mau was intelligence, and the formation of Police Special Forces incorporating pseudo-gangs and native irregulars to provide highly effective intelligence and hunter/killer capability. As a result, by October 1956 the Mau Mau threat was virtually over. The move towards independence continued over the next few years, Jomo Kenyatta being freed in 1961 and becoming the first president of Kenya after it became a republic in 1963.

In many ways, the Mau Mau insurgency was unnecessary. If the British colonists and administrators had made more concessions to African tribal customs and more fully understood the tribal philosophy of land ownership, it is quite possible that the Mau Mau would never have found more than a few recruits among chronic malcontents. However, the condescending view taken by most of the colonists towards the African, along with the refusal to acknowledge the Mau Mau threat until it had grown past easy containment, forced the police and military to deal with a full-blown terrorist campaign. In some ways the Mau Mau were their own worst enemies, committing such atrocities that much of the population was appalled by their methods. Intelligence proved critical, as in all counter-insurgency campaigns, and the decision to bring in Sir Percy Sillitoe, the former head of MI5, at quite an early stage, helped prepare the way for future successes. The use of the pseudo-gangs was an important tactic, not just because of its success in Kenya, but because the Selous Scouts who perfected this tactic in the Rhodesian War were influenced by the Kenya Police Reserve pseudo-gangs.

On Cyprus, the British again found themselves facing an insurgency supported by the bulk of the population. Only 40 miles from the Turkish coast, yet with about 80 per cent of its population Greek and 18-20 per cent Turkish, Cyprus found itself under British rule, even though 96 per cent of the Greek population favoured 'enosis', or merging with Greece. Traditional hatreds between Greeks and Turks did not help matters, as both Greece and Turkey supported their populations on the island. Into this volatile situation in 1951 came George Grivas, a Greek Cypriot officer with counter-insurgency experience in the Greek Civil War. Grivas soon became the head of the Cypriot exile group in Greece, where he began planning a campaign to bring about 'enosis'. Experienced in guerrilla warfare, Grivas realised that Cyprus was not well-suited to a traditional guerrilla campaign. Only the mountains in the central part of the island really offered the type of terrain where guerrillas could hide, while good roads made troop movements easy. Moreover, the island could easily be blockaded. As a result, Grivas decided to combine acts of sabotage with passive resistance by the bulk of the population.

For the next three years Grivas attempted to accumulate arms and explosives in Athens and smuggle them to Cyprus. Greece, though sympathetic, would not lend active support. The difficulties Grivas faced in launching an insurgency can be gauged by the fact that, when he finally landed, in late 1954, only seven pistols, 47 rifles and ten machine guns had been smuggled on to the island. Undaunted, Grivas set about training guerrillas, hiding his precious weapons, and organizing sabotage units. These tasks begun, he next selected targets in the island's main cities.

The Ethniki Organosis Kyprion Aginosial (EOKA) began its guerrilla campaign in April 1955, with fewer then 100 active fighters. The active campaign received impetus from the fact that, in 1954, the British had moved their Middle East headquarters to Cyprus, indicating their intent to stay on the island indefinitely and thus increasing opposition among the Greek population. British unwillingness to listen to the desires of the bulk of the population drove Archbishop Makarios, the foremost religious leader on the island, to support Grivas, and British intransigence also caused overt support in Greece. As a result, on 1 April, 1955, EOKA attacked government, police and military installations around the island, taking the British completely by surprise. In the wake of the attacks, thousands of leaflets were distributed announcing the aims of EOKA. The attacks were followed by demonstrations by students, then by more attacks in June to gain additional publicity.

After his opening salvoes, Grivas, along with his hard-core followers, moved to the mountains to form guerrilla bands, with the hope of drawing in the British Army. Simultaneously, EOKA carried out a guerrilla campaign against military targets in the countryside and a terror campaign within the cities. The police and army, meanwhile, got little co-operation from the Greek Cypriot population. Grivas, a student of guerrilla warfare, realized the importance of popular support, and so, with the exception of informers, EOKA treated the population quite well.

It soon become obvious that the police were incapable of dealing with the insurgency. In October 1955, therefore, Field Marshal Sir John Harding, the new governor, was empowered to negotiate with Archbishop Makarios and to use whatever force he deemed necessary to defeat EOKA. In February 1956, however, a security team snatched Makarios on his way to Athens and deported him, giving Grivas even more power by default and turning the population even more against the British. Harding, as a result, was left with his military solution. On the surface this should have been simple, as there were 25,000 military and police personnel to counter 273 hard-core guerrillas backed up by about 750 part-time fighters in the villages. The latter were responsible for ambushes. Grivas could count on additional support from youth and civil organizations. One of the greatest problems facing the security forces at this stage was poor intelligence. In fact, intelligence estimates were that only 5 per cent of the population supported Grivas, a gross underestimate, though one that would have been true in many typical insurgencies.

Operating under a state of emergency, Harding enacted harsh rules governing the population, including collective punishments and curfews. British troops went out of their way to harass the Greek population, alienating them even further. In the spring of 1956 two EOKA terrorists were executed, and Grivas responded by executing two British soldiers. British patrols were having some success in keeping Grivas's guerrillas on the run, but they were still too inflexible to corner and eliminate the guerrillas. An attempt was made to find the guerrillas by using tracker dogs, but EOKA used pepper to distract the animals from their scent. 'Q Patrols' composed of British and Turkish personnel were also used to intimidate the population and gather data from informers, but EOKA's intelligence was too good, owing to the overwhelming support of the population.

British counter-ambushes were among the most successful tactics, according to Grivas, who later wrote in his work *Guerrilla Warfare* that helicopter sweeps and counter-ambushes were the two British tactics which worried him the most. Grivas found Harding an inflexible opponent, while Grivas himself was adept at adjusting tactics to suit a situation. Most of all, however, Harding proved arrogant and continued to underrate Grivas as an opponent. As a result he relied on conventional tactics, always a mistake in an unconventional war. In fact, Harding had so many troops crammed on the island that they presented ubiquitous targets of opportunity. Although British sweeps of the island grew more skilled, there were invariably gaps through which Grivas and his men could slip, aided by local farmers. Greek hostility led the British to use torture and intimidation, too, thus turning the population overwhelmingly against them and engendering even more hostility.

When some British troops were pulled out of Cyprus for the Suez invasion in November 1956, EOKA launched 416 attacks on the island's weakened defences that month. In response, by early 1957 the British had eliminated 60 EOKA fighters, causing Grivas to ask for a ceasefire in exchange for Makarios's release. As the NVA/VC would do in Vietnam, Grivas used ceasefires as rest periods to rebuild his strength. Makarios was released, but he was not allowed to return to Cyprus. Finally realizing that some attempt to address the aspirations of the population would have to be made, the British began offering the possibility of independence for Cyprus rather than enosis with Greece. Nevertheless, Grivas launched a new wave of attacks in late 1957.

In March 1958 Grivas began a new campaign of passive resistance, including a boycott of British goods. In retaliation, the British tightened curfews and fired Greek Cypriots from jobs on British military bases. Both sides were now feeling the economic effects of the conflict, the Cypriots through loss of income, the British through the expense of keeping substantial forces on the island. The British were also receiving bad publicity owing to the large number of Cypriots under detention. The United States, meanwhile, was more concerned with keeping NATO viable, and wanted to remove this bone of contention between three allies - Britain, Greece and Turkey. Pressure was therefore put on the Turks and Greeks, especially, to work out a solution. At this point, too, Archbishop Makarios was ready to negotiate,

Thus, early in 1959, Grivas ordered his forces to stop guerrilla warfare, though he opposed any settlement which did not include enosis. Still, he disbanded EOKA and retired to Greece as a hero. Unsettled issues between the Greek and Turkish population, however, would eventually lead to civil war on the island.

In retrospect, Grivas proved one of the ablest guerrilla commanders of the post-war years, accomplishing a great deal with limited resources, no border to retreat across, and only limited rough terrain from which to operate. In addition to his own ability and flexibility as a commander, Grivas benefited most from the British lack of intelligence and flexibility in countering him. The overwhelming support which Grivas could count on from the population was also an absolutely critical factor in his success. The British would probably not have swayed the Greek population even if they had attempted to win their hearts and minds, but their harsh treatment of the Greeks ensured that even those who might have tried to stay neutral supported Grivas. As in Palestine, this was a counter-insurgency campaign the British would have been hard pressed to win because of their inability to address the political desires of the population.

British problems with insurgencies in Asia had not ended with the defeat of Ch'en Ping in Malaya, though the next campaign would be fought to assist Commonwealth allies rather than as a colonial power. This gave the British a substantial political advantage, as they were helping a local, duly constituted government. At the end of 1961 a plan for the political Federation of Malaya was announced. The new state of Malaysia would comprise Malaya, Singapore, Sarawak, Brunei and North Borneo. The Sultan of Brunei, however, sitting on incredible oil wealth, preferred his country to remain an independent protectorate of Great Britain.

Indonesia, the powerful neighbour of Sarawak, Brunei and North Borneo, was led by Sukarno, who opposed the Federation as neocolonial, though in reality he wanted to create his own empire incorporating these states. In December 1962 an insurgency broke out in Brunei which played into Sukarno's hands. Of Brunei's 85,000 citizens, about half were Malay, a quarter were Chinese and a quarter were Dyak tribesmen. The Sultan was autocratic, though relatively popular with the people. The opposition, the TNKU, had a nationalist army which tried to establish a Confederation of Borneo, which would be linked politically with Indonesia and Communist China. When the Sultan agreed to form a legislature, the People's Party, the TNKU's political arm, won all of the sixteen seats contested, but the Sultan appointed seventeen seats and thus kept control.

As a result, the TNKU resorted to force under Yassin Affendi, the military leader. To conduct the guerrilla campaign, Affendi planned to raise fifteen companies, each of 150 men. However, this rather ambitious force was poorly armed, and from the beginning lacked support, as the political leader of the TNKU, Azahari, left Brunei before operations began. The rebels' objectives were quite well thought out. They planned to seize the Sultan, capture major police stations to gain weapons, and take over the oilfields at Seria. Poor communications kept some companies from striking during the initial revolt, which began on 8 December 1962.

Nevertheless, police stations, the Sultan's palace, the Prime Minister's residence and power stations all came under attack, while the oilfields were occupied and at least one of the police stations at Seria was captured. Fortunately, the insurgents had not occupied the airfield at Brunei City, so two companies of Gurkhas were quickly flown in as reinforcements. The Sultan remained free, having taken refuge at one of the police stations. Once Brunei City was secure and the Sultan's safety assured, the Gurkhas began the 60-mile drive towards Seria. After facing the tough Gurkhas, many of the insurgents quickly surrendered, while reinforcements from the 1/2 Gurkha Rifles and the Queen's Own Highlanders continued to arrive by airlift. At Seria, an assault party from the Queen's Own Highlanders carried out a daring air-landing to recapture the oilfields and free hostages being held there. That still left the town of Limbang in insurgent hands, but a river assault carried out by members of 42 Royal Marine Commando re-took it.

TNKU fighters were now forced to take to the jungle, where they found themselves facing irregulars from the Kelabit tribe raised by Tom Harrison, the curator of the Sarawak Museum, who had commanded Kelabit irregulars in World War Two. Answering the call of Harrison and the Sultan, the Kelabits proved masters of the jungle in harrying the TNKU insurgents.

Indonesia had assisted the Brunei insurgents, but both soon found themselves facing a formidable opponent in Maj Gen Walter Walker, who arrived as Director of Operations on 19 December 1962. A veteran of the Malaya campaign, Walker realized the importance of intelligence and mobility, as well as control of the jungle and winning hearts and minds, in fighting a successful counter-insurgency. He immediately took aggressive action against the TNKU. Throughout early 1963 extensive jungle patrols were used to eliminate as many insurgents as possible. When the Gurkhas captured Yassin Affendi in May, the revolt was for all practical purposes over.

The Brunei counter-insurgency campaign was a relatively fast and easy one. This was due to Walker's firm and intelligent leadership, and also to the facts that the Sultan had not been captured initially and the insurgents had failed to occupy the airfield, allowing rapid reinforcement.

Beginning in 1963, though, Walker faced a new challenge as Sukarno began a campaign to separate Sabah and Sarawak, which surrounded Brunei and bordered Indonesian territory, from the Malaysian Confederation. Gen Abdul Nasution, Indonesia's Defence Minister and an expert in Mao-style guerrilla warfare, was put in charge of the 'insurgency' inside Sarawak and Sabah. The plan called for alternating military and political pressure, with guerrillas able to operate from safe bases inside Indonesia. In West Sarawak the Clandestine Communist Organization (CCO) offered a source of recruitment for guerrillas, but Indonesian 'volunteers' would still make up the bulk of the guerrilla force. The guerrilla campaign began in April 1963, when 30 Indonesian Border Terrorists (IBTs) crossed into Sarawak and attacked a police post. In an attempt to obscure their origins, they left documents indicating that they were TNKU.

Once again Walker acted quickly and decisively, recalling 3 Commando Brigade to Borneo. He also ordered an immediate crackdown on the CCO, seized firearms throughout the country and declared a curfew along the border. In a referendum on confederation in the summer of 1963, an overwhelming majority of the citizens of Sarawak and Sabah voted in favour, showing that Sukarno and his IBTs had little real support. Nevertheless, IBT operations were stepped up and CCOs were brought into Indonesia for training.

To intimidate the population of Sarawak and Sabah, IBT raids led by Indonesian regular troops were stepped up, but on 16 September the State of Malaysia was proclaimed. Thereafter, counter-insurgency operations became a Commonwealth affair. By the fall of 1963 Walker had five infantry battalions as his mobile defence force, plus about a dozen helicopters at any given time for airlift. The security forces still could not anticipate where infiltrations would occur along the 1,000-mile border, but additional surveillance ability was gained when a squadron of 22 Special Air Service (SAS) Regiment and the Gurkha Independent Parachute Brigade were sent in to operate four-man border patrols. The SAS also worked with local tribesmen to train them as irregular sources of intelligence. 'Border Scouts' were formed from the tribesmen. These eventually numbered about 1,000, and were mostly used for intelligence or as trackers/guides for the SAS, Gurkhas and security forces. One disadvantage faced by all of the security forces was the lack of accurate maps of the border area.

The security forces now began to show marked success in dealing with incursions. In one IBT incursion, for example, the infiltrators were pursued by helicopter-borne Gurkhas who killed 33; others died in the jungle while attempting to escape. Not only did this rapid response show the population that security forces were in control, but the brutality the infiltrators displayed in killing villagers turned the border population against the IBTs.

By the end of 1963 Sukarno seemed likely to commit more conventional forces. In December, 35 Indonesian regulars and 138 'volunteers' launched a successful attack against inexperienced members of the Royal Malay Regiment, but a reaction force from the 1/10 Gurkha Rifles hunted down all but six of the raiders. Among those captured were Indonesian Marines, some of that country's most élite troops.

The year 1964 saw world opinion shifting very strongly against Sukarno, especially among Third World countries, which saw him attempting to undermine the emerging state of Malaysia. On 23 January 1964 a ceasefire was announced, but the IBTs used it to infiltrate more men. Then, in March, raids began again in force, by regulars launched from camps just inside Indonesia. Hampered by their inability to cross the border, the security forces had to remain on the defensive. Walker sought permission to enter Indonesia in 'hot pursuit', but was turned down. Through 1964, however, Walker did receive additional Commonwealth forces as reinforcements. Each of the eight Gurkha battalions served a six-month tour. The Gurkhas proved especially adept at operations in the jungle and at ambushes. Many British troops, on the other hand, had to undergo extensive training at the Jungle Warfare School in Malaya before deployment.

To exert even more border control, platoon patrol bases were established every six miles in the areas most likely to face infiltration. Later, larger company 'forts' were built with punji stakes, Claymore mines and other defences. Artillery with interlocking fields of fire was also spread along the border at fire bases, while 105mm howitzers were moved from base to base by helicopters. From these bases aggressive patrols were carried out. Normally each patrol comprised twelve men, in two six-man elements. In turn, each element consisted of two two-man surveillance elements and a two-man communications element. If a large group of infiltrators was spotted, one of the two-man units followed them until they could be fixed and annihilated.

During the jungle fighting, the L 1A1 rifle was found to be too heavy and too unwieldy. As a result the Armalite rifle (similar to the US M-16) was adopted for jungle use. Since Indonesian special forces were already using rifles from the Armalite company, this rifle, made famous in Vietnam, saw action on both sides in Borneo. Other needs were lighter radios and lighter patrol rations more suited to the jungle environment. These same requirements were faced by US forces in Vietnam.

On 17 August 1964 over 100 raiders, primarily Indonesian élite troops, launched an incursion into Jahore on the Malayan mainland, but they were quickly rounded up. A drop by 200 Indonesian paratroopers also proved abortive, as members of the 1/10 Gurkhas and 1st Royal New Zealand Regiment soon mopped them up. These attacks resulted in the security forces finally receiving approval to conduct operations across the Indonesian border to a distance of 5,000yd. SAS units had already been penetrating the border on surveillance operations, but the new policy permitted more aggressive operations. For example, the SAS began to set ambushes and booby traps along infiltration routes on both sides of the border. The US Claymore mine proved a devastating weapon on both types of operation. Infantry attacks, code-named 'Claret' operations, were also launched to prevent Indonesian cross-border operations, and were highly successful.

With the security of their cross-border bases eliminated, Indonesian troops and IBTs began to suffer heavier and heavier casualties. Sukarno's credibility also suffered, as he had publicly vowed to crush Malaysia by 1 January 1965. Consequently he could not very well complain to the UN or the press about the incursions which were decimating his troops. By 1965, British Intelligence estimated that there were 24,000 Chinese Communists and 22,000 Indonesian troops on the Indonesian side of the border, as well as 2,000 CCO terrorists on the Malaysian side. Facing these forces were about 10,000 Commonwealth troops. Ably led by Gen Walker, however, these troops were defeating more than four times their numbers. In March 1965 Walker was replaced by Maj Gen George Lea, another veteran of Malaya, where he had commanded the Special Air Service.

Along the border, defences had developed more depth, now comprising three layers to warn and allow response. Artillery and mortars could now cover large portions of the border, interdicting all likely infiltration routes. Most of all, however, the 'Claret' operations and ambushes had removed the initiative from the Indonesians, and by early 1966 the campaign had really been won. In late 1965 Sukarno had virtually been removed from power by Gen Suharto after an attempted Communist coup. Sukarno was officially removed from power in August 1966.

The Borneo campaign offers an example of a very efficient and effective counter-insurgency operation, even though the Indonesians had the advantages of manpower and equipment resources, as well as sanctuaries across the border. Once Indonesia had been driven back from the border, the campaign was well on its way to being won. Also, the fact that the security forces were for the most part facing external invasions rather than an internal insurgency meant that they received broad support from the population. Both the British and the Malaysian government were for the most part popular with the population of Sarawak and Sabah. The tribesmen along the border especially hated the Indonesians and therefore gave active support against them. The Indonesians suffered from poor logistical support and also from the misconception that they would find large-scale assistance inside Sarawak. World opinion, too, was against Indonesia. The British, in this case, were the good guys helping a newly formed country fight for its independence. Once again the availability of superb professional soldiers such as the Royal Marines, the Gurkhas and the Special Air Service also played an important role.

The support of the Royal Navy and Royal Air Force should not be underrated either, as they helped to prevent water-borne infiltration, countered the Indonesian Air Force and flew surveillance and supply missions. The use of helicopters for quick reaction proved extremely important, just as it would in Vietnam. Another important factor was the previous experience of Walker and Lea in fighting counter-insurgency wars. They had already learned from others' mistakes, and did not have to make them again. Nor should the availability of Singapore as a massive logistical support centre be forgotten. Finally, as with so many campaigns, the fact that Commonwealth morale was high and Indonesian morale was low was a telling factor. As mentioned earlier, the Commonwealth forces were the 'good guys' in this case, and that made fighting the Indonesians, the IBTs and the CCOs much easier. Popular support was on the side of the security forces, and that is a huge plus in any counter-insurgency campaign.

While dealing with insurgencies in Cyprus and Borneo, the British also found themselves facing another insurgency in Aden; one that bore many similarities to the situation on Cyprus. In 1958 South Yemen consisted of twenty small states, seventeen in western Aden and three in eastern Aden, as well as the crown colony of Aden. Only Aden was actually British territory, though the rest had treaties with Britain. In February 1959 six of the territories formed the Federation of South Arabia (FSA), to be joined by the end of 1963 by ten more of the small states, plus Aden. Only the three members of the Eastern Aden Protectorate and one from the Western Aden Protectorate did not join. In this atmosphere, Egyptian and Yemeni agents infiltrated into Aden from across the border with Yemen. As a port at the entrance to the Red Sea, Aden was important to British strategic interests. Consequently, both Egypt and the Soviet Union were interested in it.

The original intent was that Britain would have a continued presence after independence, but Arab nationalism and Yemen's support of the nationalists began to change these plans. The two primary nationalist groups were the National Liberation Front (NLF) and the Federation for the Liberation of Occupied South Yemen (FLOSY). The NLF was pro-Egyptian and was the primary anti-British force. In any case, the British planned for the independence of the FSA by 1968.

The nationalists wanted to wrest control as soon as possible, however. Therefore, they first set out to discredit the FSA and intimidate the locals into co-operation. The nationalists also wanted to force the British withdrawal, which had now been brought forward to 1966 or 1967, when the FSA would achieve independence. The British intended to pull out in November 1967, leaving the population at the mercy of the NLF and FLOSY. It was therefore hardly surprising that most of the population reached an accommodation with the nationalists and gave the British little support.

Nationalist tactics included sniping, assassination, arson, sabotage and bombings. Attacks on isolated police stations and ambushes of patrols, standard guerrilla tactics, were also widely employed. Stand-off attacks against targets such as the airport were carried out using bazookas and mortars. Grenades were used in attacks on British troops. As the campaign progressed, insurgent bomb makers became more and more sophisticated until they were employing a wide array of improvised explosive devices (IEDs), including letter bombs, booby traps and electronically detonated bombs. As on Cyprus, attacks were alternated with civil demonstrations, which were sometimes used as a ruse to lure security forces into an ambush, but mostly for publicity and propaganda.

One of the biggest advantages the nationalists had was the nearby border with Yemen, which allowed access to a sanctuary and source of weapons and supplies. The large open spaces also allowed the guerrillas freedom of movement outside the urban areas. Especially important were the Radfan mountains, a perfect fastness for guerrillas and a source of tough recruits for guerrilla bands. In general, insurgents controlled most rural areas, relying on mined roads and snipers to harass any British patrols that ventured nearby. When security forces were deployed into the countryside in substantial numbers, the nationalists used the tactic of hitting them just before sundown to allow themselves a retreat in darkness. With the exception of the SAS, most British troops failed to become sufficiently acclimatized to the desert environment to operate effectively.

The security forces also faced a population which, either actively or through coercion, tacitly supported the nationalists. As a result, the gathering of intelligence was very difficult, particularly as there was no uniform command and, until 1965, ten different intelligence agencies were operating in Aden with little co-operation. Furthermore, the various small sheikdoms and states were often so wrapped up in their own rivalries that they had little time to co-operate with British security forces. A director of intelligence was eventually appointed, but the police special branch never proved very effective at infiltrating nationalist groups.

Most intelligence was gathered primarily by British troops manning checkpoints, patrolling, or in observation posts. The SAS was highly effective at operating in small patrols and gathering information. Cordon and search operations were used with varying degrees of success, but never made a real dent in the nationalist groups.

In the countryside, the tribesmen's lifelong familiarity with the area made them extremely difficult opponents, as they could hit and then fade away. In any case, with only two brigades available the British were spread too thinly to secure large parts of the country. Within the cities SAS 'Keeni Meeni' undercover patrols were successful in countering assassins from the nationalist groups. Using personnel dressed as Arabs, the SAS would often engage and kill terrorists just as they were preparing to carry out an assassination or bombing. The work of the SAS was one of the brightest spots in the operations of 'Radforce' in Aden.

Despite the wide experience in counter-insurgency gained by the British during the post World War two years, many mistakes were repeated in Aden. One of the greatest was a failure to take the insurgency seriously and, thus, a failure to act rapidly. In addition, far too few men were committed to enable the 100,000 square miles of the Aden Protectorate to be secured. SAS reconnaissance and patrol operations were very effective, but their success in carrying out ambushes or calling in air or artillery strikes were too few to turn the tide. The combination of the nearby Yemeni border and the fire of Arab nationalism made winning the hearts and minds of the population an impossible task, and prevented the British from carrying out a truly effective counter-insurgency campaign.

The creation of the new state of South Yemen (also known as the People's Democratic Republic of Yemen – PDRY), from Aden and the former Aden Protectorate, foreshadowed new problems to the east in Oman. Sultan Said had purposely kept Oman as backward as possible to avoid 'corruption', even to the extent of not allowing those who left for an education to return to the country. Said was also very tight with revenues, refusing to make expenditures on medical or educational facilities. Despite his attempt to keep the twentieth century out of Oman, however, some of those who had left did sneak back into the country. By 1962 popular dissatisfaction had resulted in an embryo insurgency, and by 1965 this had become the Dhofar Liberation Front (DLF). Dhofar, the Omani province bordering on South Yemen, was ripe for revolution and offered a safe haven for guerrillas just across the border.

Guerrillas were trained in the PDRY and then infiltrated back into Dhofar. The 'liberation' movement soon grew more ambitious, too, changing its name to the People's Front for the Liberation of the Arabian Gulf (PFLOAG). This movement did not do a really good job of winning the population of Dhofar over, however, as the insurgents often resorted to torture to convince Dhofaris, especially those living on the rugged Jebel Akhdar, to deny Allah. On the positive side, PFLOAG could rely on strong tribal ties among the Jebelis for a certain amount of support.

Over the next few years the Sultan's Armed Forces (SAF) virtually ceded the Jebel and much of Dhofar to the insurgents, but in July 1970 Said's son, Qaboos, with British assistance, deposed his father. Qaboos, a Sandhurst graduate, was far more progressive than his father. He immediately instituted plans for improved medical and educational facilities and announced an amnesty for those who had been taking part in the insurgency. At least 200 accepted the amnesty, many becoming irregular counter-guerrilla fighters in the Firqats which would be formed with SAS assistance. Owing to Oman's oil wealth, Qaboos had sufficient money to spend on the armed forces.

Qaboos also realized that educational and agricultural reforms were necessary to win back the population of the Jebel, but until the area was cleared of insurgents the civic action teams could not move in. Therefore the plan formulated between the Sultan, his British contract officers and his advisors was to regain control of Dhofar province from east to west, while interdicting enemy supply lines as far to the west as possible. As a prelude to the other operations it was necessary to establish permanent positions on the Jebel. The first interdiction line established was the Leopard Line, comprising barbed wire, mines and patrols. Although insurgents still breached the line occasionally, it did stop the free passage of camel trains, and thus prevented the easy resupply of insurgents. The establishment of this line also pushed the insurgents into the July 1972 attack on Marbat, in which ten SAS men and a few Omanis held off 200 insurgents, inflicting heavy casualties in the process.

For the next two years, operations in Dhofar remained primarily reactive, though the SAS made good progress in forming irregular tribal units, the Firqats. The insurgents apparently lost confidence, because they changed their name again, this time to the Popular Front for the Liberation of Oman (PFLO). PFLO members were tough, and were used to the conditions on the Jebel, operating well on little water and food. They also proved quite fierce in small unit actions, artillery and air power often being needed to defeat them. Other PFLO strengths were their ability to set ambushes and their willingness to carry mortars or rockets to good positions for attacks on SAF installations. Their weapons were standard Communist Bloc guerrilla arms, particularly the AK-47 family of weapons. The arms flow had been dammed to some extent in 1972, when the Shah of Iran persuaded the Chinese to cut back aid to the PFLO, but the Soviet Union, Libya and Cuba continued to send assistance. The Sultan's forces had continued to score some successes, too. In 1972 and 1974, for example, the PFLO had tried to move into Northern Oman, but the Oman Intelligence Service had identified and eliminated the agents.

Throughout the early 1970s the PFLO numbered about 2,000 full-time guerrillas and 4,000 part-time militia. Radio Aden continued to blast propaganda across the entire Jebel in support of PFLO. One of the few modern conveniences to be found in profusion on the Jebel was the transistor radio, which the insurgents made good use of.

The forces facing the insurgents were diverse. The Sultan's Armed Forces had British contract officers, and many of the best enlisted troops were Baluchis from Pakistan. At various times, too, assistance was lent by Jordanian Special Forces and members of the Iranian Army. As in previous insurgencies, the SAS, capable of working in small units and staying afield for long periods, and skilled at working with indigenous populations, proved invaluable. One of the primary SAS tasks was organizing the Firqats, the irregular counter-insurgency force which often included many former guerrillas. Royal Engineers and medical personnel worked closely with the SAS on civic action programmes to win the hearts and minds of the Jebelis.

The Leopard Line was strengthened into the more effective Hornbeam Line, and quite effectively stopped rebel supply movement. By the fall of 1974 the PFLO were primarily concentrated into three areas. The first of these to be cleared was south of Tawi Atair, to clear the road to Marbat. Owing to the tribal nature of those living on the Jebel, the Firqats proved most effective operating in their own tribal areas, where they could count on support and on denying support for the insurgents. As the Firqats and SAF gained control of an area, civil action teams would come in to drill wells and set up schools, mosques and medical facilities. The system developed into a quite effective counter-guerrilla strategy. The SAF would secure an area, then the Firqats would move in to defend it. Military engineers would build a road, allowing the well drilling team to arrive. Once the well was drilled, civilians would be drawn to the area for security and water, thus denying them to the enemy.

Although they disliked the idea of killing the animals, the Sultan's Air Force would hit camel supply trains on the Jebel, denying the enemy his primary form of transport. The PFLO was still very active, however, especially in laying mines and firing rockets against SAF positions. As the installation of the Firqats in tribal areas became widespread in October 1975, guerrilla surrenders increased, bringing in more intelligence about the enemy, including the fact that enemy morale was very low through lack of food and supplies. On 26 October the only major crossing of the Hornbeam Line occurred when about 80 guerrillas slipped across carrying mines and rockets.

As control of the Jebel was regained, roads which had been closed for years were reopened, allowing the Civil Aid Department to continue to expand its operations. In addition to well drilling, education and medical assistance, programmes to encourage the Jebelis to increase beef cattle production and plans for the government to buy the cattle to distribute meat more effectively were implemented. Each programme showing that the Sultan and the government cared about the welfare of those in Dhofar Province eroded guerrilla credibility.

As the strategy of retaking the province from east to west continued, the Iranians established another line to the west of the Hornbeam Line. Although their aggressiveness left something to be desired, they eventually recaptured areas which had been under rebel control since 1969. Operations in 1975 had also seized ground dominating the enemy's east-west supply lines, while other sweeps located and captured stockpiles of rockets and mortar bombs, munitions very hard to replace with supply lines so heavily interdicted. As the SAF took the initiative, the PFLO proved very slow in their command response. The SAF also had the advantage of airpower and armoured cars, which allowed them to use rapid movement to disorient the enemy. One tactic which proved highly effective was to assign a single bulldozer to a group of armoured cars. The bulldozer would move ahead of the armoured cars, creating a track as it went. As is usually the case with irregular units, the Firqats proved most effective as scouts for these operations or for infantry operations by the SAF. By February 1976, with static positions dominating the Jebel secured, the SAF could launch even more of these mobile operations to harry the remaining enemy and secure more ground. Harrying the enemy also kept them on the run, allowing them little time for operations against the SAF or the population.

Rocket and mortar attacks had become the principal PFLO offensive tactic, but helicopter assaults were now used quite effectively to clear rocket-firing sites once they were spotted. Air strikes were also effective against stand-off attacks. The PFLO declared 9 June the 'Anniversary of the Revolution', and as a result the first half of the month saw an increase in stand-off attacks.Otherwise, however, the SAF was now so much in control that the enemy was rarely encountered. Even with the massive civic action programme, though, many civilians still sympathized with the rebels, primarily because of tribal loyalties.

During the later part of 1975 the SAS continued to encourage defections, and on 21 October Operation Hadaf was launched to establish a new security line which would cut off all enemy supply. This operation was successful within a few days, thus completely isolating the PFLO from their supply source in the PDRY. Artillery firing from across the border still presented a problem, however, so airstrikes across the border were authorized to silence the guns.

The mopping up of any unsecured areas continued through the first months of 1976, but after 4 December 1975 Dhofar had been declared secure for civil development. Over the next few months most of the remaining guerrillas surrendered, and on 30 April 1976 the last rounds were fired from inside the PDRY.

The SAS continued to provide valuable training and assistance to the Firqats as they took over much of the responsibility for security on the Jebel. The SAS's popularity with the population was also drawn upon as they acted as the liaison between Jebelis and the SAF. To help prevent a future insurgency, the Sultan instituted substantial rewards for turning in weapons during this period, thus eliminating stockpiles which might have caused a problem in the future.

The counter-insurgency campaign in Dhofar had proved effective through a combination of sound strategy on the part of the security forces and some very bad tactics on the part of the enemy. Of extreme importance was the large cushion of money available to the Sultan through Oman's oil wealth. This allowed him to build up the armed forces as needed and to undertake massive civil action programmes. Replacing Sultan Said with his son Qaboos had, of course, been a necessary first step to carrying out other reforms. The civil action campaign was highly effective, and focused on the needs of the Jebelis. The strategy of retaking the Jebel east to west, thereby eliminating enemy supply lines while securing areas for civil development, was especially well suited to the terrain of Dhofar. The sound use of air power, particularly helicopters, and good intelligence also proved major assets.

Perhaps the greatest enemy mistake was to try to force the Dhofaris to abandon Islam for Communism. Had the guerrillas appealed to nationalism or tribalism alone, they would have kept the support of the population much more fully. Rather than building upon the strong tribalism, the guerrillas attempted to break it down, substituting Communism. This proved a grave mistake, though another point in favour of the counter-insurgency effort was that the SAS used the tribalism of the Jebelis in forming the Firqats. The insurgents' poor command and control structure and reliance on the single supply line from the PDRY also proved fatal for the guerrillas.

Perhaps the most important lesson to be learned from the French and British experience in countering insurgencies in colonies or protectorates was that, the more the security forces pursued the political and domestic goals of the population, the more likely the counter-insurgency was to succeed. Insurgencies need support from the population, and, to be successful, counter-insurgencies must remove that support.

CHAPTER III

Vietnam

The Geneva Accords ending the French Indochina War established a Demilitarized Zone at the 17th Parallel, a division which overjoyed Ho Chi Minh and his followers, as they gained a much larger portion of the country than they had hoped for. The Viet Minh, however, expected soon to gain control of the entire country through popular elections. In 1955 Ngo Dinh Diem became the president of South Vietnam, but in 1956 he refused to honour the agreement to hold elections throughout Vietnam because those in the north would not have a free vote. Over the next three years the Viet Minh infiltrated more cadre into the south to reinforce the thousands who had remained when the country had been divided. By 1959 the Communists felt strong enough in the south to begin a new guerrilla war.

Physical conditions in the south were well suited to a guerrilla army. The jungle and mountains which made up much of the interior offered a secure base area, while in the far south of the country the MeKong Delta offered another type of terrain suitable for hiding and supplying guerrillas. Supply, in fact, would never be completely interdicted owing to the long border with Laos and Cambodia to the west. To counter the experienced Viet Cong, as the Viet Minh were now called in the south, the Army of the Republic of Vietnam (ARVN) fielded conventional forces with little counter-insurgency training. The task of local defence fell mostly on local regional militia forces. The Viet Cong, on the other hand, experienced from the long war against the French, were organized into Main Force full-time guerrillas supported by part-time village fighters. By 1959, in the south, the Viet Cong could count on 5,000 regulars backed by 100,000 supporters within the population. This would grow by 1964 to 40,000 active personnel. So quickly did Viet Cong strength expand during the 1960s that, at times, they could absorb 50 to 100 per cent casualties within a year and still maintain their strength or even grow.

Had the insurgency continued unchecked at the pace of the early 1960s, it is highly probable that South Vietnam would have been absorbed by the north by 1965. The United States began its massive commitment, however, and thus staved off the fall for another decade. As early as 1957, advisers from the US Army Special Forces had been sent to South Vietnam to train that country's Rangers, and in 1960 more than 100 'Green Berets' had been sent to Laos to train Muong tribesmen to fight as irregulars against the Communists.

More conventional forces arrived in Southeast Asia in 1961, when President Kennedy ordered a US Marine brigade to Thailand. The combination of this unit and the Special Forces advisers in Laos led to complaints which resulted in the 'demilitarization of Laos', though the Communists really did not comply. Although Communist successes were growing in Vietnam, the institution of the 'Strategic Hamlet' programme in the central highlands began to turn the tide in favour of the South Vietnamese government. As part of this programme, US Special Forces raised and trained local militias, the Civilian Irregular Defence Groups (CIDGs), from local Montagnard tribesmen. To back up the CIDGs, full-time strike forces were formed to act as reaction teams for villages under attack. So successful was the programme that, by August 1962, 200 villages were already protected. Throughout 1963 and 1964 more and more villages came under the programme, which was also expanded to include special long-range patrols comprising indigenous personnel and Vietnamese and US Special Forces. In addition, camps were established along the Cambodian and Laotian borders to interdict infiltrators.

Diem and representatives of the US had been growing apart, and the rift was made even wider by the problems with the Buddhists during 1963. Eventually the US let it be known that, if there were a coup, it would not cause the US to remove support for the government of South Vietnam. After that, Diem's days were numbered, and he was finally removed in a coup by Gen Duon Van Minh. Despite new leadership, the ARVN continued to lose ground in 1964, and in August the Tonkin Gulf incident, in which North Vietnamese gunboats supposedly attacked US warships, offered the US a reason for expanding its involvement in the war if it chose to do so. By October 1964, at least partly in response to the successes of the CIDG programme, North Vietnamese Army (NVA) units were being infiltrated into South Vietnam, forcing the US to make a choice. It would either have to pull out the 20,000 troops already in South Vietnam as advisors, or it would have to expand its commitment to shore up the government of the Republic of Vietnam.

The ARVN had been growing to counter the enhanced threat as well. By 1963 it consisted of 192,000 troops divided into four corps, nine divisions, one airborne brigade, one special forces group, three separate regiments, eighty-six ranger companies and nineteen separate battalions. The expansion would continue, especially in the 'Ruff Puffs' (the Regional and Popular Forces), the light infantry militia units charged with countering much of the Viet Cong threat.

US commitment to the counter-insurgency war was signalled in February 1965 by a combined air raid against North Vietnam by US and South Vietnamese pilots, and by the deployment of a US Marine brigade to Da Nang in March. This initial deployment of conventional troops would grow until it reached almost 550,000 in 1968.

The Communist strategy was highly workable, and showed Ho's and Giap's genius at guerrilla warfare. While using conventional guerrilla warfare tactics in the Mao mode, the North Vietnamese leadership showed an astute grasp of what it would take strategically to win. Basing their strategy on three main points - time, space and cost - they were willing to take a decade or more to achieve their ends, while the US historically has been an impatient nation. By drawing out the war, the Communists could erode their enemies' will to win, while making the cost in men, supplies and cash too high. It was not really necessary to control large portions of South Vietnam, only to threaten the government throughout the country, thus requiring large numbers to be tied down in the defensive role. When the US commitment began to grow in 1965, Ho Chi Minh had to decide whether to pull back or to pursue the war. His choice to pay the price and draw out the war was based on a clear perception of his followers' will to win.

It should also be borne in mind that, although the North Vietnamese and the Viet Cong used negotiations as a tactic to gain time, a negotiated settlement was not desirable from their point of view. By periodically engaging in negotiations, however, the Communists kept the US off balance and avoided a situation in which the Americans decided to pursue a true victory.

The Communists saw four principal routes to victory: 1. failure of US will to win; 2. failure of South Vietnamese will to win; 3. failure to develop an effective counter-insurgency strategy; 4. failure of South Vietnam to build a stable popular government. The North Vietnamese would eventually win by a combination of the first, second and fourth of these routes. Though the counter-insurgency strategy was at times flawed, it did prove effective at wiping out the guerrilla threat, as the war was won by a conventional invasion from the North.

The South Vietnamese faced many problems in pursuing the war, not the least of which was widespread corruption in the government. Perhaps the greatest problem, however, was the diverse nature of the population in the south, which led to splits between the Catholics and Buddhists, between the central government and the religious sects such as the Hoa Hao and Cao Bai, and between the Montagnards and other minorities such as the Nungs and the Vietnamese. To some extent, too, there was a class split, with many wealthy Vietnamese sending their sons to Paris or elsewhere to avoid military service. This would be mirrored in the US as wealthy families helped their sons avoid the draft in large numbers.

Once the US became committed to preventing the spread of Communism in Southeast Asia, US prestige rode heavily on the war and the country's involvement continued to grow. Unfortunately, though the involvement grew, the commitment to win did not, and the US continued to follow a defensive strategy. While the one-year tour of duty for US Army personnel (thirteen months for Marines) rotated conscripts home quickly, it prevented the troops from ever really developing a deep reserve of experience in fighting a counter-insurgency war. As someone said, the US armed forces did not develop eight years of counter-insurgency experience in Vietnam; they developed one year's experience eight times. Of course, the constant need to rotate new troops in and out of Vietnam required an increasing number of conscripts, which led to growing disillusionment with the war in the US. The US attempt to use overwhelming firepower did not really prove effective in a counter-insurgency war, either. Theoretically, this was part of a US strategy of attrition, a strategy which proved ineffective once it became apparent that the Communists were much more willing to suffer casualties than was the US.

Through 1965 the US Army build-up brought in the 173rd Airborne Brigade, 101st Airborne Division and 1st Cavalry Division (Airmobile). These were élite light infantry units capable of moving quickly, but they were trained for conventional warfare. As they gained experience, however, each would become a skilled quick-reaction force, but the key word is 'reaction', as the US remained in a reactive mode. The US Marine Corps continued to build up too, particularly in the northern provinces, reaching a strength of almost 40,000 troops by the end of 1965.

To support the infantry effort, the US Air Force (USAF) began hitting the Ho Chi Minh Trail with B-52 raids in 1965, as the importance of the trail was finally recognized. Surface-to-air missile (SAM) sites in North Vietnam were also hit. Perhaps most effectively in the counter-insurgency role, the AC-47 gunship, 'Puff, the Magic Dragon', began flying in 1965. The following year saw B-52 strikes into North Vietnam beginning in April, and in July an air offensive against the North Vietnamese rail network began, in an attempt to impede the flow of supplies south. The Ho Chi Minh Trail was hit more frequently, too. As well as the USAF effort, the US Navy had five carriers operating in the South China Sea.

As the US Army build-up began, the initial plan was that US Army units would deal with NVA units entering South Vietnam, while the ARVNs would deal with the VC. This plan did not last long, however, as by 1966 division-sized sweep operations involving US and ARVN forces were taking place. The successful Special Forces effort to train local defence forces and establish protected hamlets, a sound basic counter-insurgency strategy, now took second place to providing intelligence for US conventional forces. As a result, Special Forces patrol and reconnaissance units, such as the MIKE Forces, took precedence. Special reconnaissance units such as Projects Delta, Sigma and Omega, which carried out combat reconnaissance patrols inside Vietnam, and the Military Assistance Command Vietnam/Studies and Observations Group (MACV/SOG), which performed reconnaissance patrols outside Vietnam, also assumed increasing importance. One of the more effective techniques employed by these units was the use of pseudo-guerrillas known as 'roadrunners', though it was never as widely used as it would be later, in Rhodesia.

ARVN strength was forced to grow along with the increasing American presence, reaching 277,363 regulars by the end of 1966, while Ruff Puff strength rose to about 320,000.

As the war progressed, it quickly became obvious that the North Vietnamese understood American politics far better than American generals did. Guerrilla warfare is political, and military and counter-guerrilla warfare must be carried out in the same dimensions, yet the US consistently failed to address the political shortcomings in South Vietnam. The North Vietnamese and the Viet Cong frequently timed important operations to coincide with presidential election years or periods during a change of power. In contrast, even though massive air strikes against North Vietnamese economic and logistical targets would have severely hampered their ability to pursue the war, President Johnson kept halting the air offensive as the 1968 elections approached.

Even more obviously, the Tet Offensive was timed to catch the South Vietnamese unprepared and to accomplish multiple goals. Although the offensive, which began on 30 January 1968, was really a massive defeat for the Viet Cong, the Communists turned it into a massive publicity victory. At the same time, the North Vietnamese made sure that the Viet Cong's power was broken, so that there would be no force to oppose them when they did conquer the south, as they were sure they would eventually do. It was the sight of a few VC infiltrators inside the US Embassy compound on American television that turned this massive defeat into victory for the Communist cause. It should be remembered, too, that there really was not a rising in the south in support of this Viet Cong offensive, despite expectations of massive support.

The 'living room war' played an important part in the erosion of US will to pursue the Vietnam War. As film of US troops in combat was shown each evening on the news, the war became much more personal and distasteful to large segments of the American public. The class division between those whose sons served in Vietnam (normally the sons of lower and lower middle class families) and those who sent their sons to graduate school or found other ways to help them avoid service, also became more marked in the years after the Tet Offensive. The actress Jane Fonda, still hated by Vietnam veterans two decades later, became the symbol of the anti-war movement, using her public persona to preach against the war, even to the extent of travelling to North Vietnam. Many of those who supported the war believed she should have been tried for aiding and abetting the enemy. Others supported her for taking a public stand against the war. The point was that the US became more divided over the war as time passed. Those who opposed it certainly operated to a double standard. United States prisoners of war were viciously tortured by the North Vietnamese, yet any harsh interrogation by US troops was labelled a war crime. The My Lai massacre and the subsequent trial was a lasting black mark against the US Army, yet at Hue, during the Tet Offensive, the Communists executed over 5,000 people.

Tactically, the US continued to rely too heavily on firepower and technology, and not enough on light, deep penetration patrols, though the long-range reconnaissance patrols (LRRPs) did prove effective at gathering tactical intelligence for divisional commanders. The use of firebases grew between 1965 and 1968, allowing US forces to receive artillery support almost anywhere within South Vietnam. Since US artillery was for the most part unopposed, this allowed heavy ordnance to be called down upon any VC/NVA units encountered. One firebase, the Marine base at Khe Sanh, became a symbol during the months following the Tet Offensive when it was besieged by NVA forces in I Corps. There is still much argument as to whether Khe Sanh tied down too many US forces or too many NVA forces. In either case, the US was obsessed with it not becoming another Dien Bien Phu, while it does not seem to have been a critical target to the NVA.

One thing that helped the US maintain its hold on Khe Sanh was the use of sophisticated electronic sensors around the base, which warned of NVA build-ups and infiltration. Such sensors were also seeded along the Ho Chi Minh Trail as part of Operation 'Igloo White', a massive surveillance effort which enabled large quantities of Communist supplies and trucks to be destroyed by US aircraft. There was even consideration given to establishing a high-tech line to inhibit infiltration along South Vietnam's borders, but the cost would have been prohibitive - the war was already costing thirty billion dollars per annum - and the length of the borders would have meant that it would have been quite vulnerable.

The US found the helicopter an extremely valuable tool in allowing rapid reaction, but the dependence upon it often meant that in bad flying weather, or in other conditions inhibiting its use, US operations were cancelled or endangered. Still, the 1st Air Cavalry Division was moved around the country as needed. In 1968, for example, the division acted as a deterrent to infiltration from Cambodia in III Corps. The 101st Airborne Division was also converted to an airmobile unit during 1968.

While the US was relying on high-tech surveillance, heavy air power and helicopters, the Communists used guerrilla tactics which had proved effective for two decades. Booby traps and rocket or mortar attacks allowed them to inflict casualties from a distance, while small, highly mobile infantry units moved about the countryside, engaging in combat only when they found it advantageous. These tactics proved so effective that, after the Tet Offensive, Gen Westmoreland asked for 200,000 more US troops. This request, which would have brought the US troop commitment to the 750,000 mark, would have required activating reserve units or increasing the draft even more, at a time when conscription was already a political hot potato. In fact, throughout the war, the unwillingness of American presidents to call up reserve forces was based on reluctance to send the message to the Soviet Union that US resources were stretched, even if they were, rather than upon military needs. By 1968, however, the US strategic reserve at one point consisted of only two brigades of the 82nd Airborne Division.

One programme which proved highly effective began in July 1968. Eventually known as the Phoenix Programme, this intelligence effort was primarily aimed at identifying and eliminating the 65,000-80,000 members of the Viet Cong infrastructure. One indication of the effectiveness of the Phoenix Programme was the vilification it received in the liberal press in the US and other countries. In some cases the Phoenix Programme did use assassination, but in far more cases members of the VC were arrested or turned. The 'teeth' of the Phoenix were provided by the Provincial Reconnaissance Units (PRUs) and the National Police Field Force, which actively hunted down the VC once they were identified. Members of the PRUs often proved especially effective, since many were former Viet Cong.

Cross-border operations for reconnaissance and raids by AC-47 and AC-130 gunships against the Ho Chi Minh Trail slowed the flow of supplies to the Viet Cong and later to the NVA, but many astute students of the Vietnam War have speculated about the effect had the US occupied Laos in force in 1965, blocking the Ho Chi Minh Trail. Certainly the outcome could not have been any worse. In 1968 alone, for example, 100,000 NVA regulars came down the Ho Chi Minh Trail. Had they been deprived of this relatively safe approach route, substantial casualties could have been inflicted on them before they reached their intended areas of operation. The 1970 invasion of Cambodia by US and Vietnamese troops actually set back the planned invasion of the South by at least a year, illustrating the advantage of denying the Communists a safe haven just outside South Vietnam's borders. The US, of course, was afraid of spreading the war and endangering the governments of Laos and Cambodia, yet both fell to the Communists anyway. There is one final, interesting point in relation to the Ho Chi Minh Trail. In 1968, owing to US airstrikes and surveillance, it took troops or supplies a month to make the journey down the Trail. By 1973, during the period of 'Peace with Honour' after the US pull-out (or sell-out, as some viewed it), it took just a matter of days to zip down the Trail.

As US troop strength began to decline after 1968, opposition to the war grew even more at home, culminating in massive protests against the invasions of Cambodia and Laos, and the Kent State massacre of students. The 'Green Beret Murder Case' and the even more publicized trial of Lt Calley for the My Lai massacre polarized the country even further. Anxious to get out politically unscathed, President Nixon now pushed for his programme of Vietnamization. Unfortunately the ARVNs, though they were improving, had been relying heavily on the Americans for years. Being thrust rapidly into the principal combat role, therefore, some ARVN units did very well, notably the 1st Division, the Rangers and the airborne troops. Others did not perform so well. After the Tet Offensive, too, the ARVN had been re-equipped with more modern weapons including the M-16 rifle.

US troops, realizing that a rapid withdrawal was under way, could not see any reason to get themselves killed, and developed a live-and-let-live attitude towards the enemy. For the most part, too, the enemy tried not to goad the US into massive reaction. The enemy now was primarily the NVA, the Viet Cong having been virtually destroyed by a combination of the Tet Offensive and the Phoenix Programme. To give some idea of the rapid pull-out of US combat troops, their strength in 1970 was 415,000, in 1971 it was 239,000, and in 1972 it stood at 47,000.

With US troop strength so low, at Easter 1972 the NVA launched a massive offensive against the south which eventually involved four-

teen divisions. This offensive was, in fact, an indication of how effectively the counter-insurgency war had been fought, since there was
now virtually no VC activity to hamper the pacification programme in
the south. The combination of more effective ARVN resistance than
expected, especially under the leadership of Gen Truong, and the massive use of US airpower stopped the offensive and inflicted heavy NVA
casualties. The renewed bombing offensive against the north, this time
including the mining of Haiphong Harbour, drove the North Vietnamese back to the negotiating table.

Once again they effectively used negotiations as a guerrilla tactic,
for, had the US combined with the South Vietnamese to push north, it
is quite likely that they could have driven deep into North Vietnam.
Or, had the US continued an unlimited air offensive, North Vietnam's
energy would have been devoted to survival rather than contemplating further invasions of the south. Instead, however, Henry Kissinger,
representing the US, agreed to a peace which allowed the NVA to
leave substantial forces within South Vietnam.

Theoretically, the US agreed to continue to supply South Vietnam
with equipment and to intervene should the south be threatened.
However, this promise was conveniently forgotten, and deliveries of US
military aid were soon cut back. Under American tutelage the Vietnamese had become heavily dependent on the helicopter, but after
1972 the NVA had SAM-7 missiles which were very effective against
the helicopter. Furthermore, massive US air support was no longer
available to stop an NVA armoured thrust. Having lost the political
will to pursue the war to victory (a victory which might have brought
China into the conflict), the US left South Vietnam to its fate when the
North Vietnamese invaded once again in 1975. Ironically, the guerrilla war had been won, but South Vietnam could not stand against a
conventional invasion.

In evaluating the Vietnam War as a counter-insurgency campaign, the first point which must be made is that the US and South
Vietnam had won the guerrilla war by 1969. South Vietnam fell to a
conventional invasion from the north. In pursuing the guerrilla war,
the NVA and VC had certain real advantages. Perhaps most importantly they had a well-established guerrilla movement which had
achieved a victory against the French. Ho Chi Minh and Giap understood the precepts of guerrilla warfare quite well, particularly the relationship between political and military action. The US, on the other
hand, though showing a good grasp of the military aspects of counter-
insurgency, often seemed naive about the corruption within the South
Vietnamese government and the dissatisfaction among much of the
population. Within South Vietnam, much of the northern portion of

the country was well suited to guerrilla operations, as was a large portion of the MeKong Delta.

The Communists also had the advantage of long borders with South Vietnam, particularly where the Ho Chi Minh Trail ran along the border in Laos. This ready source of resupply and manpower transport allowed the VC/NVA to suffer casualties and loss of weapons with seeming impunity. Strong support from China to the north of North Vietnam and from the Soviet Union was also of immeasurable assistance. The fact that the Soviet Union acted as a force in being throughout the world, particularly in Europe, prevented the US from committing its entire military force to the war, keeping the war within limits the Communists could tolerate. Finally, Communism and Ho's breed of nationalism united those fighting against the South Vietnamese and the US.

The primary weaknesses of the Communists were those inherent in the Communist system. With an economy geared almost totally to war, North Vietnam was highly dependent upon support from China and the Soviet Union. Also, as pacification efforts and civil development projects began to work in the south, the Communists proved less appealing. The fact that many in the south were relatively staunch in their religious beliefs gave them an incentive to battle the 'Godless' Communists. On the negative side, religious beliefs also divided the south between Catholics, Buddhists and other religions. Ethnic divisions were another negative factor legislating against the South Vietnamese. The Montagnards, who fought valiantly as part of the US Special Forces irregular units, had an anti-Vietnamese underground which remained active throughout the war. Vietnamese prejudice against the 'Yards' more than justified this movement, however, and it is understandable why the Montagnards were especially unenthusiastic about fighting for the South Vietnamese after the Americans had left.

In pursuing the war, the US initially took the right tack by providing members of the Special Forces as advisers. Highly trained in the precepts of guerrilla warfare, Special Forces did an excellent job of forming local defence forces and indigenous counter-guerrilla units. Once the US began committing conventional forces, however, this self-defence effort was neglected, as the Special Forces' trained irregulars were used as scouts or intelligence sources for US or Vietnamese heavier formations. The US also tried to substitute high technology for light infantrymen, attempting to kill guerrillas by bombing areas of jungle. Perhaps the biggest enemy the US and South Vietnamese faced was the US press, not necessarily because the coverage of the war was slanted, but because the war was so well covered that the American public was more aware of its horrors and grew disenchanted with it. By tradition, the US has not been a patient country, and the fact that the war dragged on for longer than any recent conflict certainly helped to make it unpopular.

As the war shifted from counter-insurgency to multinational conflict against North Vietnam, the US was unwilling to make the commitment to defeat the North Vietnamese, and thereby possibly precipitate a war with China, or even the Soviet Union. As a result, the US was really fighting a holding action, one which the ARVN would be hard pressed to maintain. US intelligence operations certainly received mixed reviews. There are indications that some gross errors in intelligence estimates occurred, but the Phoenix Programme was certainly a highly successful operation. The in-country and cross-border special reconnaissance programmes carried out by the Special Forces were also quite successful. Perhaps, however, even more pseudo operations should have been mounted.

The importance of the will to pursue victory regardless of cost has already been mentioned. The North Vietnamese had the will to continue suffering casualties, while the US reached the point where, politically, the war could not be pursued. Seemingly, the South Vietnamese will to fight also became eroded, particularly as they saw their US support evaporate. Once the Viet Cong had been defeated, the war should have been won, but it was not. The US and the South Vietnamese never developed a viable strategy for dealing with a conventional invasion from North Vietnam. Admittedly, the 1972 invasion was stopped by US airpower, but that airpower was not available after 1973.

For the US, the aftermath of the the war had many negative factors. The country remains divided to this day, as evidenced by the criticism of President Clinton for failing to serve during the Vietnam War. The large number of Vietnamese who had to flee their homeland and are now resident in the US also testifies to the failure of that country to keep its word to an ally. Perhaps most noteworthy is the fact that, for more than a decade after the pull-out from Vietnam, the US remained very reluctant to flex its military muscle, even in situations such as the seizure of the US embassy in Iran, when harsh action was called for. Other counter-insurgencies since Vietnam have also felt the effects of that war, because US veterans of that campaign, serving in the Special Forces, in the CIA or as mercenaries, have been involved in the counter-guerrilla or guerrilla campaigns in Rhodesia, South Africa, Nicaragua, El Salvador, Afghanistan and elsewhere.

Right: Greece, with its mountains and many bays, lent itself well to partisan warfare against the Germans by guerrillas such as this one.

Below: In many of the occupied countries, the Germans found mounted troops highly effective in counter-partisan operations.

Above: Partisans such as this one have often had to use dated weapons, but have countered this disadvantage by using them to kill a better-armed enemy and take his weapon.

Left: This inexpensive Liberator pistol, produced for less than $2.00 in World War Two, was intended to be parachuted to guerrillas fighting the Axis. The .45 calibre pistol would then be used to kill a German or Japanese soldier in order to obtain his weapon.

Right: Burmese tribesmen of the Kachin and Jingpaw were trained by US OSS agents as guerrillas to operate against the Japanese. (National Archives)

Below: An OSS radio operator assigned to the Kachin Rangers in Burma. (National Archives)

Above: French troops in Indochina look over the destruction inflicted by a Viet Minh ambush on a mobile column. (ECP)

Left: A mortarman of the French Foreign Legion paras in Indochina. The paras and Legion carried a heavy burden of combat in Indochina, but could not overcome the static French tactics. (ECP)

Right: Tough French paras such as this one fought valiantly in Indochina, but could not defeat the Viet Minh. (ECP)

Below: French Foreign Legionnaires on a patrol in Indochina. (ECP)

Left: Members of the Rhodesian SAS patrol the jungle in Malaya to deny it to the Communist guerrillas.

Below: Members of the Rhodesian SAS leave on a patrol during the Malayan Emergency.

Right: To insert troops into inaccessible areas in Malaya, the SAS used the tactic of tree jumping into the heavy jungle canopy, then lowering themselves via ropes. (IWM)

Below: In an attempt to bring more indigenous troops into the Indochina War, France formed Vietnamese parachute units. (ECP)

Above: French paras in Algeria acted as a mobile reserve, and were carried by helicopter to wherever they were needed. (ECP)

Right: French Legionnaires being inserted to harry guerrillas in Algeria. (ECP)

Top right: France has used her airborne forces as her premier counter-insurgency force for the past half-century. French paratroopers are seen here conducting a drop from an RAF Transport Command Argosy transport aircraft. (ECP)

Left: Members of long-range reconnaissance patrols, such as this sergeant, were among the most effective counterguerrilla forces in Vietnam. (US Army)

Right: US Army Rangers instructors train Vietnamese Rangers in counterinsurgency warfare. (US Army)

Left: LRRPs and other special operations troops were often inserted by fast rope or rapel directly into operational areas in Vietnam. (US Army)

Right: US Special Forces fighting camps such as this one were located to interdict infiltration routes into Vietnam and, as a result, often came under attack.

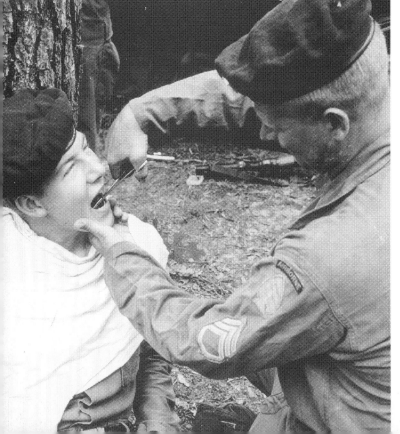

Above: A US Ranger advisor supervises hand to hand combat training for Vietnamese Rangers. (US Army)

Left: US Army Special Forces medics training to take care of their own personnel in the field, and to perform medical civic action duties to win hearts and minds. (US Army)

Above: US Army Rangers have often been known as 'snake eaters', as this Ranger instructor prepares to demonstrate for his South Vietnamese counterpart. (US Army)

Right: Booby traps can be an effective element of guerrilla psy warfare, but they can also be deployed against guerrillas by well trained CI troops.

Above: US Navy SEAL teams proved to be highly competent guerrilla fighters in Vietnam. (US Navy)

Left: A member of the New Zealand SAS moves through the jungle on a patrol in Vietnam.

Top right: Controlling possible guerrilla supply routes is important in counter-insurgency, in this case in the waterways of Vietnam's MeKong Delta. (US Army)

Right: US Navy SEALs being inserted for an ambush in Vietnam. (USN)

Above: Selous Scouts in Rhodesia beside one of the makeshift armoured vehicles built in that country. (David Scott Donelin)

Below: Home-made armoured cars such as this one were used in Rhodesia to counter guerrilla ambushes. (David Scott Donelin)

CHAPTER IV

Revolution and Counter-Revolution in Latin America

Although Latin America has experienced revolutions throughout its post-colonial history, probably the most important event in fomenting post-World War Two insurgencies was the Cuban Revolution. Though it was the fourth most prosperous country in Latin America during the mid-1950s, Cuba still had 500,000 impoverished peasants, and thus offered fertile ground for an insurgency. Ironically, however, this peasant base proved of only marginal importance during Fidel Castro's guerrilla campaign. Other factors, too, had prepared the ground for Castro. President Batista had seized power, and had little legitimacy in the eyes of the population, while corruption in the army and police was rampant. Castro himself, when he was a law student, had been very political, later even going to court to show that the Batista regime was unconstitutional.

Simultaneously with his legal efforts against Batista, Castro had begun to form a group of armed insurgents, which on 26 July 1953 attacked two military posts in Oriente Province. As a result of this abortive 'revolution' Castro and most of his followers were captured and imprisoned, Castro receiving fifteen years. Batista also took harsh measures against other dissidents. In 1954, partly through fear of internal unrest and partly to court the McCarthy faction in the US, Batista even formed a special anti-Communist secret police, the Buro de Repression alos Actividades Communistos (BRAC). In May 1955 Fidel Castro, who had been freed in a general amnesty, returned to the Cuban political scene.

Realizing that he was not ready for further actions in Cuba, Castro went to the US to raise money, and then to Mexico, where he raised and began to train a group of Cuban exiles under the tutelage of Col Alberto Bayo, an ex-Cuban Air Force colonel. Among those joining Castro in Mexico was Che Guevara, who was already a Communist revolutionary. While training his guerrilla force, Castro continued to build support inside and outside Cuba, the Batista regime's widespread infringement of civil rights helping the cause in Cuba itself.

Although other dissident groups were operating in Cuba during 1955-56, they were so fragmented that they were easily controlled. Meanwhile, Castro was being harassed by Mexican security police at Batista's request. He did gain one especially valuable backer while in Mexico, however. Former Cuban president Prio Socamos provided funds which allowed him to purchase a yacht and arms in preparation for November 1956, when Castro and 82 guerrillas set sail for Cuba. The plan was for the group to land and join with other guerrillas to attack the Manzanillo army garrison to obtain arms. Urban terrorism and a general strike were to coincide with Castro's 'triumphant' return. In the event, however, 70 of the insurgents were captured or killed and Castro, his brother Raul, Che and a few other followers escaped to the Sierra Maestra mountains.

There, in good territory to support guerrilla operations, Castro established his revolutionary base and developed a strategy of combining urban and rural warfare. As part of this strategy, urban terrorism, strikes, and riots in Santiago and Havana tied down the army in the cities, keeping them from coming after the guerrillas in the mountains while they built up their strength. Urban followers also sent money, arms, supplies and recruits. Meanwhile, rural units expanded their mountain base and began training fledgling guerrillas. As soon as possible they began striking at isolated army posts, goading the army into repressive reaction. Although Castro and Che would later claim that the Cuban revolution was a classic guerrilla campaign, they never really established the rural base that Mao felt was imperative. Instead, the urban units were always the most important of Castro's followers. Peasant support did grow, but very slowly.

Things were going so badly for the revolutionaries that in December 1956 it was widely reported, and believed, that Fidel Castro had been killed. Additionally, the Cuban economy was in good shape, undermining potential support for Castro. Then Castro discovered publicity. In February 1957 a *New York Times* interview turned Castro into a romantic hero who was 'fighting for a democratic Cuba'. Not only was he obviously alive, but he was achieving worldwide notoriety. Although the publicity was useful, the new commander in Oriente Province, Col Barrera Perez, appeared very dangerous, as he implemented a truly effective pacification programme. Fortunately for Castro, the corruption in Batista's army could be relied upon to undermine an effective officer, and Perez was soon transferred. Their heavy-handed dealings with much of the population continued to make Batista's army and police Castro's best recruiting agents.

Castro's supporters were still primarily the disaffected middle class, who continued to send recruits. As the new recruits arrived and were trained, they were organized into platoons, some of which now began independent operations. Agitation and propaganda were used to gain peasant support. Through these various efforts, strength continued to grow until the revolutionaries felt confident enough to undertake large offensive operations.

Terrorism in the cities drove the police and army to excessive reactions in an attempt to re-establish security. Then, in the summer of 1957, a plan was evolved to seal the guerrillas in the Sierra Maestra and destroy them. At this stage there were still only 200 hard-core guerrillas in the mountains, but they had been hardened by the rough life and proved much more formidable than expected. Moreover, the Cuban army's troops had received little or no training in counter-insurgency tactics. Batista also faced a rearguard action against the US press, which now highlighted the evils of the Batista regime. Even the US government's support became ambivalent. Nevertheless, Batista's policies became still harsher, thus alienating even more moderate Cubans. In retrospect, it seems that this would have been the time for the US to throw its support behind more moderate anti-Batista elements. It did not, however, and most other opposition groups sought an accommodation with Castro.

Batista's control continued to slip away, even amongst his military. In the autumn of 1957 there was an attempted mutiny by naval personnel who supported Castro. Though this failed, it was obvious that Batista was in trouble. Castro continued to launch ambushes and raids against the army and police, and now controlled 2,000 square miles of Oriente Province. He now felt confident enough, in fact, to send units to other provinces. Neither did he forget the propaganda effort, and in February 1958 rebel radio began broadcasting. Prominent professionals began expressing open support for Castro. Realizing the power of the giant near Cuba's shores, Castro continued to focus on building support within the US as well, and US disenchantment with Batista led to an arms embargo against his regime.

However, Castro may have grown too confident too quickly. A general strike in April 1958 proved a massive failure. Castro began renewed guerrilla operations in the aftermath, and the Batista forces countered with indiscriminate violence. Hoping to deal Castro a death blow, the army launched 'Operation Summer' at the end of May 1958. Employing 4,500 troops, this operation was the largest attempted to date, but it faced difficulties from the outset. The combination of squabbles among incompetent commanders, lack of training in counter-guerrilla warfare and poor morale among the troops doomed the operation to failure. Nevertheless, at one point Castro and his closest followers had been boxed into a four-square-mile area. Castro's intelligence system proved superior to the army's, however, and he managed to avoid capture and even went on the offensive, launching ambushes against his opponents.

These ambushes inflicted heavy casualties and forced the army into frustrated retreat. With the army tied down, Raul Castro kidnapped a group of Americans and carried out raids in the north. Ever careful of US opinion, Fidel Castro made sure that the Americans who had been kidnapped were treated well and eventually set free. The kidnapping was, in fact, intended to show Batista's lack of control. Rebel radio made Batista's forces look ridiculous, too, as it recounted the fiasco in the countryside. Castro's control had grown so much in the wake of the failed Operation Summer that he even received an income from the sugar cane crops in areas over which he exerted influence.

Now well into the second stage of guerrilla warfare, Castro's forces expanded into other provinces, cutting communications and ambushing army patrols, and eroding Batista's base of support even further. By December 1958 more and more towns were falling to the guerrillas, while Santiago was surrounded. Che Guevara then moved to cut the island in half, forcing Batista, who now faced certain defeat, to flee into exile.

Although Fidel Castro and Che Guevara would play upon their image as people's revolutionaries, the Cuban revolution certainly did not follow the typical 'people's war' pattern. It was essentially a middle-class revolution fuelled by dissatisfaction with the government and aided by the incompetence of Batista's security forces. Particularly noteworthy was the way Castro used the media to develop his 'heroic' image at home and abroad. Castro's reluctance to abandon this carefully cultivated image is illustrated by his clinging to his military fatigues and beard for three decades. The Cuban revolution also shows that consistently corrupt and brutal security forces can make revolutionaries out of a population not particularly interested in revolution. Just as the Nazis proved particularly adept at creating guerrilla movements in World War Two, so did Batista's Secret Police during the later 1950s.

Another interesting point about the Cuban revolution is the fact that Castro was really not a Communist - at least not overtly – during its early stages. As the US attempted to isolate Cuba after the revolution, particularly in response to the nationalization of US holdings, Castro was driven into the arms of the Soviets. Ironically, a US naval installation remained operational on the Cuban mainland throughout more than 30 years of Castro's domination, and for most of that time there was a substantial Soviet presence on the island. While Cuba was often portrayed as the greatest threat to US security in the

Western hemisphere, its citizens continued to be employed at a US military installation.

In the wake of the fall of Batista, Castro began attempting to export his revolution, though the facts first had to be rewritten to make it a peasant's rebellion. Che wrote his work *Guerrilla Warfare*, important reading for those involved in counter-insurgency warfare (one must know one's enemy), but certainly not in the same class as Mao's work on the subject. As Cuba's dependence on Soviet aid increased, the Cuban revolutionary line became more Communist.

Che Guevara became the Cuban international ambassador of revolution. First he travelled to the Congo with 125 guerrillas, and then, in the autumn of 1965, he went to Bolivia to foment revolution there. In late 1966 and early 1967 he began training Bolivian guerrillas. The US, however, had learned its lesson, and did not intend to allow another Latin American neighbour to fall under the sway of Cuban Communism. US Special Forces personnel were dispatched to train Bolivian Rangers in counter-insurgency. Along with their Special Forces advisors, this force provided formidable opposition for Che and his guerrillas, who were hunted down and destroyed. Although Che Guevara would become a martyr for some revolutionaries, as a guerrilla leader he had proved especially inept. His guerrillas did not know the terrain over which they were operating, whereas the Bolivian Rangers were fully at home in the wild. Most importantly, Che's force never really developed any support among the local peasants, who were actually quite happy with the Bolivian government and informed the security forces of guerrilla movements. It appears that, despite Che's posturing as an expert in people's war, he had never really grasped the most basic principles of successful insurgency warfare.

Ironically, considering Castro's attempt to portray his revolution as a rural-based people's war, Latin America was becoming more urbanized, and it was therefore more likely that guerrilla warfare would be based in the cities. Perhaps the most important theorist of Latin American urban guerrilla warfare was Carlos Marighela, who, in his work *The Handbook of Urban Guerrilla Warfare*, modified many traditional tenets to fit the urban environment. Among the important precepts was the point that, by luring security forces into urban areas, the rural guerrilla would be free to establish a base. Marighela also believed that violence was a key tactic to bring about revolution, but that revolutionary violence had to be carried out in front of a large audience for it to be effective. Theoretically, this violence would force the regime to be so repressive that society would be polarized, thus laying the foundations for a revolution. Marighela's tactics included murder, kidnapping, bombing, strikes, sit-ins and demonstrations, maximum publicity being important in all cases.

One of the earliest of the post-Castro Latin American revolutionary groups was the FALN in Venezuela. The FALN used violence as proposed by Marighela, but overdid it and soon lost any support they might have had among the population. Furthermore, Venezuela's president was popularly elected and had broad-based support, and this made the counter-guerrilla effort easier. Guatemala also saw an early urban campaign of violence by the FAR after a rural guerrilla movement had foundered. The FAR did manage to goad the security forces into repressive measures, but they had not counted on the fact that the Guatemalan security forces would use draconian measures to identify and eliminate them. Right-wing death squads arose as well, and killed a large number of FAR members as well as anyone likely to support them.

Perhaps the most widely known urban guerrilla group from this period was Uruguay's Tupamaros. Originating as a group of students and workers, the Tupamaros carried out a campaign of kidnapping designed to show the ineffectiveness of the government, but avoided killing whenever possible. As a protest movement the Tupamaros were relatively popular, though they never really had much chance of toppling the government.

Argentina also faced urban guerrillas, in the form of the ERP and the Monteneros who carried out widespread acts of violence in the 1970s. However, the March 1976 military coup, and the ensuing willingness of the army to be as repressive as necessary to do away with the guerrillas, marked the end of these movements as forces to be reckoned with. In Brazil, Marighela's own movement, the ALN, carried out urban violence in the late 1960s but was fragmented, then infiltrated and destroyed.

None of these movements was really successful because they never progressed beyond urban violence to develop a workable political programme. Moreover, Latin American governments were prepared to use as much repression as necessary to destroy the guerrillas. In most cases, one of the urban guerrillas' objectives was to goad the government into restrictive actions, but these actions often destroyed the guerrillas. As it transpired, Latin American dictatorships or oligarchies used repression more effectively than the urban guerrillas had expected. In Guatemala, Brazil and, later, Argentina, right-wing death squads helped eliminate the left-wing guerrillas, but themselves proved a far greater threat to democracy. Other Latin American nations, including Chile, would eventually fall prey to the same repressive tactics in the name of 'security'.

Uruguay, a Latin American nation with a history of democratic rule, fell prey to repression, too, when a military regime took control in response to a combination of rampant inflation and the Tupamaros. Once in control, the military suspended civil rights and patrolled rigorously, bringing about the demise of the Tupamaros and democracy as well. Uruguay, in fact, offers an object lesson to countries facing a threat from guerrillas, terrorists, drugs or crime. It often seems acceptable to give up civil rights to fight a 'threat', but once the rights are sacrificed, the government often proves worse than the former threat.

Probably the most successful guerrilla war in Latin America over the last three decades was that fought by the Sandinistas and then the Contras in Nicaragua. Anostosio Somoza's resignation on 17 July 1979 ended a guerrilla campaign which actually had its origins when the US Marines helped fight Nicaraguan guerrillas under Sandino. Somoza's father, who had also been president of the country, had been assassinated in 1956 by forerunners of the Sandinistas, and Sandinista guerrilla activity had certainly been going on since 1963. In the late 1970s, however, the Sandinistas had many advantages which led to their victory. These included wide support from Cuba and other Latin American countries, including Venezuela and Costa Rica; support among many Catholic priests in Nicaragua who were both political and leftist; and a weak US president in Jimmy Carter, who gave tacit if not active support to the Communist guerrillas.

Pedro Chamorro, the deceased husband of the president of Nicaragua as this is written, was close to many of the leftist factions in Nicaragua, and through his anti-government newspaper gave them a forum against the Somoza regime. In 1974, however, the campaign to destabilize the regime took on a new complexion when guests at a party for the former US ambassador were taken hostage by the Sandinistas. The situation was resolved when the government paid a ransom and released prisoners, giving the Sandinistas a high-profile act to garner publicity. Simultaneously, leftist priests began appealing to sympathetic US congressmen to end aid to Nicaragua.

Once Jimmy Carter took office in early 1977, his regime's hostility towards Somoza, based at least in part on a naive 'human rights' campaign which seemed to assume that only conservative anti-Communist governments committed outrages, eventually led to the cessation of arms shipments to the Somoza government, thus hamstringing their counter-insurgency campaign. On the other hand, Cuba and other Communist countries poured arms into Sandinista hands. Initially the US congress voted against Jimmy Carter on the arms embargo, but it eventually gave in. Somoza had been so pro-US over the years that his reliance on US support put his government in grave danger with a president such as Carter in office.

The Sandinistas must be given credit for carrying out an effective 'public relations' campaign, having learned from Castro the importance of the world's press. Their effective use of the liberal press worldwide had virtually isolated the Nicaraguan government by late 1977. That year also saw simultaneous raids on police stations, on an army battalion in Managua, and along the Honduran border. The proven guerrilla tactic of hit-and-run raids was used to good effect. The Sandinistas concentrated especially on recruiting teenagers, who were especially vulnerable to propaganda. Meanwhile, the guerrillas persisted with their political campaign, while the Carter government put pressure on Somoza to replace his cabinet ministers, thus hampering his government at this critical juncture.

The assassination of Chamorro in January 1978 led to widespread demonstrations, though it transpired that the Somoza regime had nothing to do with his death. In fact, Somoza and his Liberal Party were overwhelming victors in the 1978 elections. After Chamorro's death there was a general strike which lasted two weeks, though many merchants attempted to open their businesses in the face of intimidation from the Sandinistas and other leftists. Still, the strike was broken by the people, not by the government.

Normally, in a counter-insurgency campaign, a duly elected government should be able to hope for support from neighbouring governments. In the case of the Nicaraguan guerrilla war, however, many members of the OAS seemed to support the guerrillas, especially Venezuela, Panama and Costa Rica, which gave active or tacit support to the Sandinistas.

Traditionally, guerrillas select symbolic targets, and the Sandinistas were no exception. In August 1978, led by Eden Pastora, they attacked the National Palace in Managua, which contained many of the most important government bureaux. About 1,500 hostages were taken, including members of the House of Representatives, staff, and many citizens paying taxes. Once again the Sandinistas received extensive news coverage, as well as winning the release of prisoners. Afterwards, the guerrillas escaped to Panama and Venezuela.

The Sandinista attacks on major cities continued, the most notorious confrontation taking place at Matagalpa, the country's third largest city. The Sandinistas brought young guerrillas to the battle, allowing them to propagandize it as the 'Children's Uprising', thereby implying that the youth of the country was in revolt. One counter-guerrilla tactic which the Guardia Nacional found effective in this instance was the setting up of checkpoints, where they caught many guerrillas trying to infiltrate to join the battle. By constantly moving the checkpoints, this tactic proved effective throughout the battle.

The pressure was stepped up again on 9 September 1978, with simultaneous attacks on Managua and five other major cities. The intention in Managua was to knock out the outlying police and military posts, then hit the city centre. Similar assaults would be launched on the other major cities. In Massoya the Sandinista forces hit the central police station, then burned the downtown area and looted businesses. The planned attacks failed in the other cities because the police posts held. These assaults were followed the next day by major attacks along the Costa Rican border by 300 guerrillas, though they were turned back by 25 members of the Guardia Nacional at a border post. During the attacks the Guardia Nacional first secured Managua, while troops undergoing basic training were committed as reserves to reinforce other cities. At one point the Guardia Nacional was spread so thinly that the Presidential Guard Company was also sent as reserves, leaving the seat of government protected by a handful of troops.

During this critical period, one aspect of Guardia Nacional training proved of immense value. Units had been trained along US Marine Corps lines so that men of diverse units could function as squads or platoons.

Following hard on the heels of the massive Sandinista offensive, another general strike was called in September, but once again this failed. In the wake of the attacks it became apparent just how widespread was Sandinista support, as many countries had planned to recognize the 'Sandinista Liberation Government' in 'liberated cities' had the offensive been successful. With the attacks defeated, however, this strategy was never put into effect. Most of the Cuban-trained Sandinista cadre escaped to fight another day, though they left many local guerrillas to take heavy casualties.

Though not particularly successful on the battlefield, the Sandinistas continued to win battles in the world press and in the corridors of power in the Carter Administration. Intelligence indicated, in fact, that Venezuela was spending massive sums of money in the US, especially among members of the press, to destabilize the Somoza regime. The offensive was carried out over the airwaves as well, as Radio Havana continued to broadcast attacks on the Nicaraguan government throughout Latin America, including Nicaragua.

The Carter Administration continued to push for a mediated settlement, though with Carter and his bureaucrats in sympathy with the Sandinistas, Somoza's government had no chance of a fair hearing. Nevertheless, a multinational negotiating team was formed. Even amidst the negotiations, however, shelling into Nicaragua continued from Costa Rica; shelling which the Costa Rican government ignored. Every day, the Nicaraguan government become more isolated, a situation worsened by pressure from the US on the International Monetary Fund to limit Nicaragua's credit.

Like the North Vietnamese, the Sandinistas used periods of negotiation to build strength, and even to launch attacks. In May 1979 guerrilla infiltration from Honduras continued to increase, and in June attacks were again launched on major cities. Already thinly stretched to protect the population centres, the Guardia Nacional also had to face an invasion of 5,000 guerrillas from Costa Rica. As a result, troops had to be withdrawn from the cities in an attempt to counter the invaders, who were executing many captured administrators, police or military officials. Now facing a full-scale invasion much as South Vietnam had faced in 1975, the Nicaraguan government was fighting for its existence. At this point the US, which had already cut all supplies of arms and ammunition, put pressure on Israel to turn back an arms shipment on its way to Nicaragua. This virtually sealed the fate of the country, as the Guardia Nacional was running out of ammunition and the national treasury was bare.

The guerrilla forces could now bring overwhelming firepower to bear on the government forces. The fall of the city of Leon seemed to mark the beginning of the end for the Somoza regime as military pressure increased, along with political pressure directly from the OAS and indirectly from the US. On 17 July, 1979, Somoza stepped down and left the country. The Sandinistas took power and a bloodbath began as they tortured and executed those who had been loyal to the Somoza regime. Ironically, President Carter's concerns about human rights seemed to have evaporated.

The Sandinista abuses of power, the fact that a substantial portion of the Nicaraguan population had not supported the revolutionaries, and the existence of up to 6,000 former members of the Guardia Nacional along the Honduran and Salvadorean borders soon turned the tables on the Sandinista government, which now found itself fighting a counter-guerrilla war. Many of these initial 'contras', who titled themselves the 'Jackals', had been trained at Fort Bragg, Fort Benning, or at the Jungle Warfare School at Fort Gulick in Panama, and proved quite skilled at small unit tactics. This group carried out operations until 1983, when the real guerrilla war against the Marxist regime began.

The new group, the FDN Contras, were much more of a reflection of the people's dissatisfaction with the Sandinistas, and contained only a small number of former Guardia Nacional members. With the Reagan Administration far less sympathetic to Marxist governments in the western hemisphere than Carter's had been, the FDN received substantial aid from the CIA. When Honduras became worried about repercussions as a result of allowing the Contras to operate from within its borders, the FDN moved operations into Nicaragua itself, joining other anti-Sandinista guerrillas already operating within the country. These other groups included the Misorasata, an alliance of indians based along the east coast, and the ARDE, led by former Sandinista officer Eden Pastora. Most Contra political leaders had numbered themselves among the opposition to Somoza, thus removing any taint or hint that their campaign was an attempt to restore the Somoza government. This was a difficult proposition in any case, because Somoza had been assassinated while in exile.

Although at this point the US was supporting the Contras in their campaign to remove the Sandinistas from power, the principle US concern was El Salvador's counter-insurgency campaign. It was felt, quite perceptively, that keeping the Sandinista regime occupied with internal security problems would diminish their enthusiasm for supporting the guerrillas in El Salvador. Contra successes began to become rather pronounced, however, as they carried out raids within 60 miles of Managua. Sandinista human rights violations, and their failure to hold popular elections, were turning a substantial portion of the population against the government as well. In an attempt at area control, the Sandinistas had started relocating peasants away from the border, or, in some cases, exterminating them to remove potential sources of Contra recruits. However, as is often the case with this tactic, many more peasants were driven over to the Contras. The large influx of Cubans and Russians into Managua in support of Daniel Ortega's Sandinista regime was also driving many former Sandinistas, who had joined the movement out of patriotism, to ally themselves with the Contras.

The US under Ronald Reagan was a far different country from the weak giant under Carter, as the Grenada invasion illustrated, and this sent shock waves through the Sandinistas. A US invasion was a distinct possibility. September 1983 saw Managua bombed by ARDE pilots. Hit-and-run raids were launched in other parts of the country, often using mortars and recoilless rifles. Substantial numbers of Sandinista prisoners or defectors were soon in Contra hands. By treating these prisoners well, the Contras gained many new recruits with intimate knowledge of Sandintista methods.

Theoretically, the Sandinistas should have been able to take advantage of their knowledge of guerrilla warfare, but their political campaign had been more effective than their military one. Hence, they found themselves in great difficulty in attempting to fight the

Contras. They did institute one successful tactic, however, by forming BLIs, fast-moving light infantry units trained in counter-guerrilla tactics. Small border watch patrols were also used to give early warning of incursions so that Sandinista reaction forces could be brought to bear. These tactics proved relatively effective, especially against the ARDE, which was driven across the border into Costa Rica. Once again, the countries which had harboured the Sandinistas were harbouring guerrillas who could infiltrate into Nicaragua. The Sandinistas could not seal all of the borders, nor the many waterways, and infiltration continued. The FDN was now waging economic warfare against the Sandinistas, too, hitting power lines, oil depots and communications.

US advisors from the CIA and other organizations assisted the Contras with training and with equipment. The CIA also published FM 95-1A, a guerrilla warfare manual in Spanish, primarily for the use of the Contras. This was a fairly standard manual which covered propaganda, organization, tactics, the selective use of terror and other tactics of the type used by the Sandinistas during their quest for power. It was termed a 'handbook on assassination' by the liberal media in the US. CIA support for the Contras, and the publication of this manual, were undergoing severe criticism in the same liberal press which had helped bring the Sandinistas to power. This criticism peaked after the Contras mined Nicaraguan harbours.

It was obvious that the guerrilla effort against the Sandinistas would be more effective if the various groups worked together, so in 1985 a loose alliance was formed between the ARDE, FDN, and MISURA, known as UNIR. Former US Special Forces troops showed the combined guerrilla forces how to make improved mines and place them at critical points along the Nicaraguan road network. Harassment tactics to tie down Sandinista resources, such as planting old hubcaps to force Sandinista engineers to treat them as mines, were also taught.

The Sandinistas tried to take the offensive in the spring of 1985, when they attacked an FDN camp on the Honduran border with rockets, but they remained on the offensive. Contra long-range patrols continually operated against the road network, cutting various highways. These patrols often came back to their bases much stronger than when they had left, having picked up recruits along the way. Just before Easter 1986 the Sandinistas carried out a cross-border attack against an FDN base in Honduras, but were caught from behind by a returning Contra patrol. They suffered heavy casualties, and encountered diplomatic difficulties because they had violated another country's borders. October 1986 saw approval of a $100 million aid package for the Contras by the US. The Sandinista economy, on the other hand, was being bankrupted by the cost of keeping 119,000 men under arms, by far the largest army in Central America. Although the Sandinistas were deploying more and more troops along the borders, and were mining infiltration routes, their failure to address dissatisfaction within Nicaragua allowed internal support for the Contras to grow.

The Russians and Cubans continued to pour aid into Nicaragua, including Mi-24 Hind and Mi-17 gunship helicopters, but US-supplied Redeye and Stinger missiles allowed the Contras to counter this threat rather effectively.

Meskito indian guerrillas gained control of large coastal areas during 1986 and 1987, putting pressure on the Sandinistas from another side. Meanwhile, the Contras kept up their campaign against economic targets, hitting three major gold mining towns in north-eastern Nicaragua in December 1987. Substantial casualties were inflicted on the Sandinistas during these attacks, and the towns were sometimes occupied for days. Frustrated by their failure to stop Contra depredations, in March 1988 the Sandinistas carried out another border crossing into Honduras, but units of the US 82nd Airborne Division were deployed on a 'training mission', thus discouraging this operation.

Though their strength and support had grown through 1988, the Contras were still not ready for stage three of a guerrilla war, in which they would engage the Sandinista forces in pitched battle. The heavily armed Sandinistas could still bring too much firepower to bear with their Communist-Bloc-supplied weapons. The indian guerrillas along the southern coast had continued to grow in strength, opening another front against the Sandinistas, especially after the June 1987 meeting in which Yatama, the combined indian guerrilla movement, had been formed with US support. Thousands of its members had received insurgent training in the US, and this proved quite effective, especially in the numerous ambushes they set for Sandinista columns.

As Contra pressure increased during the next year, the Sandinistas, with support from the Soviet Union waning, were forced into popular elections in which Daniel Ortega lost to Violeta Chamorro in February 1990. Reluctant to compromise with the Sandinistas, the Contras had received promises from the US government which led most to lay down their arms and attempt to re-enter the political system in Nicaragua. Despite Ortega's defeat, he remained a power behind the government, while Sandinistas continued to control important police and army posts. Ortega also continued to undermine the elected government through the use of strikes. With estimates as high as 60,000 killed during the Contra war, however, everyone had hoped that the political solution would work.

President Chamorro had trimmed the armed forces from about 80,000 to 26,000, and had reduced the police force by more than half. Many who would have remained followers of Ortega had turned against him owing to his affluent lifestyle, the seeming antithesis of the Marxist philosophy he espoused. As they suffered new atrocities at the hands of the Sandinista-controlled army or police, many former Contras took up arms again and took to the jungle as 'Recontras'. Although the situation in Nicaragua now appears stabler than it was a few years ago, Bill Clinton's presidency raises a large question. If he shows similar weakness to Jimmy Carter, the situation in Nicaragua, as well as elsewhere in Latin America, could certainly become more conducive to insurgency.

The principal US concern in Latin America has remained El Salvador, and much of the aid to the Contras was designed to stop the Sandinistas supporting the Salvadorean guerrillas. By 1989, government forces in El Salvador, with extensive help from US counter-insurgency experts, had become quite proficient in counter-insurgency warfare. The Salvadorean airborne and quick reaction units in particular had performed to high standards, but they still faced a relatively strong foe in the FMLN.

In truth, the FMLN was a blanket organization of all of the guerrillas fighting against the Salvadorean government. Several groups were included in its ranks. The Popular Liberation Forces (FPL) had once been the largest of the guerrilla movements in the country, but in 1989 stood at about 1,500-2,000 combatants. A Marxist-Leninist group, the FPL made extensive use of terrorism and assassination. The People's Revolutionary Army (ERP) had originally been formed among university students, but had grown to be the largest combatant force, with about 2,000 fighters. The ERP, however, lacked popular support, and therefore made extensive use of violence in an attempt to goad security forces into repressive measures which would drive the population into their arms.

Perhaps the most political of the groups was the Armed Forces of National Resistance (FARN). An offshoot of the ERP, the FARN infiltrated unions, student groups, human rights organizations and other vocal anti-government groups. The Central American Revolutionary Workers Party (PRTC) had the smallest number of combatants, but was willing to make extensive use of terrorism to achieve its ends. As its name implies, this organization had ambitions beyond El Salvador alone. Finally there was the Communist Party of El Salvador (PCES), which, though it was not strong militarily, had the closest ties with

Cuba and the Soviet Union, and could thus help acquire arms and funds. As the Soviet Union imploded and abandoned the business of supporting 'wars of national liberation', the PCES lost much of the influence it had gained.

US aid allowed the Salvadorean élite units to win back the night from the guerrillas, using infrared optics and highly effective night ambush tactics. However, El Salvador was still tying up an immense amount of resources in the counter-insurgency war. By 1989 56,000 men in the security forces were countering 6,000 Marxist guerrillas. The election of the conservative ARENA government in 1989, on a law and order platform, seemed to indicate that most of the country supported a hard line against the insurgents.

Despite government successes, though, the Communist guerrillas retained enough power to launch an assault on 11 November, 1989, against major civilian and military targets throughout El Salvador. Lasting until 5 December, this assault cost the guerrillas dearly, the Salvadorean Airborne Battalion alone accounting for 260 guerrillas. After the manner of the Viet Cong during the Tet Offensive in Vietnam, the FMLN hit major Salvadorean cities - primarily San Salvador, San Miguel, Zacatecoluca, Usulutan and Santa Ana - but in the process reportedly lost a total of 1,773 killed and 1,717 wounded or captured. Though beaten soundly, the guerrillas had shown the ability to strike at any point throughout the country, making them still a force to be reckoned with.

Cuba claimed that it was not supporting the insurgency in El Salvador, but in 1991 evidence was found that cans of coconut originating in Cuba and shipped to El Salvador actually contained grenades. This came as no surprise to either the Salvadoreans or the US. In the spring of 1991 the FMLN penetrated into San Salvador once again to attack the presidential residence. Such attacks achieve publicity out of proportion to their actual effect, and serve as a symbolic show of power by the FMLN.

In a misguided attempt to speed up negotiations between the FMLN and the Salvadorean government, in 1991 the US congress held up half of the $85 million aid package promised to the Salvadorean government. This sent the wrong message to the FMLN, which stepped up guerrilla activity. In a typical Marxist guerrilla tactical move, the FMLN used the negotiations as a ploy to weaken the Salvadorean army while bringing in SAMs, making it dangerous for the Salvadorean Air Force to fly counter-guerrilla support missions. The length of the war was beginning to tell on government forces by 1991, even the élite quick reaction battalions now being heavily staffed with conscripts. Despite successes against the guerrillas, the army had suffered 2,000 casualties in 1990, and the FMLN continued to cut power lines, water and roads, and to harass the infrastructure almost at will.

To show government ineffectiveness, too, the FMLN had made it a practice to hit Mariana Prison periodically, and free prisoners. The prison had been attacked six times in eleven years; 150 prisoners had been freed in 1985, and 130 in the last raid. Not having learned from previous 'negotiated settlements' to guerrilla wars, the US pressured the Salvadorean government, which itself was no doubt growing weary of the economic and psychological drain of the continuing war, to negotiate. As a result, the counter-guerrilla war was declared officially over in 1992. The military forces were to be halved, while land, judicial and electoral reforms were to be implemented. A 1,000-man peacekeeping force was to monitor the ceasefire. As part of the peace accords, members of the FMLN were to be accepted into the police. Once again, whether the Clinton administration is regarded as tough enough to deal with renewed fighting will probably determine how well the two sides stick to the ceasefire.

In other parts of Latin America, government forces continued to fight insurgents, drug cartels, or a combination of the two. In Guatemala, for example, cuts in US aid actually proved advantageous, as they forced the army to concentrate on civil affairs to win as much of the population as possible to the government cause. As a result, after eight years the remaining 200-400 hard-core insurgents had been driven back to a final refuge in the mountainous Quiche area. Even so, they had enough strength to mount attacks against the army in 1990. The Organization of People in Arms (ORPA) carried out RPG-7 rocket attacks against military and civilian targets and mined roads. The Guerrilla Army of the Poor (EGP) remained active as well, though more in the political than in the military arena.

The ORPA originated in 1979 as a splinter group of the Rebel Armed Forces (FAR). It had nearly been wiped out during the early 1980s, but had staged a mild resurgence by 1990, with 150 or so members. The ORPA continued to carry out minor operations from its base in the Quiche and from a refuge along the Pacific Coast, a popular tactic being to carry out massacres which it attempted to blame on the army. In fact, this tactic showed that the guerrillas were now kept at a distance from the people, and illustrated the popularity of the army. The combination of growing democracy and an army more effective at counter-insurgency seemed to have the insurgency well in check by 1990, and this remained the case at the time of writing.

In Peru, on the other hand, the 'Shining Path' guerrillas, perhaps the most dangerous in Latin America, have continued to gain control of a growing portion of the country. *Sendero Luminiso*, as the Shining

Path guerrillas are called in Spanish, have certainly been aided by various factors, particularly Peru's rampant inflation (1,700 per cent per year by 1990), an oligarchical government, the US 'war on narcotics' against one of the few money-making enterprises in Peru, and the army's unwillingness to adjust to the necessities of full-scale counter-insurgency warfare. Formed initially in the remote mountain department of Ayacucho, the *Sendero Luminiso* were still very powerful in the higher Andes. The Shining Path wants to replace all existing Peruvian institutions with Marxist ones.

The guerrillas have established a reputation for being especially brutal, attacking religious groups or welfare workers as well as the army. One technique used in villages by the Shining Path has been to have every person inflict a knife wound in stabbing someone to death, so that all are implicated. With an estimated 1,500 active guerrillas and 8,000 sympathizers by 1989, the Shining Path's power base was quite extensive. Realizing that Peru's economy was a great recruiter, Shining Path made a point of attacking mines, thus hurting the economy even more.

In 1965 Peru had faced the danger of another Communist insurgency, but the army, as sometimes happens in Latin America, had seized the government and instituted much-needed reforms. However, they went too far with the reforms and almost destroyed the economy. In reaction they swung too far to the right, thus setting the stage for the Maoist *Sendero Luminiso*. The army made some attempts to form a peasant militia to fight the guerrillas, but normally this militia lacked arms and thus became easy prey. Perhaps the army's one great advantage was that Peru had no Communist neighbours, which made it harder for Shining Path to obtain arms and supplies and denied it a cross-border training area. To counter this disadvantage, Shining Path has reached an agreement with drug traffickers, offering it protection in exchange for arms.

On the other hand, Shining Path was well-organized into local, regional and main force guerrillas, and had a coherent strategy based on splitting the country along the Sierra spine and then isolating Lima from its food supplies. During 1989-90 this seemed to be working, as the guerrillas spread along the spine. The US anti-drug effort was not only giving the Shining Path extensive propaganda fodder ('pawns of the DEA destroying the peasants' income'), but it was diverting army resources away from counter-insurgency. Corruption and scandal within the Peruvian government also helped the guerrillas. Strikes against the infrastructure during 1991, such as blowing up pylons and knocking out 90 per cent of the power in the country, gave *Sendero Luminiso* the cachet of being able to strike at will, too.

By 1991 the Shining Path had killed about 20,000, including 91 local mayors, and had forced more than 50 per cent of the country to be placed in a state of emergency and thus under military control. Peasants had been relocated, in many cases to the slums of Lima, adding to the burdens of an economy already near collapse. To make the situation worse, in 1988 it was estimated that the Shining Path had been responsible for the loss of over $2½ billion to the Peruvian economy.

Most peasants felt that there were really four terrorist groups in Peru - the Shining Path, the Tupoc Amanu Revolutionary Movement (MRTA), the military and the police. The MRTA, a smaller guerrilla movement than Sendero, has also had some success, especially at targeting government buildings and army installations. It was born in 1983 with the support of Fidel Castro. Named after the last Inca leader to lead a revolt, the MRTA draws mostly from the middle class, while the Shining Path draws primarily from the peasant class. Both anti-American and anti-Shining Path, the MRTA considers itself primarily an urban guerrilla group, but in 1986 it had moved into the countryside. Sophisticated at propaganda, the MRTA has made good use of radio stations, which it has seized to broadcast its message to the country.

Although the Shining Path remains active, as does the MRTA to a lesser extent, US advisors have been present during the 1990s, teaching the Peruvian army the techniques of counter-insurgency, and their are indications that they are beginning to make inroads against the insurgents.

Colombia's primary problem is often believed to be the drug cartels, but it has also been mounting a counter-insurgency campaign against the M-19 guerrillas, who have both allied with the drug lords and fought them after the guerrillas attempted to enter the drug business themselves. One great advantage Colombia has is the Lancero School, often considered the best light infantry training school in Latin America. Similar to the US Army Ranger course, the Lancero School provides an excellent preparation for counter-insurgency forces.

Nonetheless, the situation was so unstable that leftist guerrillas launched attacks in the northern provinces early in 1991 which killed 40. This resulted in an attack against an FARC HQ near Bogata in which 60 guerrillas were killed, but the guerrillas retaliated themselves by assassinating 36 police officers. Judges who have passed harsh sentences against drug dealers have also become the targets of assassins. At the time of writing, the Colombian army and police are waging a campaign against the drug cartels and the guerrillas, both of whom remain interrelated through mutual self-interest.

Other Latin American countries, Chile and Bolivia among them, still face insurgencies or threats from the drug trade, but none seem to be threatened to the extent of Peru, or to be facing the extended counter-insurgency campaigns which have been fought in Nicaragua, El Salvador or Guatemala.

Marxist insurgencies in Latin America have traditionally been aided by the poverty endemic in many countries, the rigid class systems and oligarchical governments, the tendency of the armies to dabble in government (often on the far right), and the ability to arouse sentiment against the US. Until recently the ready availability of arms and training in Cuba has also assisted Latin American insurgencies, while the coastlines have allowed weapons to be smuggled in with relative ease. The failure of most Latin American insurgencies can be attributed to their tendency to lose track of the political aims of the population. Those revolutions which are urban based, with a few exceptions, have not managed to build a true peasant base of support, while most of those which have strong peasant support have not displayed the political sophistication to take over and run a country.

In many cases, Latin American guerrillas have proved their own worst enemies, using terrorism so readily that the security forces have felt free to retaliate with draconian measures such as death squads and torture. However, although these methods might seem effective in the short term under military regimes, such repression normally creates an atmosphere of fear which separates the population from the government. Perhaps most frighteningly, insurgencies have often toppled relatively democratic governments in Latin America and replaced them with repressive military regimes which justify their actions in the name of 'security'. The US has often hurt itself among emerging nations by its support of right-wing military juntas in Latin America, a choice that was often made to protect American business interests. One problem seems to be that moderate governments are not that common in Latin America, and the choice often comes down to a Marxist government or a military dictatorship.

The US realizes the importance of Latin America to its own security and so is normally quite willing to give counter-insurgency assistance. One policy the US has traditionally followed is that of pairing promising Latin American officers at West Point with promising American cadets, assuming that a few of these officers will eventually rise to positions of power in their countries. Their former West Point room mates will then be available to act as military liaison, whether on counter-insurgency or other matters relating to US security.

Over the last decade, Latin American military units, often trained by the US Special Forces, have proven apt students of counter-insurgency. The best of the light infantry, airborne, ranger or special forces units in Latin America have shown themselves capable of harrying guerrillas and destroying them, while an increased awareness of the value of hearts and minds has allowed many armies to gain popularity and achieve much greater support among the rural populations than they enjoyed hitherto. Cuba has lost the support of Russia and faces a bankrupt economy, so Castro's support for Latin American insurgencies has waned. This may well prove to be the greatest aid to counter-guerrilla operations in the next decade. Without Cuba's support it will be much harder for any of the Latin American insurgencies, especially those in Central America, to reach the second or third stages of guerrilla war.

CHAPTER V

Ragged Wars Without End: Ongoing Religious Conflicts Around the World

Amidst the more clear-cut counter-insurgency or counter-terrorist campaigns there are a few ongoing conflicts, normally based on religious or ethnic strife, which seem unlikely to end in the foreseeable future. One of the most obvious aspects of these continuing conflicts is the difficulty in determining right or wrong, as both usually exist on each side of the conflict. Much partisanship around the world, by countries or by expatriates, also normally marks these conflicts. The following are the most long-lasting, or of most current interest, among such conflicts.

NORTHERN IRELAND

The origins of the conflict in Ulster date to Elizabethan times, when the country was conquered by English Protestants. However, the most recent serious outbreak of violence can be traced more directly to 1969, when Protestant violence against Catholics and the resulting retaliation reached a point where British Army units had to be deployed to help restore order. Almost a quarter of a century later the British Army is still serving in Northern Ireland. The cycle of murder and counter-murder has continued amid periods of relative calm, but violence is always just below the surface. Catholic bitterness has simmered owing to the historic memory of English invasion, discrimination against Catholics in Ulster, and bitterness between Catholics and Protestants. Ironically, one of the causes of the increased violence in 1969 was an attempt to grant more rights to Catholics in Ulster, and the ensuing Protestant backlash.

During the first decade of the current 'troubles' about 2,000 lives were lost on both sides among civilians, police and military personnel. By 1991 the number had risen to 3,000. Both Protestant and Catholic terrorist/guerrilla groups (in this case the two terms can almost be used interchangeably) have used assassination of selected individuals as a tactic, while the Irish Republican Army (IRA) has specialized in the use of bombs. IRA bomb making has grown more sophisticated over the years, ranging from radio controlled bombs to letter bombs, and from car bombs to 'sleeper' bombs of the kind that almost killed Margaret Thatcher. Although the IRA has Semtex, 'field expedient' explosives manufactured from fertilizer have been most commonly used. Perhaps the most infamous of the IRA's bombings was that which killed Lord Mountbatten in 1979, though others have accounted for more casualties. The IRA has also proved willing to take its bombing campaign abroad, striking at English cities during various 'offensives' over the years. Actually, the IRA had been in long decline since the glory days of the Easter Uprising and then the independence of Eire in 1922, but Protestant violence in Ulster led to its resurgence as a defensive organization. That mission has now been replaced by modern terrorism and urban guerrilla warfare.

The IRA has been a remarkably successful guerrilla movement, partly because it won great popularity with the Catholic population owing to its initial defensive mission. Later it became more indiscriminately violent, became involved in crime (especially extortion to raise money), and developed distinctly Marxist views. This change resulted in some loss of popularity, but the fear of reprisals, which the IRA metes out harshly, has ensured at least tacit loyalty on the part of many Irish Catholics. It should be pointed out that Republican forces claim that most of the accusations of IRA crime and leftist politics can be attributed to British disinformation. Probably some truth and some anti-IRA propaganda are mixed. The IRA certainly has some distinct advantages, including strong support from abroad, the border with Eire, and the religious loyalty of a substantial portion of the population. The IRA has also maintained ties with other terrorist groups as part of 'terror international', though the group with which the IRA has co-operated most is the ETA, the Basque separatist group operating in France and Spain. Interestingly, the IRA has also shown strong support for the African National Conference.

Particular IRA targets have been members of the Royal Ulster Constabulary (RUC) and the Ulster Defence Regiment (UDR), the locally raised army unit. The UDR is especially hated, to some extent because it is still associated with the old 'B-Specials' who served as a police reserve used to repress the Catholic population. The British Army has suffered over 3,000 casualties in Northern Ireland, making it a more costly campaign than the conflicts in the Falklands and the Persian Gulf. Beginning in 1971, many Republicans were detained without trial, and there were accusations of abusive interrogations. That year also saw the first British soldier killed in Northern Ireland. By 1972 21,000 British troops were deployed to Ulster, but they had yet to develop a real counter-guerrilla strategy. Massive sweeps in July 1972 failed as IRA members crossed into Eire. Over the years, however, the Army developed an effective combination of intelligence operations, ambushes, checkpoints, surveillance and foot patrols. Reasonable co-operation has been received from the Irish Republic, though it has remained necessary to maintain security operations along the borders to prevent arms smuggling and infiltration. It should be pointed out, too, that, despite the heavy British Army presence, the RUC has remained the principal security force. A 1985 agreement granting the Irish Republic more say in the affairs in the North, in return for tighter border security, has also helped to cut infiltration.

In 1974 the British tried to establish a government shared by Protestants and Catholics, but the Protestants instituted a massive strike. In addition, pub bombings resulted in 21 deaths. 1975 saw a ceasefire between the IRA and the Army, but 247 people still died in that year. Relations between the IRA and the Army again took a downward turn in 1976, when the British government stopped treating IRA prisoners as Prisoners of War. This led to a string of prison protests which won the IRA substantial sympathy at home and abroad. The 'Blanket Protests', in which prisoners refused to wear prison uniforms and wore only blankets, began in 1980, to be followed in 1981 by the death of ten IRA members in hunger strikes. Eventually the British authorities did grant some concessions in treatment of prisoners to stop the deaths. The attempt on Margaret Thatcher's life at Brighton in 1984, along with the previous bomb attack on Guardsmen in Hyde Park, London, and the abortive bombing attack on Gibraltar, illustrated renewed IRA willingness to take the war to the British anywhere in the world. 1991 almost saw the greatest IRA success of all, when a mortar attack was carried out against the British Cabinet at 10 Downing Street.

In 1991 the IRA claimed about 500 active members who could rely on the support of about 40 per cent of northern Catholics and about 20 per cent of southern Catholics. If the figure of 500 is correct, which seems likely, the IRA has been incredibly successful in tying down many thousands of security personnel. Some IRA recruits join as a result of harassment of themselves or their families by the Army or the RUC, while others come from families with long histories of IRA involvement.

After 1977 the IRA was organized into cells or Active Service Units (ASUs), each comprising from three to ten members. Each cell specializes in bombing, assassination, sniping or intelligence gathering. ASU leaders report to a brigade commanding officer. Normally, each ASU draws arms as needed, though 'commando units' which operate along the border for weeks on end, on the IRA equivalent of long-range reconnaissance, carry pistols, rifles and explosives at all times. In addition to acting as the control for the ASUs, the brigade provides policing for Irish Republican enclaves within its area, since many Catholics do not recognize the authority of the RUC. Normally, each county has two brigades. The most active brigade is in Belfast, though the toughest is usually considered to be in South Armagh. The brigades report to a Northern Command in Ulster, and to a Southern Command in Eire. Overseeing all of these units is the GHQ, which reports to the seven-member Army Council, the supreme IRA authority. The Bible for IRA matters is the *Green Book*, the official manual of the organization.

The IRA considers itself a guerrilla movement rather than a terrorist organization, and in some ways it follows traditional guerrilla tactical doctrine (i.e., striking at isolated Army or police posts). Beginning in 1985, the IRA concentrated on levelling British barracks and then intimidating contractors not to rebuild them. Flamethrowers have also been used against barracks. During 1990-92, to draw soldiers out of their hardened barracks and make them more vulnerable, the IRA disrupted the Dublin-Belfast Railway to force soldiers to provide security.

The Army's presence has shrunk over the years, however, as responsibilities have been turned over to the RUC and UDR. In 1972, for example, the British Army had 31 regular battalions in Northern Ireland and 11 UDR battalions. By 1992 this was down to ten regular battalions and nine UDR battalions. This still made the UDR the largest regiment in the British Army. It was far more common, though, for UDR soldiers to be assassinated off duty rather than be killed on operations. In 1991 the RUC had 8,250 personnel. Perhaps most active in the war against the IRA and other extremist groups are the Mobile Support Units of the RUC. A total of 277 RUC members have been killed during the 'troubles'.

Although attacks against the UDR and RUC continued, attacks against the British Army had decreased by the early 1990s. The cycle may well begin again, however, with attacks taking place anywhere in the world where the British Army is stationed. Battalions recently withdrawn from Northern Ireland have frequently been targets. It would be unfair and simplistic to imply that all acts of terrorism are carried out by the IRA. There are still active Protestant terrorist groups as well, the most noteworthy being the Ulster Defence Force and Ulster Volunteer Force, both of which kill Catholics in revenge for IRA killings, though the revenge counter-revenge killings have established a vicious circle which is hard to break. More political is the Orange Order. A frightening commentary on the contemporary US, however, is that despite the 'troubles' Northern Ireland is still much safer than most American cities. The homicide rate, for example, is usually about one-tenth that of Detroit.

Perhaps the most effective but misunderstood aspect of British Army operations in Northern Ireland has been the deployment of the SAS, who are viewed as trained killers by the IRA. There has been a tendency to blame the SAS for any killings of IRA members in Northern Ireland, and even some in Eire, but there is no doubt that the IRA has a healthy respect for the SAS. The SAS was initially deployed to Ulster in 1969, when D Squadron was sent to counter gun-running along the border, but the special operations troops were soon sent back to the UK. They did not return until 1976, when they were brought back after eleven Protestants were taken off a bus and executed. To some extent the SAS has been used to train other units to carry out the type of undercover tasks at which it excels. As a result, the RUC and Military Intelligence have developed units which now perform tasks initially carried out by the SAS. The Mobile Reconnaissance Force was one such unit which worked with ex-terrorists, who pointed out former colleagues. Perhaps the best intelligence operation, however, was the establishment of the Four Square Laundry, which operated a successful laundry service in the Catholic areas of West Belfast, collecting laundry and testing it for traces of explosive in order to locate IRA bomb making facilities. The use of communications intelligence units to scan frequencies and detonate bombs has also resulted in some IRA members being blown up by their own explosive devices.

The SAS has also helped to train the various infantry reconnaissance battalions to carry out surveillance missions. It is generally accepted that the SAS has operated in the south on occasion, reportedly to carry out snatches and a couple of assassinations, but its primary role has been surveillance and ambush in the north. The SAS presence is also somewhat psychological, as the IRA has such paranoia about the Service. For example, before the SAS deployment in 1976, 21 civilians had been murdered in six months, but none were murdered in the next twelve months. The SAS, it should be noted, operates against both the IRA and the UVF.

Owing to SAS successes, the RUC formed their own special units, such as E4A for surveillance and Special Patrol Group, Bronze Section, for 'active measures'. This unit was later known as the Special Support Unit. SAS commitment continued, though, and two squadrons were deployed to Northern Ireland by mid-1977. Over the next year there were some highly successful ambushes, but also at least one mistaken killing, on which the PIRA capitalized in the press. In the aftermath, SAS operations became much more secret.

Secrecy covered SAS operations in Northern Ireland for the next decade, with SAS successes often mixed with successes by Army Intelligence. In May 1987, however, the SAS carried out a masterly ambush of eight IRA members who were preparing to attack an RUC station using the methods adopted to attack twelve other stations during the year. In revenge against the Army, the IRA bombed the War Memorial on Remembrance Day, 1987, thus turning sentiment overwhelmingly against themselves. The SAS has continued to achieve successes in the secret war, including the killing of three members of another Active Service Unit. Most controversial was the killing of an IRA group in Gibraltar, to prevent them detonating a car bomb. This was an excellent operation, showing good intelligence and sending a pointed message to the IRA that, just as the IRA can attack the British Army outside Ulster, the SAS can attack the IRA outside Ireland.

The 'troubles' in Ireland are of such long standing and are so deep-seated that, even though most of the population of Ulster would like to see the violence stop, the attainment of a political solution acceptable to all parties seems an elusive goal. The most viable solution would probably be to allow the north to join with the south, where Protestants seem to have little objection to the government, but it is unlikely that either Britain or the Protestant majority in Ulster would find this acceptable. The IRA's tactics are an interesting mixture of astute guerrilla operations and senseless terrorist attacks which lose them much of the ground they have gained.

The IRA's greatest assets remain their substantial support at home and abroad, and the historic basis for their struggle. With a relatively small number of active personnel; money supplied by supporters, counterfeiting and extortion; and a sufficient supply of arms and explosives, the IRA manage to keep their campaign going without moving beyond the first stage of a guerrilla war. This is one reason why it is hard to consider this a counter-insurgency, rather than a counter-terrorist, war. There remain, too, the Protestant terrorist groups. These show even fewer characteristics of a guerrilla force than the IRA, and add another dimension to the security effort, as a substantial element of the population will oppose whatever actions may be taken for security.

The British Army and the UDR and RUC have not always shown the best diplomacy in dealing with the Catholic minority, though the long stay of the Army in Northern Ireland seems to have given British soldiers a better understanding of the population. A surprising number of the soldiers are actually Catholics themselves. The threat of bombings and assassinations, as well as the delays at checkpoints, seem to have become so much a part of life in Ulster that the population has become reconciled to a status quo of violence and fear. IRA bombings in London often seem especially counter-productive, as they appear to harden British will to stay in Northern Ireland. But the bombings, too, seem to be part of the mindset of the Ulster terrorist groups, to whom violence and counter-violence seem to be ends in themselves, rather than tactics in reaching a goal.

The British security effort has proved adequate to prevent IRA or UVF influence from growing too widely, but after 25 years of operations in Northern Ireland the British Army, the UDR and the RUC are nowhere near declaring Ulster secure. As a result, this remains one of the world's festering trouble spots.

ISRAEL-PALESTINIANS

Although the Arab-Israeli conflict does not date as far back as the English-Irish troubles, like the Ulster problem it has certainly continued to defy solution. The current problems in Palestine date back to the 1880s, when Zionist settlers began arriving in Palestine. Their numbers swelled until, by 1914, they accounted for nine per cent of the population. At this point the local Arabs and Christians began to worry about those who they viewed as interlopers, even though the land had been legally purchased. Immigration was encouraged, however, after the British captured Palestine from the Turks in 1917.

When the British Mandate over Palestine was granted in 1922, the Jewish Agency wielded more political clout in Great Britain than did the Palestinians, who boycotted talks about problems and thus weakened their position even more. Vicious attacks by Arabs on Jewish settlements in 1920 and 1921 gained sympathy for the Zionist cause, and also led to the establishment of Jewish defence forces which evolved into the Haganah. By 1929 even more serious attacks were taking place against Jews, to some extent influenced by the Mufti of Jerusalem's calls for the Zionists to be expelled. Initially, the British caved in to Arab pressures and agreed to stop Jewish immigration, but they soon reverted to their previous policy. As a result, by 1940, 33 per cent of the population of Palestine was Jewish.

The Holocaust which killed millions of Jews in World War Two gained international sympathy for the appeal for a Jewish homeland, while the Haganah, Palmach and other guerrilla forces carried out acts of terrorism against the British forces occupying Palestine and against the Arabs. When the British finally agreed to leave in 1947, the plan called for a Jewish zone, an Arab zone, and an international zone for Jerusalem and certain other areas. The Arab Palestinians, however, found that the Jews, who represented 33 per cent of the population, were going to control 54 per cent of the land.

In the 1948 war, which was fought primarily to determine control of the land in Palestine, the Jews gained additional areas, and when the conflict ended 73 per cent of the land was under Jewish control. Moreover, 725,000 Palestinian Arabs were left homeless. The areas remaining under Palestinian control were primarily the West Bank and the Gaza Strip, which were now controlled by Jordan and Egypt respectively.

The Palestinians, as well as sympathizers from the surrounding Arab states, began launching raids into Israel. These led to retaliatory raids by the Israelis, and this cycle has continued to some extent until today. Another war, in 1956, did little to right perceived wrongs or gain Israel security. Tensions continued to grow again, particularly after Fatah began launching raids in 1965. In 1967 the Israelis demonstrated their military superiority by defeating the surrounding Arab states decisively in six days, regaining the rest of Palestine as well as other territory including the Golan Heights and much of the Sinai.

The Israelis began establishing settlements in the occupied territory, thus sending the message that this land was now part of Israel, and would not be returned. Arab states took a harder line, the Palestine Liberation Organization (PLO) stepped up raids, and UN resolutions called for Israel's withdrawal from occupied territory. However, Old Testament nationalism, which caused the Israelis to desire borders matching those of Biblical Israel, combined with the need for buffer zones to provide security, strengthened Israel's determination to keep the territory.

Palestinians driven from Palestine had been a problem for the Hashemite Kingdom of Jordan for some years, but their acts of terrorism, particularly the hijacking and blowing up of three airliners in Jordan, finally caused King Hussein to become disenchanted. In 1970 he turned the Arab Legion loose on the PLO, driving them from Jordan. As a result, Black September was formed to carry out acts of terrorism in revenge. The most notorious was probably the massacre of Israeli athletes at the 1972 Munich Olympics. Carried out in front of the entire world, this act certainly drew attention to the Palestinians' plight, but it also branded them as terrorists in the minds of most westerners. In fact, many western anti-terrorist units were formed in direct response to the Munich massacre.

In Egypt, at least, the military balance had begun to tilt towards the Arab states, and during the 1973 war Israel received a frightening reawakening to the fact that it was a small state surrounded by enemies. Israel mobilized its reserves and once again rolled over its enemies, but in the process suffered substantially greater casualties than in the past. In the wake of this last war, the Palestinian National Council continued to view armed struggle as the only path to liberation. As a result, the Palestinian was viewed, for the most part, as a villain in the west and as a freedom fighter among Arab states. Now operating primarily out of Lebanon, PLO raids into Israel grew in intensity, provoking Israeli retaliation and, as a result, the disintegration of Lebanon. One sad outcome of the Arab-Israeli conflict is that Lebanon, formerly the financial capital of the Middle East and a centre of tolerance, has become engulfed in a long civil war, itself another seemingly solutionless conflict.

Finally, in 1978, Israel invaded Southern Lebanon to destroy the PLO. Ironically, in the same year Egypt and Israel signed the Camp David Accords which ended the decades-old war between those two states and returned the Sinai to Egypt. The rise of militant Islamic fundamentalism in the late 1970s and early 1980s would add a new dimension to relations between many Arab states and Israel, and to their relations with the USA and other western countries as well. Supported by most of the rest of the Arab world, which had isolated Egypt after the peace accords with Israel, the PLO continued to use Lebanon as a springboard for raids into Israel. In an attempt to end this threat, Israel invaded Lebanon again in 1982, and with the help of Christian militias drove the PLO from Beirut. Under great pressure, PLO chief Yasser Arafat agreed to the withdrawal in order to save as many PLO members as possible, but the slaughter of some women and children after the fighters had gone, combined with the perception that their leader had caved in to the Israelis, caused fighting among PLO members, and some high-ranking members loyal to Arafat were assassinated.

After being forced from Lebanon, the PLO set up its headquarters in Tunis. However, in 1985 the Israelis demonstrated that they were still able to exact revenge. An Israeli F-16 strike devastated the quarters of Force-17, Arafat's personal bodyguards, in retaliation for the killing of three Israelis in Cyprus.

Arafat now seemed to be attempting to accomplish through negotiation what he had been unable to accomplish through military action. He sat down with Jordan, Israel and the US, but the negotiations broke down when the PLO continued to carry out terrorist acts such as the hijacking of the *Achille Lauro*, and Israel bombed the PLO headquarters in Tunis. Beginning In 1987, however, a PLO resurgence started as various warring factions reconciled and focused on their primary objective.

It was not through the direct action of the PLO that the world became aware of the PLO cause once again, but through the spontaneous uprising in the occupied territories. The 'intifada', or shaking off, as the demonstrations came to be known, drew attention to Israel's treatment of the Palestinians and gave them a human face. As the demonstrations spread, so did Israel's use of force to put them down. By September 1988, 257 Palestinians had been shot dead during demonstrations, while another 89 had died from tear gas, beatings, or other directly related causes. At one point all of Gaza was under curfew, with 500,000 Palestinians confined to their homes. Israel, a country formed in the wake of the attempted genocide of the Jews, now faced growing accusations of carrying out a genocidal war against the Palestinians. Political repercussions at home and abroad were felt by the Israelis, who continued to treat the intifada purely as an internal security matter.

In April 1988 Israeli Commandos assassinated Abu Jihad in Tunis, eliminating the PLO leader in charge of the occupied territories. Intelligence sources indicate that Jihad had been targeted for some time by the Israelis in retaliation for previous acts against Israel, but the fact that he was planning to form a shadow government in the occupied territories to erode Israeli authority even further may have sealed his death warrant. One has to admire Israel's willingness to take draconian action when necessary, though in this case the intifada did not go away. Palestinians who performed many of the menial jobs in Israel now resorted to strikes, while Israel countered with economic pressure against Palestinians.

Ever since the end of the British Mandate, the Palestinians have shown a seeming self-destructive urge, and in the months leading up to the Persian Gulf war this urge seemed to exert itself once again when the PLO backed Saddam Hussein. Not only did this act alienate many of the moderate Arab states which had been the economic support of the PLO, but for security reasons many Palestinian workers were not allowed to enter Israel. As a result, when the Gulf War ended fewer than 200,000 of 1.7 million Palestinians in the occupied territories had jobs. Soviet Jewish immigrants now undertake many of the menial jobs in Israel that were formerly performed by Palestinians, while Kuwait and Saudi Arabia, formerly the most lucrative job markets for Palestinians, have expelled large numbers of them.

By 1991 the heat of the intifada was being turned inwards as Palestinians slaughtered each other, often after accusations of collaboration. More Palestinians were now being killed by their own kind, in fact, than by Israeli soldiers. Nevertheless, the intifada had shown that the Palestinians could perhaps achieve more with an unarmed civil rebellion than they had been able to accomplish with almost half a century of terrorism. Passive resistance does not seem to be consistent with Islam, though, so there is little likelihood of this becoming a coherent strategy.

In the post-Gulf War era, US strength in the region has allowed the possibility that Israel might barter land for peace, but the importance of the West Bank and Golan Heights, and the poor record of the US in keeping its word to allies as administrations change, may cause Israel to balk at giving up all of the occupied territory. The Golan Heights allow an aggressor to command too much of Israel with artillery or rockets. Obviously, the Palestinians are not simply going to go away, though perhaps most of the world wishes the problem would disappear.

The increasing immigration of Soviet Jews will create even more demand within Israel for land, making it unlikely that the Palestinians could regain their former lands without the total destruction of Israel. Lebanon has already been destroyed by the conflict, and Jordan has been threatened. Consequently, few other countries are prepared to assimilate the Palestinians, who from frustration will continue to strike out through acts of terrorism. These will bring retaliatory action, just as they have for the past four decades.

THE BALKANS

Another lingering conflict which has loomed especially large during the last two years is that in the countries which used to form Yugoslavia. Animosity dating back thousands of years has unleashed ethnic and religious bitterness, resulting in widespread bloodshed and suffering. Moslems, Catholics and Eastern Orthodox have renewed centuries-old attempts to exterminate each other, but modern weapons make the task much easier.

The most recent eruption of this smouldering conflict was generated in 1991, when Slovenia and Croatia declared their independence from the central government of Yugoslavia. The Yugoslav army, controlled by Serbs, moved into position to dominate both Slovenia and Croatia, and by the summer of 1991 the country was moving towards full-scale civil war. In addition to Croats, Serbs and Slovenians, other ethnic groups included the Macedonians, Albanians and Montenegrans. Long-simmering feuds existed between many of these groups, especially the Serbs and the Croatians. As Yugoslavia disintegrated, the army, with 90 per cent of its officers Serbs, could not afford to lose Slovenia and Croatia, economically the strongest areas of the country. One of the most important considerations in the attempt to force these two provinces to remain part of the Communist state was that customs duties collected on their borders with the West accounted for up to a third of the government's income.

As a result, Serb minorities in these provinces who fought against the Croats or Slovenians received air and armoured support from the Yugoslav army, the country's last bastion of Communism. In many instances, the Serbs and Croatians attempting to slaughter one another had been neighbours for years. There were 600,000 Serbs in Croatia when independence was declared. Fearful of their status under the control of their traditional enemies, they began fighting, and 7,000 had been killed by the end of 1991. In late 1991 both sides had agreed to accept UN Peacekeepers.

Despite the presence of the 'peacekeeping force', which was too weak to enforce anything, the Yugoslavian army launched armoured thrusts against Croatia in 1992, and instituted a naval blockade of its coastline. To exacerbate things from the point of view of the Serb/Communist government, Bosnia-Herzegovina and Macedonia were also moving towards independence.

The Croats, who are Roman Catholic, and the Serbs, who are Eastern Orthodox, view each other as pagans and, as is always the case with 'holy wars', the fighting is especially bitter. Both, of course, view the Moslems with disdain, even hatred. Croatia managed to field about 100,000 fighters, though they lacked heavy weapons other than a few captured tanks and artillery pieces. The Serbs, on the other hand, could draw from the modern arsenal of the Yugoslav government. Air raids by jet aircraft were a common tactic, particularly against the Croatian city of Zagreb. To aid Croatia, many expatriots returned from abroad to fight for their motherland. Sniping was a key tactic throughout the country, and accurate rifles with telescopic sights became greater status symbols than the ubiquitous AK-47s.

Former American special forces soldiers advising the Croats taught them to use platter charges to counter Yugoslavian/Serb armour with some success, but the Serbian government continued to focus on controlling the lines of communication. The best fighters for Croatia proved to be the Hrvatska Stravka Prava (HOS), the Croatian Party of the Rights. Quite a few international volunteers were also fighting for Croatia, some because of their heritage, others simply because it was the only war going.

Even more bitter has been the bloodletting in Bosnia, where the fact that the majority of the population is Muslim has made the fighting even worse. The Bosnian population at the beginning of the conflict was 44 per cent Moslem, 39 per cent Serb and 17 per cent Croatian. Bordered by Serbia and Croatia, Bosnia offered an appealing source of territory to both of its neighbours. Consequently, the Moslem population have been assailed from all sides. They have often been the victims of atrocities committed in revenge for those carried out by the Turks centuries ago. Despite the constant pounding of Bosnian cities, and the passing of UN resolutions, no UN troops had been committed by the autumn of 1992, though estimates of the number killed by late that year ranged from 10,000 to 50,000. Hundreds of thousands had been displaced.

Although Serbia achieved military victory over Croatia and Bosnia, it found itself in a terrible economic plight by the end of 1992, facing sanctions and massive unemployment. As a result, even the Serbs were reluctantly forced to listen to UN suggestions for peace.

The plan unveiled at the beginning of 1993 called for Bosnia-Herzegovina to be divided into ten semi-autonomous provinces. Under this plan the Serbs would control only about half of the country, but they want more, and simply argue: 'We deserve what our tanks and soldiers control'. Torture, starvation and rape have all been used by the Serbs, and to a lesser extent by others involved in the conflict. The systematic use of rape to degrade and demoralize the Moslem population was, in fact, one of the primary reasons that world attention became focused on trying to end the conflict. In retaliation for Serb atrocities, some Mujahideen from Afghanistan and other countries are reportedly fighting for the Moslems in Bosnia, and have shown themselves willing to use terror tactics. The atrocities on all sides, both currently and for generations past, have created a circle of revenge which is hard to break.

Even though 6,600 UN peacekeepers had been deployed to Bosnia, they proved ineffective at stopping the killing. As a result, from April 1993 NATO aeroplanes were scheduled to enforce a no-fly zone over Bosnia, and at the time of writing the US and her allies were contemplating committing troops there. Ironically, one of the key factors influencing President Clinton's decision whether or not to send in US troops is his own failure to serve in Vietnam, which lays him open to criticism for committing troops to another 'internal conflict not affecting US security'.

However, any attempted solution which fails to address the ethnic make-up of the provinces and the political aspirations of the various ethnic groups is doomed to failure, either immediately or later. Minorities who managed to live relatively happily among other ethnic groups while Tito ruled the country with an iron fist will find it very difficult to return to their old homes. Furthermore, the Serb superiority in military equipment must be addressed if an equitable solution is to be reached. If Croatia, Slovenia, Bosnia and the others are to survive as independent states, they will need to have the ability to stand up to the Serbs, who inherited the entire military hardware of Yugoslavia. The US normally wants to send in military forces for a few months, achieve a 'quick fix', and leave. The important point to remember in any attempted solution of the problems in the former Yugoslavia is that they have not existed for two years, two decades, or even two centuries. They are far older than that.

SRI LANKA

Another ongoing counter-insurgency, but one that is far less in the news, is that being waged in Sri Lanka. After the country had achieved independence from Great Britain, the Sri Lankan majority, the Sinhalese Buddhists, passed various laws which were highly distasteful to the Tamil Hindu minority. These laws included the establishment of Buddhism as the state religion, and the specifying of English as the state language for those holding positions in the government. Tamils were thus deprived of the chance to work in the civil service and, in most cases, the opportunity to attend universities. Anti-Tamil riots in 1983, combined with the discriminatory policies of the government, resulted in the rise of various guerrilla groups, the most effective of which was the Liberation Tigers of Tamil Eelam (LTTE). The Tigers and other guerrillas had received extensive support and training from India, which felt that Sri Lanka was proving too pro-Western, and had 50 million Tamils in India applying political pressure. India's intelligence agency, the Research and Analysis Wing, had helped train many of the guerrillas in the Tamil regions of India.

In July 1987, however, after concessions from the Sri Lankan government, an Indian Peacekeeping Force was deployed to help enforce peace between the Tamils and the government. The Tamils wanted a separate state known as Eelam, but this was unpalatable to India as well, as it was thought that it could have a destabilizing influence on the Tamils in that country. The Tigers refused to abide by the peace, and India soon found itself engaged in a counter-insurgency campaign against the guerrillas it had previously armed. As a result of pressure from India, the Sri Lankan government had given semi-autonomy to two Tamil provinces. However, the government then found itself engaged in another counter-insurgency conflict against members of the Sinhalese majority, who opposed concessions to the Tamils. The rising dissatisfaction culminated in an assassination attempt against President Jayewardene, while the Sinhalese Marxist group, the People's Liberation Front (JVP), began a rebellion of its own.

To counter the various guerrillas, the best Sri Lankan army unit was the Special Task Force, which had been trained by the SAS. When a group of Tamil leaders was captured while running guns, they committed suicide, a standard Tiger practice. The Tamil rioting which ensued resulted in the death of 200 Sinhalese villagers. Under pressure from the Sri Lankan government to keep the peace, the Indian army attacked the Tamils, especially the Tigers, who they found much tougher than they expected. As a result the Indian Peacekeeping Force had to be increased from 10,000 to 30,000, including élite Gurkha and paratroop formations.

The Tigers, who considered death preferable to surrender (most carried a cyanide suicide capsule), began resorting to Middle Eastern-style tactics, including suicide bombers. Now faced with a bloody counter-insurgency fight against its own monster, India used other Tamil guerrilla groups to help combat the Tigers, in particular the TELO. Other guerrilla groups included the EPRLF, the PLOT, the ENDLF and the pro-Tiger EROS. The Indian Peacekeeping Forces were accused of rape and looting in retaliation for losses suffered to the LTTE, as well as using torture in an attempt to identify LTTE members. As is normally the case in counter-insurgency operations, such actions created fertile breeding grounds for more guerrillas seeking retribution for atrocities against their families. Operating in a foreign country, the Indian Peacekeeping Forces felt little compunction about clearing and destroying villages in retaliation. One principal cause of losses, both to the Sri Lankan government forces and to the Indians, has been the homemade mines the Tamils proved so adept at making.

Partly due to dislike of the Indians and the Sri Lankan government, and partly through belief in the cause, the Tigers retained substantial support from the population and managed to continue operating successfully. By 1990 the Sri Lankan government forces had their hands full with the JVP, 700 to 1,000 deaths per month resulting from this conflict. Although the Indian peacekeepers were bearing much of the burden against the Tamils, the Sri Lankan government forces were still periodically in action against Tamil guerrillas as well.

The Sri Lankan forces were quite well organized for counter-insurgency, having adopted a reinforced battalion organizational system in which each battalion comprised seven companies, each company consisting of five 30-man platoons. Each platoon was divided into three sections, each led by an officer. This force proved highly adaptable for counter-insurgency operations, and was adept at cordon and search, raids, ambushes, road blocks and other standard tactics. However, the reluctance of the Sri Lankan government to tackle the causes of insurgent concerns, especially among the Tamils, doomed the military effort. The combination of government corruption, bureaucracy and unresponsiveness fuelled unhappiness among the Sinhalese as well as the Tamils. Through 1991 the government had also continually failed to develop a plan of military and civil action to deal with the insurgency. Coupled with increasing economic problems, this provided fertile ground for an insurgency.

There seemed to be some reason for hope on New Year's Eve, 1990, when the Tigers began a unilateral ceasefire, but fighting soon erupted even more violently. During 1991 4,270 LTTE members were killed, and government losses totalled 1,100. Renewed government offensives had received impetus from the People's Republic of China, which no doubt became involved, at least in part, to counter Indian influence. A Tiger suicide bomber managed to kill Indian Prime Minister Rajiv Gandhi in May 1991, and the Tamils continued to make effective use of mines, using one to kill nine senior Sri Lankan officers in July 1992.

Despite government successes, the Tigers remained a formidable foe, and shortly before this account was written they assassinated Sri Lankan President Ranasinghe Premadasa using a suicide bomber. Other prominent officials have also fallen prey to suicide bombers, as the Tigers resort to assassination and terrorist bombing to carry their fight to the Sinhalese hierarchy.

Once again, the conflict in Sri Lanka illustrates the precept that, to counter a guerrilla movement, some attempt must be made to separate the guerrillas from the population and to accede to the political aspirations of the population. In the case of the Tamil minority, present government abuses, religious differences and bad feelings concerning the past continue to fuel the conflict. The added dimension of the presence of the Indian army, which no one really seems to want, creates even more potential for a protracted conflict. As in Ireland and Palestine, it seems likely that the confrontation will turn into counter-terrorism rather than counter-insurgency as the Tamils, feeling betrayed by India as well as by the Sri Lankan government, strike at the leadership of both countries.

Bitter religious rivalries can even arise in countries with long traditions of religious freedom. It is not surprising, therefore, that counter-terrorist or counter-insurgency campaigns generated by religious differences are among the most difficult to carry through. Even though these conflicts are often the result of political inequalities as well as religious ones, the religious aspects seem to make it much harder for those charged with developing a workable military/political/social/economic solution to achieve success.

CHAPTER VI

Africa, Mostly Southern

RHODESIA

Much as in Kenya before the Mau Mau rebellion, in Rhodesia a policy of racial separation existed throughout much of the twentieth century. Land ownership remained a critical issue, with most native Africans living in tribal trust lands. As Great Britain divested itself of former colonies in the 1960s, the Crown began moving towards political and land reforms in Rhodesia, but the Europeans who controlled the country made a Unilateral Declaration of Independence from Great Britain in November 1965, establishing an independent government under Ian Smith. The seeds for an insurgency against the new government were already sown, however, as the Zimbabwe African People's Union (ZAPU) had already been formed in 1961, followed by the Zimbabwe African National Union (ZANU) in 1963. ZANU drew its members from the dominant Shonas, who comprised about 70 per cent of Rhodesian Africans, while ZAPU drew from the minority Matabeles. Robert Mugabe led ZANU, and ZAPU was led by Joseph Nkomo.

Five members of ZANU had undergone initial guerrilla training in the fall of 1963, when they went to the People's Republic of China. This group formed the nucleus of ZANLA, the military arm of ZANU. The equivalent military arm of ZAPU was ZIPRA. The initial strategy followed by both groups was to frighten Europeans into making concessions and/or bring about British intervention. White paranoia after the Mau Mau rebellion, however, made the minority in Rhodesia unlikely to compromise. The next step in the guerrilla campaign was an attempt to destabilize the white government and in the process gain as much African support as possible. The first clash of the guerrilla war occurred in April 1966, with ZANLA the first to see combat against the security forces. What really signalled the opening of the campaign to white Rhodesians was the slaying of a European couple by ZANLA in May. Although the security forces eventually killed or captured thirteen of the fourteen ZANLA guerrillas involved, infiltration attempts would increase.

ZIPRA began its campaign with larger infiltrations. In August 1967, 90 came in as a group but were reported by local Africans, resulting in 47 being killed and 20 captured during the ensuing weeks. ZIPRA continued to attempt massive incursions, and 123 crossed the Zambesi River early in 1968 to establish base camps. Within a couple of months, though, these bases were destroyed and 60 of the guerrillas were killed. By 1969, security force successes caused both groups to halt infiltration.

Unfortunately, from the point of view of developing an overall counter-insurgency strategy, these early successes gave Rhodesian leaders a false sense of security. As a result, neither political reforms nor increased military spending took place. Meanwhile ZANLA, astute students of Mao's precepts, began politically educating the local African population. ZIPRA, more Soviet in orientation, continued to emphasize military action, especially the planting of land mines. Both groups were based in Zambia, but ZANLA, through ties with FRELIMO, also had the use of bases in Mozambique. In addition to giving the Rhodesian security forces multiple border areas to cover, this access to Mozambique allowed ZANLA to infiltrate the mountainous areas of north-eastern Rhodesia, where more secure bases could be established.

With its political bases better established, ZANLA began attacking white farmers again in December 1971. ZANLA was, in fact, now moving freely across the Rhodesian border, while the fragmented Rhodesian intelligence services, which included the army, British South Africa Police (BSAP), Special Branch and Internal Affairs, suffered from their lack of sources in the tribal lands. So poor was intelligence at this point that, while ZANLA was operating from Mozambique to infiltrate Rhodesia, Rhodesia's two best military units, the SAS and the Rhodesian Light Infantry (RLI), were in Mozambique in support of the Portuguese.

What was worse from the long-term point of view, the ZANLA proselytizing began to pay dividends in north-eastern Rhodesia, the local Africans becoming much more reluctant to betray guerrilla parties operating in their area. Consequently, the Rhodesian security forces finally began to take the threat seriously, establishing a Joint Operations Centre designated 'Hurricane' to co-ordinate counter-insurgency efforts. The tactics employed included the establishment of a security zone along the border (including a 20-klick no-go area and surveillance devices), vigorous patrolling, population and resource control, protected villages, and martial law. The combination of border closure and population control was sound, but was indicative of the tunnel vision which kept the Rhodesian government focused on an external threat throughout the war. Population control included

102

removing the population of an area, whether or not they wanted to go, and then 'sterilizing' the area. Once it was deemed sterile, guerrillas would be channelled into it and destroyed. Eventually 750,000 people would be relocated to 'protected villages'. The Zambian border was closed in 1973, too, in another effort to stop infiltration.

These military measures were sound, but little effort was made to address African political aspirations, and collective punishments against villages alienated substantial portions of the population. To show the government's inability to protect the population, and to gain future recruits, the guerrillas adopted the tactic of kidnapping school children during 1973.

One problem facing the white minority became apparent very early – the finite pool of white manpower to serve in the security forces. By the end of 1973 national service had been extended from nine months to twelve, and in 1974 call-ups were doubled. Loss of civil liberties also followed in the wake of guerrilla activities. Suspects could now be detained without trial for up to 60 days, and residents could be ordered to build defensive works. In an attempt to obtain intelligence, rewards were offered for information leading to the apprehension of guerrillas. Morale in Rhodesia was already eroding when, in July 1974, the Portuguese announced that they would pull out of Mozambique and turn it over to FRELIMO, thus showing that a guerrilla movement could depose a white regime.

Realizing the importance of farming to the Rhodesian economy, the guerrillas struck at isolated white farmers throughout 1974. Militarily, however, the Rhodesian armed forces and BSAP were doing an excellent job. Their kill ratio was ten to one in their favour, and early pseudo-operations involving fake guerrillas proved so successful that the Selous Scouts were formed to carry out even more of these operations. 'Fire Force' tactics employing helicopters and Rhodesian Light Infantry troopers were also highly effective.

Fortunately, as is often the case, there was dissention among guerrilla forces which blunted their effectiveness. Nevertheless, while the security forces continued to score impressive military successes, politically they continued to lose ground, internally and externally. By 1976 relations with Mozambique were so bad that the countries appeared likely to go to war. FRELIMO troops had, in fact, crossed into Rhodesia. Guerrilla incursions increased as well, while about a thousand guerrillas were operating inside Rhodesia, supported by another 15,000 undergoing training in Mozambique. One of these training camps was the target of the most successful raid of the war, when the Selous Scouts struck into Mozambique in August 1976 to kill hundreds of terrorists, perhaps even a thousand, at a ZANLA camp.

Despite the military successes, however, the Rhodesian economy was having trouble sustaining the war effort. The civilian workforce was being eroded as more men served for longer periods. ZANLA continued to apply pressure as well, moving southward. As ZANLA's area of operations expanded, Rhodesia's rail link with the outside world was threatened. Despite being thinly stretched, however, the Rhodesian government avoided increasing the number of Africans in the security forces. Civil liberties suffered even more as journalists faced censorship to prevent the publication of anything which might adversely affect morale. Taxes were increased to help meet costs, and loans or grants from South Africa paid for an ever increasing percentage of the war. National service was lengthened again, to 18 months, double what it had been at the start of the counter-insurgency war. The flight of Europeans now began, too, with substantial numbers leaving each month.

Though the Rhodesian security forces were still showing marked success in military terms, the guerrillas seemed to be achieving their three primary goals: the destruction of European morale, the over-extension of the security forces, and the crippling of the Rhodesian economy. Cross-border operations were highly appealing to the security forces because they were both impressive and detrimental to guerrilla morale, but the political aspirations of Rhodesia's black majority were not being addressed. In fact, cross-border operations helped perpetuate the idea that the insurgency was an external rather than internal problem. South Africa, Rhodesia's chief economic supporter, opposed cross-border operations, too, and threatened financial retaliation if they continued.

Following a pattern which often occurs in democracies facing terrorist or guerrilla threats, harsher internal control measures had been put into effect in Rhodesia. Internationally, the election of Jimmy Carter in the US did not bode well for Rhodesia, as he was strongly committed to black majority rule. With the Zimbabwe Patriotic Front, an alliance of ZANLA and ZIPRA, representing the black majority, a Geneva Conference had begun in October 1976 under Henry Kissinger's aegis, though infiltration and guerrilla activities continued. The surrounding black African states had declared their support for the Patriotic Front, but the Ian Smith government rejected the conference in January 1977, isolating Rhodesia internationally to an even greater extent.

The pressure from all sides finally forced the Rhodesian government to make some concessions, however. In March 1977 blacks were allowed to purchase land, though cynics pointed out that this may have come about because so many white farmers were selling out and leaving that it was necessary to allow black purchases or there would be no one to buy the land.

1977 also saw ZIPRA begin military activities again, probably to build credibility in anticipation of an eventual victory in Rhodesia. Although only a small guerrilla force was sent into Rhodesia, ZIPRA had an army training in Zambia in preparation for a full-scale invasion when the war moved into the third phase. Cuban and Soviet advisors were training this army.

With over 2,500 guerrillas operating in the country and a full-blown insurgency raging, a Combined Operations HQ was formed by the Rhodesian security forces in March 1977. In command of this HQ was Lt Gen Peter Walls, an experienced counter-guerrilla fighter who had served with the SAS in Malaya. Some concession to the need to win over the black population was finally made, too, with the formation of a Psy Ops unit, but its successes were minimal.

In the face of American and British pressure, in November 1977 Ian Smith reluctantly admitted that majority rule was a necessity to end the insurgency. The number of insurgents had doubled within a year, and urban terrorism had grown. The ability of the white population to provide manpower had reached its limit as well, with virtually all white males aged between 18 and 60 serving in some capacity.

In an attempt to salvage something, the Smith government talked with moderate black leaders in late 1977, and on 15 February 1978 an agreement was reached which would lead to a majority rule government. A transitional government was formed on 31 March 1978, but ZANLA and ZIPRA members continued to commit acts of terrorism, including bringing down an Air Rhodesia airliner with an SA-7 missile on 4 September. This caused the Smith government to abrogate the agreement to grant majority rule at the end of 1978. Both ZIPRA and ZANLA expected to gain more power through a military solution, and wanted to discredit the Smith government and the moderate black factions; hence, this decision suited their ends.

With more and more whites emigrating – 13,700 in 1978 – the Rhodesian government was forced to use blacks in the counter-insurgency role to a greater extent, thus making the war a more common effort. Black militias were formed in many locales, and were trained in rudimentary infantry tactics and weapons handling. The guerrillas, however, were now striking at will at economic targets such as the oil depot in Salisbury, which they blew up on 11 December 1978. Their current strategy was to make the war too costly in manpower and money, and they were succeeding.

The number of insurgents operating in Rhodesia continued to grow as well, with 11,000 guerrillas inside Rhodesia by early 1979.

Demoralization of the white population and intimidation of the black population remained high guerrilla priorities, and another Air Rhodesia aircraft was shot down in February 1979, demonstrating the guerrillas' ability to cut even this tenuous link with the outside world. Still looking for an external solution, in April 1979 the Rhodesian SAS came close to killing Joshua Nkomo on a cross-border raid, and another external raid destroyed the ferry between Botswana and Zambia. Although these raids were good for Rhodesian morale, they did little to win the war.

After elections in April 1979, Bishop Muzorewa's United African Council brought a moderate majority government to power. In an attempt to revitalize the Rhodesian economy, many whites were demobilized from the security forces and returned to civilian jobs, but this drastic reduction in manpower allowed the guerrillas almost free rein. Although Zimbabwe-Rhodesia came into existence on 1 June 1979, the true struggle was still going on between supporters of Muzorewa and Robert Mugabe. Eventually, through further negotiations under the auspices of Lord Carrington of Great Britain, Robert Mugabe took power, thus granting ZANU/ZANLA the final victory.

The counter-guerrilla campaign in Rhodesia is worthy of note for many reasons, not the least of which being that it is the classic example of winning a guerrilla war militarily, but still losing politically. The Rhodesian Army was one of the best counter-insurgency forces ever created, a fact obviously appreciated by South Africa, which absorbed certain elements of the Rhodesian Army almost in their entirety into the South African Army when they left Rhodesia. Nevertheless, it was, at best, naive to concentrate on cross-border operations and search and destroy operations, assuming that the minority government did not need to address the political aspirations of the majority black population.

Even some of the effective counter-insurgency tactics were implemented in a way that caused negative consequences. The protected village plan, which had been so successful in Malaya, was handled in Rhodesia in such a way that it drove recruits into the arms of ZIPRA and ZANLA. Rather than offering an incentive to those being resettled, as in Malaya, where they considered their life-style improved in the protected villages, in Rhodesia such villages were often viewed as akin to concentration camps. Protected villages work best, too, when they are protected by local militia with a stake in the safety of the village and its inhabitants. In Rhodesia such militias were not organized until late in the war. Racial separation in the Rhodesian Army was another factor which inhibited the effectiveness of the overall effort, as black Africans did not regard those fighting the war as 'their soldiers'. There were, of course, exceptions. The Selous Scouts were the best example. Here was a unit with blacks and whites serving together, the white members highly dependent for survival on the black members, many of whom had been former guerrillas. The Rhodesian African Rifles was a fine unit which fought very well in Rhodesia, but except for white officers serving with the regiment it was a black regiment.

The front-line Rhodesian units, especially the Rhodesian Light Infantry, Rhodesian African Rifles, Grey's Scouts, the SAS and the Selous Scouts, were all outstanding, but they were used heavily in a search and destroy strategy which made little allowance for pacifying areas and then expanding government control. There is no doubt that the Rhodesian Army could dominate any area of operations, but they were too few to dominate the territory of the entire country. The Rhodesian government had, in effect, chosen a war of attrition (a strategy, it should be noted, which had failed for the US in Vietnam despite its massive resources), yet found itself dependent upon a dwindling pool of white manpower. As a result, large portions of the tribal lands were, in effect, given up to guerrilla domination.

Rhodesia faced other problems which made a successful counter-insurgency difficult, if not impossible. The independence of Mozambique and Angola in 1974 established guerrilla refuges on Rhodesia's borders; refuges with governments highly sympathetic to the guerrilla cause and highly antipathetic to the white government in Salisbury. Mozambique and Angola also stood as nearby examples of former colonial states which had passed to black majority rule. Pressures from nations that should have been Rhodesia's three staunchest supporters - the US, Great Britain and South Africa - often forced concessions which hurt the Rhodesian cause. South Africa, of course, with the fall of Rhodesia, now finds itself the lone white minority state remaining in Africa.

Other important lessons to be learned from the counter-insurgency war in Rhodesia can be gleaned from the Selous Scouts' experience. Trained to operate in enemy controlled territory, and employing ex-terrorists mixed with black and white Rhodesians, the Selous Scouts turned pseudo operations into a high art form. Their fake terrorist bands exerted an influence far out of proportion to their numbers. They eroded confidence between guerrilla bands, which when they met were always suspicious that they were encountering Selous Scouts. Many shoot-outs between guerrilla bands resulted from such suspicions. Although they had little real impact on the final outcome of the war, the highly successful cross-border operations carried out by the SAS and Selous Scouts are also worthy of study as examples of effective special operations. Many white Rhodesians made particularly good counter-insurgency troops because they had grown up in rural Africa and were used to living off of the land to some extent. The influx of US Vietnam veterans and British veterans of other counter-insurgency campaigns brought in some outside expertise which melded with the basic fitness and bush sense of many Rhodesians.

The Rhodesian war is also a good example of a counter-insurgency campaign fought on a shoestring, yet executed relatively effectively. Locally produced armoured vehicles for isolated farmers, for example, form a subject for study in themselves. Grey's Scouts were also an interesting anachronism, as they showed that dragoons could still provide an effective counter-insurgency force in the late twentieth century.

Most of all, however, the lesson to be learned from the Rhodesian war is that political and civic action are as important as military action in winning a counter-insurgency campaign. A counter-insurgency cannot be fought in a vacuum; the political aspirations of the population must be considered, as should external political pressures.

ANGOLA AND MOZAMBIQUE

Although South Africa was also engaged in a counter-insurgency campaign in south-west Africa, against the South-west African People's Organization (SWAPO), the most interesting counter-insurgency campaigns in Africa after the fall of Rhodesia were those in Angola and Mozambique. This is because they were typical of the Marxist regimes that went on the defensive during the hard-line Reagan administration's support for anti-Marxist guerrilla groups.

In Angola, the guerrilla campaign against Portugal had been carried out by three main groups; the MPLA, UNITA and the FNLA. Although the MPLA was Marxist and the others were not, their political differences had taken second place to driving the Portuguese from Angola. However, once the MPLA came to power in 1974, the other two groups continued their guerrilla campaign against the Communist government. Before the Carter administration took office, the CIA had been supporting UNITA and the FNLA, but in 1976 the funds were cut off. The MPLA continued to receive massive Soviet support. The Carter administration proved as much an enemy to the anti-Communist guerrillas as the MPLA, as US aid was granted to Angola, and Zaire and Zambia were pressured not to assist the anti-Communist forces.

Of the two groups, the FNLA initially appeared to be the one most likely to succeed. Under Holden Roberto, an able leader, the FNLA had operated from sanctuaries in Zaire to tie down many of the 25,000 Cuban troops who had been sent to Angola during the weak Carter presidency. The FNLA also harassed the Marxist regime throughout northern Angola in whatever ways possible.

UNITA, which had initially seemed a less viable movement under Jonas Savimba, proved to have a better grasp of the importance of winning over the population before waging a successful guerrilla war. In part, this was due to the fact that Savimba had received his initial guerrilla training in China, and was well-versed in the precepts of Mao. Savimba also realized the importance of finding support to replace that lost when the CIA funds dried up. As a result, he came to an understanding with South Africa, whereby he helped inhibit SWAPO raids into Namibia in return for aid. By 1981, UNITA successes, combined with Roberto going into exile, caused the FNLA operations to be cut back, and this moved Savimba's group to the forefront. In fact, by that time UNITA was in control of about a third of Angola.

Savimba, a PhD and a very intelligent man, realized the need to put a strain on the Angolan economy. He interdicted the Benguela railway line, stopping the flow of copper from Zambia and Zaire as well, and caused substantial losses to the Marxist regimes. The hated Cubans made especially appealing targets, and the cities where they were concentrated became hotbeds of UNITA urban guerrilla activity. Although the East Germans, often thought to be the best intelligence operatives in the Communist world, had helped establish the Angolan intelligence service, UNITA was so strong among the population that government intelligence sources were scant. Because of the widespread popular support for UNITA, and despite the presence of 50,000 government troops, more than 20,000 Cubans, 3,000 East Germans and 1,500 Soviets, the Marxist regime was constantly losing ground. During daylight hours the heavy Angolan and Cuban columns, shielded by air support, could move freely about the countryside. At night, however, UNITA controlled the roads in at least half of the country. This forced the government into concentrating on retaining the population centres, the Cabinda oilfields and the main communications lines. Reopening the Benguela railway remained a high priority, as the war was an ever-increasing financial drain on the Marxist government.

One disadvantage the government faced was that, as UNITA controlled increasing areas of countryside, government troops had to be drawn from urban areas. As they operated poorly in the countryside, this allowed UNITA to establish even tighter control of these areas. The government attempted to establish an élite Long-Range Penetration Unit, with the assassination of Savimba as its primary mission, but this unit received virtually no local support and did not fare well because the locals reported its movements to UNITA. The Marxist regime tried to discredit Savimba by stressing his ties with South Africa, but the presence of the Cubans was just as distasteful to the population, and counteracted any anti-Savimba propaganda.

In parts of the country the UNITA forces had virtually moved into the third stage of guerrilla warfare, as they were operating in 500-man regular battalions south of the Benguela railway. These battalions were part of Savimba's 16,000 regulars, some of whom had been in combat for 15 years and were therefore quite hardened. North of the railway, guerrilla units of about 50 men operated. Among the regulars were some Portuguese Angolans who supported Savimba. UNITA members were well motivated and well trained. After an initial five-month training course, they returned for a three-month training session each year. They were especially adept at ambushes and small-unit tactics. After the withdrawal of US aid, China, Morocco, France, Saudi Arabia and other conservative Arab states continued to provide financial assistance.

Savimba needed the money to meet his expenses, but the war was even more expensive for the Marxist government, running to $1.6 million per day. Moreover, as costs increased, the Angolan economy grew weaker owing to guerrilla attacks on the diamond, coffee, and iron producing areas and interdiction of the railways.

In 1981-82 South Africa moved into Angola on operations against SWAPO, supplying UNITA with captured weapons in return for their allowing the raids to be carried out. The presence of the arrogant Cubans, who were hated by the people and by the Angolan government troops, hurt the government's cause more each month. UNITA propagandized about the Cubans whenever possible, too. One advantage the Cubans gave the Marxist government was airmobility, though UNITA deployed heavy machine guns against helicopters whenever possible. The government also used napalm against UNITA concentrations when attacking garrisons.

Again illustrating Savimba's intellect and grasp of the precepts of guerrilla warfare, the areas under his control were well-organized politically and economically. Although the Marxist government was forced to import half of its food, the areas controlled by Savimba were self-supporting. Hygiene and logistics were also relatively efficient within 'Free Angola'. By 1983 UNITA boasted 35,000 regulars and guerrillas, linked by a comprehensive radio network. At Jamba, Savimba's capital, there was a school for clerks and a machine shop to produce spare parts for captured Soviet weapons.

The government's position grew worse each day, with only about a third of the country really under Marxist control. When they moved at all, Cuban convoys had massive support, but they were still ambushed constantly. The distances between Angola and Cuba and the Soviet Union were so great that logistical support for the Cuban and Angolan government troops was stretched to the limit. By late 1984 UNITA was cutting power to Luanda, the capital, at will, while the FNLA was still operating in northern Angola. The Cabinda oil-fields were so threatened that foreign security personnel had to be hired, and even more of the hated Cubans arrived to bring their total to more than 30,000.

One combined strategy which worked quite well was a South African cross-border strike which drove the Cubans back. As the South Africans withdrew, UNITA would occupy those areas. In the autumn of 1985 the desperate Angolan government launched an offensive intended to break UNITA's power. UNITA did suffer heavy casualties, but not as many as the MPLA. Throughout 1986 and 1987, UNITA continued to carry out operations with the South Africans, forcing the government on to the defensive and necessitating an airlift of 10,000 more Cuban troops at the end of 1987 and beginning of 1988. Using Stinger missiles, which had proved so effective in Afghanistan, UNITA brought down dozens of aircraft operating in support of the Cubans. With South African artillery support, UNITA's string of victories grew throughout 1988. In one battle alone, 70 Soviet tanks were either captured or knocked out. Suffering losses in combat, disliked by the people and hit by a massive AIDS epidemic, Cuban troops began withdrawing in 1989. An agreement with South Africa was supposed to ensure that all had left by 1991.

Without the Cubans, the Marxist regime was in serious trouble, and direct MPLA and UNITA negotiations took place in July 1989. On the negative side, the South Africans were supposed to withdraw their support for UNITA when the Cubans had withdrawn. Finally, in the autumn of 1991 the MPLA and UNITA signed a peace accord, with free elections to follow.

In carrying out their campaign against the MPLA, UNITA had many advantages, the most important being Jonas Savimba himself. Remaining within the country and providing dynamic leadership, Savimba proved a natural leader with an understanding of the precepts of guerrilla warfare. Support from South Africa was important, but UNITA performed quite effectively even when outside support was not available. The massive Cuban, Soviet and East German support for the MPLA kept the government in power, but also turned much of the population against the MPLA, creating Mao's sea for UNITA to 'swim in'. Renewed US clandestine support under the Reagan administration was also important, of course, especially for the availability of

Stinger missiles to counter Angolan and Cuban air power. From the US point of view, UNITA's success was important not only because it discredited the Marxist government of Angola, but also because it discredited the Cuban troops deployed there.

FRELIMO, the Marxist regime which had driven the Portuguese from Mozambique, found itself facing RENAMO, another anti-Marxist guerrilla group, after 1977. Initially RENAMO operated out of Rhodesia with support from the Rhodesian SAS and the Central Intelligence Organization (CIO). However, FRELIMO was so unpopular that, by 1979, about a thousand RENAMO members had moved into Mozambique. Although support from Rhodesia ended in 1980, South Africa filled the vacuum. Many of the South African troops working with RENAMO had really just changed uniforms, as they were members of 5 Reconnaissance Command, which comprised former Selous Scouts. SAMI, the South African intelligence agency, supplied captured arms to RENAMO, too. As in Angola, the support for RENAMO gave the Marxist regime other things to worry about besides aiding SWAPO.

During the 1980s RENAMO operated successfully throughout Mozambique, normally from small bases, with supplies coming from local villagers sympathetic to the cause. Much support came from people who felt that the growing Soviet presence in the country threatened to turn it into another Cuba. By 1982, for example, there were between 4,000 and 5,000 Soviet 'advisers' in Mozambique. Although RENAMO was effective it continued to rely on traditional guerrilla tactics, ambushing government forces, cutting communications and mounting hit-and-run raids against economic targets.

1984 saw an agreement between South Africa and FRELIMO, under which South Africa agreed to stop arming RENAMO in return for FRELIMO ending its support for SWAPO. In fact, SAMI had delivered large quantities of weapons before the agreement, so it really did not hurt RENAMO as much as it appeared at first. Nevertheless, RENAMO strength grew, with government deserters providing a substantial portion of the fresh manpower. In many provinces RENAMO controlled the countryside where capitalism was encouraged, thus gaining popularity for RENAMO and increasing production. Sabotage was carried out very effectively, and provincial capitals were isolated.

Despite the removal of overt South African support, RENAMO strength had grown to more than 15,000 fighters by 1985. On the other hand, FRELIMO was in such trouble that it required 20,000 troops from Zimbabwe just to keep the railway links to neighbouring countries open. To isolate the regime even more, in January and March 1985 RENAMO struck at the airport at Quelimane. FRELIMO found itself increasingly isolated and forced to remain in heavily fortified garrisons. Even with large numbers of foreign troops to help keep routes open, FRELIMO had to use heavy convoys just to move between garrisons. Freedom of movement was virtually non-existent, and FRE-LIMO found itself in the reactive mode.

Under Alfonso Dhlakama, RENAMO had formulated a very clear-cut summary of what it was fighting to achieve. Its manifesto set forth five main goals: removal of the Communist dictatorship; establishment of a government of national unity; free elections; respect for the people's traditions and customs; and respect for human rights and liberty.

So popular was RENAMO that FRELIMO tried 'black' operations, such as masquerading as RENAMO while committing atrocities against villagers. With FRELIMO definitely on the run, it seems likely that, had the US, Great Britain and South Africa given RENAMO their full support, the Marxist regime would have been toppled by 1986. Even without aid, by 1986 provincial capitals were so isolated that they could only be supplied by air. Also aiding the RENAMO cause was the death, in October 1986, of FRELIMO strong man Samora Machel. In the aftermath, as high-ranking FRELIMO members jockeyed for power, RENAMO controlled up to 85 per cent of the country, deploying 25,000 full-time fighters and appearing ready to move into the third phase of its guerrilla war. Following Viet Cong practice, special shock units equipped with recoilless rifles and mortars were used against FRELIMO garrisons and other important targets. These 850-man units came directly under the command of President Dhlakama.

FRELIMO's retention of certain areas of the country could be attributed primarily to the aid of outside troops. As other African regimes tired of propping up the discredited Marxist government, they pulled out their troops, often allowing RENAMO to move into towns as they left. Zimbabwe kept most of its troops in Mozambique through the end of the 1980s, but Tanzania and others had removed theirs. Though RENAMO had not achieved final victory at the time of writing, its power base among the population remains intact, and it appears that FRELIMO will either have to compromise on popular elections or face eventual defeat.

NORTHERN AFRICA

Insurgencies have raged further north in Africa as well, most notably in Ethiopia, where the Eritrean People's Liberation Front (EPLF) and other separatist or guerrilla groups fought against the Marxist Dengue government. By 1988 the EPLF controlled the northern third of Ethiopia. A true people's movement, about 30 per cent of its fighters were female, and it was armed almost completely with captured weapons, including about 150 tanks and other armoured vehicles. Facing the Marxist government forces, the EPLF could muster about 40,000-50,000 guerrillas. Although government forces totalled 300,000, they were opposed by six successionist movements, and were also waging a war against Somalia. As a result, they resorted to the standard tactic of shaky Marxist governments in Africa, and brought in Cuban troops.

The last government attempt to wrest control of Eritrea from the EPLF had been in 1985, but like the previous eight attempts it had been unsuccessful. Despite superior armoured firepower, these attacks had proved unsuccessful primarily because of the EPLF's broad-based support. It actually is a national liberation front, and is viewed as such by the people. The EPLF has also made good use of its radio station, the 'Voice of the Masses', to broadcast in five languages throughout the Horn of Africa. The EPLF's advantages include the highly effective use of mortars, allowing hit-and-run raids; the use of female soldiers, even as infantry or armoured vehicle crews; and a highly developed medical service. As with the successful anti-Marxist insurgencies in southern Africa, the EPLF has established a sound economic and social infrastructure within the controlled areas, making conditions there substantially better than elsewhere in Ethiopia, which is officially recognised as the poorest country in the world.

By 1991 the EPLF and other guerrilla forces such as the TPF were taking more and more territory, and by the summer they were closing in on Addis Ababa. As a result, President Mergistu fled the country, allowing the rebels to topple the Marxist government. As the former guerrillas met to form an independent government, which promised numerous reforms, the interim government agreed to Eritrean independence if access to the Red Sea were guaranteed, and at the time of writing Eritrean independence had been granted. The new government, realizing that it could not support a massive army, planned to trim the military to about 10 per cent of its former strength. This reform, however, could not be fully implemented because the Ethiopian People's Revolutionary Democratic Front, which had taken Addis Ababa, found itself facing Moslem fundamentalist rebels.

Another recent trouble spot, this time in western Africa, has been Liberia. The Liberian Civil War began immediately after Christmas 1989, with a rebellion led by Charles Taylor and his National Patriotic Front (NPF) against President Doe, who had assumed power in a 1980 coup. Many of Taylor's followers had fled Liberia after a fraudulent election in 1985, while Taylor himself had been trained in Libya. Fighting continued for the next sixteen months, into 1991. It is necessary to understand that there are sixteen different tribes in Liberia. For the purpose of understanding the fighting, the most important of these are the Krahn, to which Doe and most government officials belonged; the Mindingo, which supported Doe; and the Mano and Gio, which in simple terms were opposed to the other two tribes.

Although the relationship between the US and Liberia had been a long and close one since the country had been established as a home for freed slaves, the US gave Doe little support against the insurgents. Many deserted from Doe's army as well, thus eroding his power. The US was drawn in, however, in March 1990, when Liberian embassy guards threatened to burn the US embassy and kill personnel. Further threats led to the evacuation of non-essential Americans, and US Marines were put on standby for deployment to evacuate others. By May 1990 Taylor's forces controlled much of the country outside Monrovia, the capital.

By 1991, Prince Johnson of the Independent National Patriotic Front of Liberia was the acting president. Johnson, who had originally been a comrade of Taylor's, now opposed him in a power struggle for control of the country. Amidst the continued fighting, starvation and disease were rampant in Monrovia. To make matters worse, Johnson, who had brutally tortured former President Doe to death, roamed the city with death squads. Although Doe was dead, his loyalists continued to oppose Taylor in the fall of 1991, driving him into Sierra Leone. Finally, in early 1992, a West African Peacekeeping Force moved into Liberia, and in the spring of 1992 elections were scheduled. The repercussions of the Liberian Civil War continued, however, as in the summer of 1992 a military coup took place in Sierra Leone, stimulated at least partly by cross-border raids by Taylor's supporters.

The rest of Africa was not calm, either. The autumn of 1991 saw separatist rebels in Senegal and a rebellion in Rwanda. In the Sudan, the Iranians were using the country as a fundamentalist training camp for the rest of North Africa, but by the fall of 1992 the Islamic Sudanese government was attempting to subdue Christian and Animist guerrillas. By the spring of 1992 Somalia was facing a civil war, with rival war lords jockeying for control of Mogadishu and the countryside. The commitment of US forces to protect food shipments exerted a certain amount of control but, without a strong central government, chaos is likely to return when US troops are pulled out.

It is likely that various guerrilla movements will continue to threaten national governments in Africa. The tribal nature of many African states almost guarantees that one or more groups will oppose the government in power unless it is truly representative of the make-up of the population. As in Latin America, the armed forces are often the most organized political unit in the country and, as a result, they feel the need to step in and take control when it appears that anarchy is about to reign. Occasionally, such coups render a positive service to the population, but they often provide the impetus for an anti-government resistance movement as well. The loss of the Soviet Union as a backer of resistance movements may lend some stability to Africa, but Libya retains the potential to stimulate insurgencies across the continent. The vast quantities of arms which have poured into Africa over the last three decades have also created a plethora of warlords, who function much as guerrilla chieftains in their unwillingness to accept central government authority. Finally, it must not be forgotten that a substantial number of Africans are Moslems, and the rise of Islamic fundamentalism, combined with Iran's foothold in the Sudan, offers the possibility of Islamic guerrilla movements arising in many African states.

CHAPTER VII

The Middle East

Lack of stability attracts insurgencies, and for the last half-century the Middle East has certainly been unstable. Add the incredible oil wealth available to some states, and the rise of militant Islamic fundamentalism, and one certainly has a volatile mixture. The Iranian Revolution not only caught the US by surprise, forcing a rapid reassessment of the balance of power in the Persian Gulf region, but the Islamic regime which replaced the Shah presented myriad problems. In addition to taking the personnel of the US embassy hostage, creating a lengthy loss of face for the Carter administration, Iran also began exporting its revolution. Among other events, this resulted in an attack on the Great Mosque at Mecca.

Iranian Revolutionary Guards soon came to hold the same position in the Middle East that Cuban revolutionaries once held in Latin America, turning up wherever the potential to create revolution existed. As a result, Iranian influence will be found in virtually all of the events which have taken place in the Middle East over the last fifteen years. However, perhaps even more influential than the Iranian revolution, as far as the rest of the world was concerned, was the invasion of Afghanistan by the Soviet Union, as this event was to play a key role in the dissolution of the Communist state.

AFGHANISTAN
Both Afghanistan and its people seem to have been designed by Allah for guerrilla warfare. The Afghans have a long tradition of resistance to central authority, even if it is their own duly elected government. Add a mountainous countryside and rugged individualists whose language lacks a word for 'submission', and it becomes obvious that even the mighty Red Army would face a formidable challenge. The people of Afghanistan are unified by their religion, Islam. It was this religion which the Communist Afghan regime and the Soviet Union tried to deny, thus making a counter-insurgency campaign a counter-jihad campaign as well. In Islam, holy warriors go to heaven if they are killed in battle against infidels.

The Soviet Union had long coveted Afghanistan and, as a result, had worked hard to develop an Afghan Communist Party. In April 1978 the Communist People's Democratic Party of Afghanistan (PDPA) seized control of the government and quickly signed a Treaty of Friendship and Good Neighbourliness with the Soviet Union. However, PDPA attempts to create a Stalinist state met with great dissatisfaction among the population. Especially unpopular were attempts to collectivize farming and impose local commissars, who were often hacked to pieces as a typical Afghan 'protest'. Although the Afghans were so individualistic that they had not formed a central guerrilla movement by early 1979, 25 of the 28 provinces were facing some type of insurgency.

The insurgents were known as Mujahideen (fighters for the Islamic faith) and were fighting a jihad, or holy war. The Afghan army was unsuccessful against the guerrillas, particularly since a good portion of the army deserted and joined the insurgents at the first opportunity. Events came to a head on on 21 March 1979, when dozens of Soviet advisors were killed during anti-PDPA violence, causing massive retaliation including air strikes, resulting in at least 5,000 killed. Blood feuds had been a basic precept of Afghan warfare through the centuries, and this act inspired the Mujahideen to fight even more bitterly in revenge. The Afghan army was committed in force against the Mujahideen, though their forté seemed to be the massacre of innocent civilians.

The Mujahideen, on the other hand, seemed to be growing more effective, ambushing and destroying a government mechanized column in July. As the situation deteriorated, the Soviets began acting to shore up the puppet regime, sending in helicopters and paratroopers to defend Bagram airfield. The Communist regime also moved against members of the professions and religious leaders to eliminate possible resistance organizers. Many of the most highly respected citizens of the country were murdered in this purge. These and other atrocities resulted in open revolt by some army units, while even those which remained loyal fared poorly in combat. Meanwhile, the Prime Minister, Hafizullah Amin, who was chiefly concerned with consolidating his power, killed his predecessor, Taraki, in October 1979. The Soviets had little faith in his ability to rule, however, and by December 1979 had mobile units in place along the Afghan border. Airborne troops had been flown in, too, to provide security at Kabul Airport.

The Soviet invasion was imminent. Advisors immobilized Afghan tanks, while the airborne troops prepared to hold the airport until reinforcements were flown in. On 27 December the invasion began. As motorized rifle divisions roared into Afghanistan, paratroopers moved out from the airport and seized control of the capital. Soviet special forces troops – Spetsnaz – took control of communications and assisted in the capture and execution of Amin. To replace him, the Soviets flew in Babrak Karmal to act as a figurehead while they took closer control of the Afghan government. The Soviets had realized that a holy war offered numerous disadvantages, not the least of which was the possibility of inflaming the Moslem minority in the Soviet Union. Karmal was therefore ordered to cease anti-Islamic activity.

The Afghan army proved even less willing to fight for the Soviets than for its own Communist government. As a result, some units fought against the Soviets, while others deserted almost en masse. More Soviet troops had to be brought in, but on 21 February 1980 there was still an anti-Soviet uprising in Kabul - the 'Night of Allah Akbar'. The Soviets put this revolt down with heavy bloodshed, but other uprisings and more desertions followed. Trained for decades to fight a land war in Europe, the Soviets were not proving adaptable to counter-insurgency operations, either. Their principal tactic at this point was large-scale mechanized sweeps, which the wily Afghan guerrillas easily avoided. More successful was a scorched earth policy, in which they destroyed as much agriculture as possible to deny the guerrillas food. The aerial deployment of PFM-1 'butterfly' mines also interfered with guerrilla movement to some extent, though more often civilians or animals were maimed by them. These tactics resulted in a substantial flow of refugees into Pakistan; refugees whose stories helped rally world opinion against the Soviet Union. This concentration of Afghans in refugee camps actually helped the resistance to get itself organized, as well.

Soviet troops were now fair game for the guerrillas, who managed to isolate some columns and hack them to pieces. Even in Kabul, Soviet troops had to travel in large groups to remain safe. As a result of their ground losses in 1980, the Soviets began to rely more on airpower in 1981. Although the open spaces of Afghanistan were seemingly well-suited to aerial counter-guerrilla operations, the effectiveness of these operations was minimal. In fact, despite massive air support, ground offensives, whether by government troops or Soviets, were normally unsuccessful. The Soviet troops and Kabul troops were normally deployed in heavy columns to secure roads leading to Kabul or other cities, but they really only controlled the ground they sat on. As they moved along in heavy columns, the Soviets often fired randomly along the route in the hope of catching guerrillas lying in ambush. They seemed to have rediscovered the futile tactics of the 'mad minute of fire' and 'recon by fire' employed by the US in Vietnam. The Soviets made their supreme tactical error, however, in conceding the

Mujahideen the high ground above their routes, allowing themselves to be ambushed from above. The Soviets had strong artillery support which they sometimes used to fire preparatory barrages along the routes they were traversing. This tactic, too, indicated that they were operating on the defensive, leaving the initiative to the guerrillas. Lacking heavy weapons, however, the Mujahideen could not move beyond stage two of their guerrilla war. Although they could occasionally destroy government or Soviet armoured columns, they normally had to be content with picking away at them.

The Red Army, despite its slowness to adjust to the war in Afghanistan, was a well-led force which did learn from its mistakes in 1981. Airmobile operations became a key part of Soviet strategy, especially against guerrilla strongholds. Continued depopulation of areas which might support a build-up for an attack on Kabul also proved effective, if draconian. The resistance movement, however, was content to harass the Soviet and government troops, attacking only when the odds seemed favourable. More importantly, the Mujahideen retained much of the initiative, cutting the power lines to Kabul at will and keeping government and Soviet troops bottled up in garrisons except for their occasional massive forays. Guerrilla training had improved, too, as the most skilled survived and passed their knowledge on to others in the training camps which had now been established.

The Soviets had now adapted their combined arms/airmobile tactics well enough to score some marked successes in 1984. Airmobile troops were landed to secure the high ground ahead of advances, helping to eliminate many ambushes, while élite airborne troops were used to advance over inhospitable terrain to harry the guerrillas. However, the guerrillas normally refused to fight when the odds were bad, and faded away. During offensives against one guerrilla group, others would normally hit Kabul or Jalalabad. Such co-operation was at least partially due to an agreement in 1984, which had created an alliance among the seven primary resistance groups. The guerrillas grew bolder, too, hitting Bagram airfield in May and destroying several MiG-21s. All of these attacks had taken place while the Soviets concentrated on clearing the Panjshir Valley, but once the Soviets pulled out of the valley the Mujahideen infiltrated back in and re-exerted their control. Soviet depredations did, however, force as many as 80,000 to flee for the refugee camps in Pakistan.

After their succesful strike against the airfield, the Mujahideen grew much more confident in attacking Kabul. Rocket attacks, attacks on fuel convoys and continued power cuts all harassed the enemy in the capital. The Soviets responded by moving their perimeter outward to establish a defence in depth. Once again, though, they were falling prey to the fortress mentality which normally conceded too much initiative to the guerrillas, as each soldier tied down in static defence was one less for aggressive patrolling. The Soviets also made an unsuccessful attempt in 1985 to seal the Pakistan/Afghanistan border. This border, which had been crossed by caravan/smugglers' routes for centuries, proved far more open than the Soviets might have imagined, especially as they were unwilling to deploy the massive number of troops which would have been necessary to control it. In fact, more weapons and supplies were crossing the borders as the US, China and Saudi Arabia, among others, sent clandestine aid.

Durinq 1985, many Kabul government garrisons were isolated and cut off by the Mujahideen. The Soviets then had to launch massive offensives to relieve the garrisons, suffering heavy casualties in the process. The garrisons then had to be evacuated or left to be surrounded once again. At this stage the Soviet high command should have been reading accounts of the French war in Indochina, for the Afghan campaign was assuming the same complexion. The Soviet strategy of food and population control, simply summarized as destroying both, had worked in that much of the population had fled to refugee camps in Pakistan, but what remained was the hard core of guerrilla fighters, their hatred of the Communists even more finely honed because of the destruction of their homeland.

Unable to seal the Pakistani border, the Soviets began a series of what the intelligence community terms 'black' operations within Pakistan, including an attempt to foment a Pathan revolt. Military moves along the border were intended to intimidate Pakistan during 1985 and 1986. The Mujahideen, however, were not tied to roads, so even the presence of Soviet mechanized forces along the border deterred them very little as they infiltrated across the border, carrying weapons and supplies by hand, by camel, or using other beasts of burden. As the US had discovered in Vietnam, interdiction tactics work much better against a mechanized foe than against one which relies on human and animal transport.

Although there was still much disunity among the resistance, the most influential resitance leader at this point, Ahmad Shah Massoud, had instituted a continuous campaign to drive the Soviets from Afghanistan. Relying on 120-man guerrilla units comprising full-time professionals, Massoud concentrated on attacking Bagram airfield, the Salang Pass highway, and the garrison at Fakhar. Massoud had, in fact, instituted a highly effective guerrilla organization of the pyramid type in the Panjshir. Within his area of operations he divided operational areas by the natural terrain of the country. Guerrilla base areas normally comprised a large valley with a population of 50,000–100,000. The political and military leader of one of these base areas was known as an 'amir'. Each base area was subdivided into from ten to twenty Mujahideen garrisons, each responsible for organizing and defending a group of villages. Villages had their own 'security groups'; farmers and other part-time fighters who acted as a home guard. Local guerrilla forces also included 'strike groups' of 30-50 men who were relatively well armed and were responsible for the defence of a certain area. Directly under the 'amir' were 'mobile groups' which were used for both offensive and defensive operations as needed. Normally, these mobile groups comprised proven combat veterans who had served in the strike groups. The élite central groups of about 25 men were under the direct command of Massoud, and also acted as training groups for leaders of other formations. In north-east Afghanistan, Massoud had also built up a highly efficient civil infrastructure to support guerrilla operations.

The Soviets scored many successes during 1984, '85 and '86 by deploying Spetsnaz as hunter-killer light infantry which could harry and kill the Mujahideen, but by the end of 1986 the guerrillas were so good that they were even achieving successes against the Spetsnaz and airborne troops.

In 1986 Kabul's ineffectiveness led to Karmal being replaced by Najibullah, chief of the Afghan secret police (KHAD). The secret police would eventually achieve ministry status as WAD, the Ministry for State Security, obviously named after their mentors in the KGB. Guerrilla successes became marked, too, as US Stinger missiles allowed them to start shooting down Hind helicopters and some aeroplanes. No longer could the Soviets bomb or strafe the Mujahideen with impunity. Astute observers also noted that Mikhail Gorbachev had begun to hint that the Soviets might leave Afghanistan. Perhaps nothing illustrated the Kabul regime's lack of viability as much as the Battle of Arghandab in 1987. Government troops suffered hundreds of casualties, and 1,200 troops deserted to the Mujahideen. At least 30 armoured vehicles were lost, too, many to anti-tank mines, and numerous aircraft fell to Stingers.

Attempting to set the stage for the Soviet equivalent of 'Peace with Honour', Najibullah, at Soviet insistence, framed a new constitution and changed the name of the country to the Republic of Afghanistan. In theory, at least, non-Communist parties would be allowed, but only approved 'parties' could take part in the political process. When elections were held, it was no surprise that Najibullah won. The Mujahideen continued their guerrilla war, while the Soviets worked to remove Iranian and Pakistani support for the guerrillas.

KHAD/WAD, as the most reliable force within the Communist Afghan government, grew in power during the late 1980s, and by 1988 it had 60,000–70,000 personnel and 100,000 informers. Much like the KGB, KHAD began fielding military units totalling 10,000-15,000 men.

Although comparisons between Afghanistan and Vietnam can be overstated, the Soviets did find themselves in a similar situation to the one faced by the US during the early 1970s. Just to maintain the status quo in Afghanistan, they would have had to commit substantial additional assets. The Stinger had added an entirely new dimension as well, forcing the withdrawal of garrisons that previously had remained in place through helicopter support. Considering that the Mujahideen's success rate with the Stinger was running at about 60 per cent, with somewhere between 150 and 200 Soviet aircraft brought down by 1987, the Soviet reluctance to continue to lose aircraft is understandable.

By this stage, guerrilla operations were showing much more sophistication than in the earlier years of the campaign. Well planned and well co-ordinated attacks now included simultaneous assaults from multiple directions, supported by rockets, mortars and artillery. Stinger and Blowpipe missile crews prevented Soviet air support, or at least made it costly. Cross-border raids into the Soviet Union itself were launched, forcing the Soviets to deploy additional KGB border guards. Interestingly, though, the Stinger and Blowpipe might not have been the most effective forms of American aid. During 1987 and 1988 the US airlifted more than 2,000 Missouri mules to the resistance, and these hearty animals, with temperaments much like those of the stubborn Afghans, proved the perfect beasts of burden for supplying the Mujahideen. Unfortunately, the guerrillas' ideas of animal care were pretty primitive, and many of the mules died.

The Soviets had not completely conceded to the Mujahideen, and late in 1987 they launched a major operation to relieve Khost, which had been beseiged for months. Using specially trained mountain infantry supported by helicopters flying below the Stinger's effective altitude, the Soviets showed that they had adjusted to the realities of combat in Afghanistan. Airmobile troops seized the high ground along the route of advance, leap-frogging from hilltop to hilltop and holding the positions until the advancing mechanized troops were well past. Khost was relieved, but, even in this well-planned and well-executed operation, Soviet and Afghan government casualties were twice those of the Mujahideen. In retrospect, it seems likely that this offensive was the Soviet swan song, an offensive which would give the Red Army a face-saving victory before pulling out. By the spring of 1988 the Soviets were pulling back to their main bases, from which, through early 1989, they withdrew into the Soviet Union. In extremely critical situations they would commit air power, as at Kandahar late in 1988 to prevent its fall. During the defence of Kandahar the Soviets also fired Scud missiles (to become familiar during Operation Desert Storm) at Afghan villages which supported the guerrillas attacking Kandahar. Soviet advisors remained, but the burden of combatting the Mujahideen would now fall on Afghan government forces. Interestingly for a non-capitalistic state, the Soviet Union seemed to believe by 1989 that, even if military and political victory eluded them, they would still reap the benefits of economic ties with Afghanistan.

By this stage of the war, Afghan military units were often stationed in a mix of four types of troops: army, interior troops, KHAD and militia. They were primarily based together to keep an eye on each other, but the KHAD troops did offer some 'stiffening', though they were so hated that they drew Mujahideen attacks and could not always count on support from other units. The WAD was also suspected of involvement in the August 1988 death of President Zia of Pakistan, as he was a staunch supporter of the guerrilla cause. US-supplied Spanish M-84 120mm mortars gave the Mujahideen far greater range from 1989, too, and they could strike at Afghan government garrisons even more effectively. As the Soviet mechanized columns streamed toward the border, the guerrillas usually, and sensibly, let them withdraw in peace.

During almost a decade of combat in Afghanistan, the Soviets had suffered over 50,000 casualties and lost more than 1,000 aircraft. Afghan government casualties were much higher. Even more telling, one and a half million civilians had reportedly died. The Red Army had suffered a loss of prestige similar to that suffered by the US Army in Vietnam, and a generation of cynical veterans returned to the Soviet Union, many addicted to drugs they had discovered in Afghanistan. Without a doubt, the frustrations of the Afghanistan campaign helped set the stage psychologically for many of the political reforms which transformed the Soviet Union during the next three years.

The Soviet Union did not abandon her erstwhile ally completely, as political pressure continued to be applied against Iran, China and Pakistan to try to prevent them giving too much support to the resistance. Probably the greatest aid to the Kabul regime, however, remained the dissension among the Mujahideen, especially with the common enemy, the Soviet forces, now gone. The atrocities committed on both sides, combined with the Afghan sense of blood fueds, did not bode well for a negotiated settlement, though the Soviet Union had given some indications that it might support a partitioned Afghanistan, with the border areas with the Soviet Union remaining under Communist control.

By the autumn of 1988 the Mujahideen had infiltrated 10,000 men into Kabul in preparation for a final battle for the capital, and Kandahar was close to falling by the end of the year. The Stinger kept the government forces from using air power against the guerrillas, while their superiority in armour was counteracted by the Milan anti-tank missile now being used by their opponents. As of early 1989, both the Communist government and the Mujahideen could deploy about 125,000 troops. Although the Mujahideen remained fragmented, this was balanced by the fact that many government troops were reluctant conscripts. It was assumed that large numbers of government troops would defect once the Soviets were gone, but all Communist Party members began to receive 15 days of military training and were issued with AKs in preparation for the final battle. Oddly, the Communist regime received support from some moderates, who feared that a fundamentalist Islamic regime might replace the Communists and be even worse.

The problems facing the Mujahideen in moving into the third stage of their guerrilla war and taking Kabul were graphically illustrated in the March 1989 attack on Jalalabad. The area was defended by 17,000 hard-core regime troops, while 15,000-20,000 guerrillas were attacking. However, owing to poor planning and lack of co-ordination, the attack failed. To defeat the Communist regime decisively, a unified command and regular forces were required. The disorganization within the Mujahideen ranks was also hurting them in a more subtle way. Thousands of regime troops who would gladly have defected were afraid to do so, as they assumed that they would immediately be executed. Had there been a strong authority to assure them of sanctuary, Communist strength would have been rapidly depleted.

Kabul, however, was in deep trouble. With most of the country controlled by the resistance, and only two routes into and out of Kabul - the airport and the Salang highway to the Soviet Union - the noose was slowly tightening around the capital.

Massoud saw the need for a true Mujahideen army, and began training his recruits for 30 days in readiness to form an Islamic army to take Kabul. Holding the Salang highway remained one of the highest priorities of the Communist regime. In January 1989 Mujahideen pressure along the route had caused food riots in Kabul. In retaliation, Soviet and Afghan government forces had devastated villages along the highway with artillery strikes, killing 400-600, mostly civilians. Regime troops then dug in along the route. In March 1989 Massoud's troops had closed the Salang again during the battle for Jalalabad, but after hard fighting the regime troops reopened the highway. The northern part of the highway fell under control of the Shi'ite militia, who allowed supplies to pass in return for supplies and weapons from the Soviet Union. At other points, however, ambushes and harassment of convoys remained the norm, providing a regular source of captured supplies for the Mujahideen. In some places, in fact, the main road had to be abandoned because the terrain allowed ambushes, and convoys on the way to Kabul had to use side roads.

For much of the war the Mujahideen had kept in contact with Moslems in the Soviet Union, but after the Red Army withdrawal fundamentalists, especially, tried to foment religious unrest within the Soviet Union. Parties infiltrated across the border to supply Soviet Moslems with copies of the Koran and audio tapes of mullahs. There were also plans to supply weapons if needed. Increased Soviet religious tolerance diffused the effectiveness of this destablization campaign to some extent, but it certainly proved an annoyance to the Soviet government.

Meanwhile, in Afghanistan, fighting among the Mujahideen factions kept them from focusing on the defeat of the government forces. The guerrillas' success against the Soviet Union had attracted Moslems from all over the world who wanted to take part in the fighting and study tactics. Among them were Palestinians and Iranians, both of whom aroused suspicions among many of the Mujahideen about their intent. More welcome were those from Chinese Moslem areas and Kashmir in India, who wanted to help spread the Holy War.

In 1991 Khost fell to a combined offensive by seven Mujahideen groups when they set their squabbles aside to assault this important government stronghold, destroying 80 aircraft on the ground and in the air during the operation. Before the attack, the guerrillas made sure that 20,000 civilians had been evacuated. Although the Soviet Union had substantial internal problems, in the north along the Soviet border some Soviet pilots were still flying missions against the Mujahideen from the Soviet Union, but this was intended more to discourage cross-border movement of the guerrillas than to influence the war.

In 1992 it finally appeared that Kabul would fall. On 1 January Washington and Moscow reached a mutual agreement to stop supplying arms. Najibullah had grown increasingly dependent upon members of northern tribes, especially the Uzbeks who comprised the 53rd Militia Division, to keep his regime intact. However, when he tried to install southern Pushtan generals, units from the north allied themselves with Massoud, depriving the regime of its most important combat troops. On 17 April Najibullah resigned.

The fighting for the capital continued, though, as the Uzbeks and other northern minorities joined with Massoud's troops to battle the Hezb-i-Islami, who were also trying to take the city. Both Massoud and Gulbuddin Hekmatyar of the Hezb were fundamentalists, but Massoud believed in representative government and was more acceptable to other Mujahideen groups. Although both groups had supporters among former government troops, those fighting alongside Massoud proved the most effective, and the Hezb were driven from Kabul. Sibghatullah Majadidi, the interim Mujahideen president of Afghanistan, then arrived from Pakistan to assume power, though his defence minister, Massoud, would truly be the most powerful man in the country. Even with the Communist regime defeated, however, it appears that factional and ethnic fighting will continue to divide Afghanistan with continuing bloodshed. The threat of groups such as the Hezb, who want to ally with Iran, may be the greatest, but after years of fighting there seems to be a reluctance to lay down arms and return to a life of farming.

The Mujahideen were successful for many reasons. The uniting and militant force of Islam was very important, as was the Pathan code of Pushtuwali, which requires revenge for damage done to one. Applied on a countrywide scale, this revenge was exacted from the Soviet Union and the Communist government. As even a duly constituted Afghan goverment had trouble ruling, an unpopular government would find it even harder. Additionally, the typical Afghan was warlike and familiar with weapons. The mountainous terrain was important to support a resistance movement, as was the nearness of Pakistan and Iran, which allowed the Mujahideen to receive supplies. The principal disadvantages faced by the guerrillas were their tendency to operate as small, relatively undisciplined units, and the fighting among various resistance groups. Moreover, teaching the Mujahideen to use modern weapons (i.e., the need to lead aircraft, and the importance of scoring a first hit with mortars) was at times somewhat difficult.

In fighting the Mujahideen, the Soviet Union found that an army trained for a conventional war in Europe was not particularly well suited to guerrilla warfare. The Red Army did adapt, however, using specialized air assault, airborne, Spetsnaz, and mountain troops to take the war to the enemy. As with the US in Vietnam, the Soviet Union found itself attempting to prop up a regime which did not meet the political aspirations of the population and, hence, would never receive widespread support. The cost to the Soviet Union was growing year by year, and showed every indication of continuing to grow, especially after the Mujahideen received Stingers and other advanced weapons. The Afghan adventure almost certainly played a part in the disintegration of the Communist system in the Soviet Union, producing a disillusioned generation of conscripts opposed to the establishment, just as the Vietnam War had done for the US.

RESISTANCE AGAINST IRAQ IN KUWAIT

Although the Iraqi occupation of Kuwait did not last long enough for a fully developed guerrilla movement to develop, there was an active and successful resistance during the occupation. Initially arising in retaliation for Iraqi atrocities, the Kuwaiti Resistance eventually proved an excellent source of intelligence. As Iraqi soldiers raped, looted and tortured in an attempt to erase Kuwait's sense of identity, the Resistance battled to retain that identity and reassert national pride. Probably the most effective resistance fighters were the Shi'ites, who already had a secretive cell system in place, in at least some cases because they were agents of Iran. Iran aided them as well, sending instructors to teach them the use of explosives with which they blew up Iraqi military compounds, barracks and AA emplacements, among other targets. Eventually there were about 60 Resistance groups, each with an average of 40–50 members, who did not know the identities of members of any other group.

Iraqi Intelligence, the Mukhabarat, had 7,000 agents operating in Kuwait, with suspected members of the Resistance as their primary targets. As with the Gestapo and Milice in occupied France, the Iraqi secret police were often the best recruiters for the Resistance, creating guerrillas with each loved one they murdered or tortured. Within Kuwait City, the Resistance sniped at Iraqi positions and also killed Iraqis in much more subtle ways. For example, nurses and doctors in Kuwaiti hospitals, forced to operate on Iraqis, administered lethal injections, while Resistance members aware of the Iraqi habit of looting food and drink at checkpoints would lace orange juice with rat poison and hide it in the trunks of their vehicles so that it would be confiscated.

Resistance members also acted as the conduit for the distribution of money which was used to bribe the Iraqis to leave many citizens alone. Once Operation Desert Storm began, the Resistance helped coalition airmen who had been shot down to escape and evade, supplied guides for coalition troops and provided intelligence on potential targets.

As the liberators entered Kuwait City, however, the Resistance turned to harsh revenge against those who had collaborated with the Iraqis, summary execution often being the punishment. About 5 per cent of the Resistance fighters had been Palestinians, but many Pales-

Above: Rhodesian troops take a break during a patrol. (David Scott Donelin)

Below: Rhodesian troops on patrol during the counter-insurgency war. (David Scott Donelin)

Top left: Members of the French Foreign Legion are often deployed when former French colonies ask for assistance against insurgents. (ECP)

Bottom left: US military personnel often work with allied units to establish relationships which can be expanded during counter-insurgency operations. Here, an 82nd Airborne Division officer and an Egyptian airborne officer discuss a joint jump. (US Army)

Above: In Afghanistan the Soviets used airmobile troops to wrest control of the high ground from the Mujahideen.

Below: Rhodesia made highly effective use of its limited supply of helicopters during its counter-insurgency war.

Above: Selous Scouts show fatigue during a selection course. (David Scott Donelin)

Below: Members of the Selous Scouts being trained on Communist Bloc weapons likely to be used by the guerrillas they will impersonate. (David Scott Donelin)

Right: Airborne troops can frequently be inserted quickly to bring force to bear early in an insurgency, or to reinforce an outpost. (US Army)

Below: Members of France's national counter-terrorist unit, the GIGN, show their various capabilities. (ECP)

Left: Members of the SAS enter the Iranian Embassy in London to free hostages. (22nd SAS)

Above: Members of Spain's GEO counter-terrorist unit.

Below: Members of the Spanish Foreign Legion are the type of élite light infantry especially well suited to counter-guerrilla operations. (Spanish Foreign Legion)

Above: Members of the Contra guerrillas armed with M1 carbines and a crossbow, the latter still an effective silent killer.

Below: These antiSandinista Contras appear to be rugged jungle fighters.

Above and below: Contras carefully infiltrating Nicaragua via the water.

Above: A Contra patrol returns to its base.

Below: A South African Reconnaissance Commando with an RPG launcher.

Above: Guerrillas raised and trained by South African Reconnaissance Commandos in Mozambique. (David Scott Donelin)

Below: AntiCommunist guerrillas in Mozambique.

Left: A member of the Selous Scouts ready to set out on a patrol, armed with a Soviet DPM light machine gun. (David Scott Donelin)

Below: South African Reconnaissance Commandos prepare charges to destroy a bridge in Mozambique. (David Scott Donelin)

Above: Although the Soviet Union deployed its élite airborne troops to Afghanistan, it still could not defeat the Mujahideen.

Right: Members of the 2nd Foreign Legion Parachute Regiment practise instinctive firing techniques with their MAT49 submachine guns. (FIRE)

Above: The French Foreign Legion has often been deployed on counter-insurgency operations. This jeep patrol of the 2nd Foreign Legion Parachute Regiment is light, well trained, and readily deployable, making it an excellent choice for CI operations. (FIRE)

Above: US Special Forces personnel practise operating as guerrillas behind enemy lines. (Special Warfare School)

Below: The sniper can be a critical element in counter-terrorist and counter-insurgency operations, as he can strike from a distance, often creating psychological trauma among the survivors as well as selectively killing enemy personnel. (US Army)

Above: US Army counter-terrorist personnel practise retaking a bus seized by terrorists.

Right: Members of Belgium's counter-terrorist unit, the ESI. (Rene Smeets)

tinians were detained because the PLO had supported Iraq, and because some Palestinians had supported the Iraqi forces and collaborated. Later, many would be evicted from the country. The Resistance would prove to be a double-edged scimitar, however, as many of its members also opposed the return of the Emir, especially when it appeared that no concessions would be made to greater political freedom.

THE KURDS

The guerrilla war being carried out by the Kurds offers some interesting anomalies. Although Kurdistan is a relatively well-delineated area with a distinct population, the fact that it extends into four nations – Turkey, Syria, Iran and Iraq – each of which has carried out campaigns to exterminate the Kurds, makes the survival of a Kurdish resistance a study in determination. The most publicized Turkish guerrilla group is probably the Pesh Menga, in the Iraqi areas of Kurdistan, which gained attention as the plight of Iraqi Kurds came to be known in the aftermath of Operation Desert Storm. The political arm of the Iraqi Kurdish resistance is the Kurdish Democratic Party (KDP), led by Massod Barzani.

Iraq's campaign against the Kurds had been constant and brutal throughout Saddam Hussein's rule. Many had been relocated to controlled villages, really concentration camps, often located in the desert far away from their mountain homes. Roads had been built into the mountains, not to aid the Kurds, but to allow Iraqi troops to be deployed more easily for operations against them. Finally, the Bekma Dam was being built to flood a good portion of Kurdistan. Villages, and even a city of 80,000, had been levelled and the survivors removed to camps. A classic counter-insurgency tactic is to remove the basis of support for the guerrillas by relocation, but few have practised this tactic as ruthlessly as the Iraqis.

Across the border in Iran, the Kurdish Democratic Party of Iran fulfils the same function as the KDP in Iraq. Ironically, during the Iran-Iraq War, while he was trying to exterminate the Kurds in Iraq, Saddam Hussein gave aid to those in Iran to help them fight against Iran, while the Iranians gave aid to the Iraqi Kurds to help them fight Iraq.

Other Kurds live in Turkey and Syria. The largest number live in Turkey, which has a Kurdish population of about eleven million, equal to the combined total in the other countries. The Kurdish Workers Party (PKK) is the principal organization of Turkish Kurds. Marxist in philsophy, it wants an independent Kurdish Middle Eastern state, but it wants this state to be Marxist. This has led to conflict with the other Kurdish guerrilla forces. However, the PKK is efficient, running numerous training camps along the border. With 10,000 guerrillas operating in Turkey, and with an average of at least one action per day against government forces, the PKK is a relatively serious threat. The basic PKK unit is the *manga*, composed of 15 fighters; three *mangas* equal a *takim*. Three *takims* are organized as a *buluk*.

The Kurds have certain definite advantages in fighting a guerrilla war. A Kurdish proverb states: 'The Kurds have no friends but the mountains', and, from the point of view of fighting a guerrilla war, mountain bases offer many advantages owing to inaccessibility. Having been raised in the mountains, many Kurdish guerrillas move and fight very well in rough terrain. The fact that Kurdistan encompasses four borders also allows the guerrillas a certain freedom of movement, though the opposition of all four governments certainly does not help. It appeared that the massive defeat of Saddam Hussein's forces offered an opportunity for the Kurds, but Iraqi forces moved rapidly to suppress them, using them as scapegoats, in fact, after defeat by the United Nations Coalition forces. The US offered a degree of protection for a time, but without strong outside support there seems little hope that the Kurds will be able carve out an independent state.

The US Special Forces has had long-standing ties with the Kurds, and should the US desire to foment trouble for Iran or Iraq, offering assistance to the Kurds would certainly be a method. The only US ally in the area is Turkey, and it is doubtful whether Turkey would support any military aid to the Kurds which could eventually be turned against them. Another point working against US support for the Kurds is the fact that one faction, al-Daawa, assisted Iran in acts of terrorism against the US, as well as against the French, Saudis and Kuwaitis in the past. In most of the West the Kurds are viewed as bandits more concerned with intramural squabbles. Furthermore, the US does not want another fundamentalist Shi'ite state, and fears that the Kurds might form one. On the other hand, the US did encourage Kurdish hopes to destabilize Iraq, and thus must take some responsibility. At the time of writing, the Kurds are continuing their struggle for independence, but in truth they are also fighting for survival.

LEBANON

The civil war that has raged in Lebanon since 1975 contains elements of terrorism and elements of urban guerrilla operations, though it is probably most closely related to China in the age of the warlords, where factionalism prevented a strong central government. At the time of writing, Lebanon does not really have a central government for all practical purposes. Instead, various factions control different percentages of the country and receive allegiance from sections of the population. The most influential groups are: the Hezbollah, which is composed of Iranian oriented fundamentalists who are pro-PLO and anti-Syrian; the Amal, the largest Moslem faction, which is allied to the Syrians and, though also Shi'ite, does not normally co-operate with Hezbollah; the Sunni Moslems, who are centred around Tripoli and are pro-PLO and Hezbollah and anti-Syrian; the Druze, who have been allied with Israel and Syria at different times; the Syrian army, which has about 30,000 soldiers and 3,000 intelligence agents in the country; the Lebanese Force Command, which is Christian and progressive, though it has been attracting some Moslems searching for stability and trying to avoid the fundamentalists; the Lebanese army, which is mixed Moslem and Christian (though many Christians have left), and is viewed with suspicion for supplying weapons to the Druze and Amal; and the South Lebanese army, which is supported by Israel but contains Moslems.

Beirut remains the centre of factional fighting, with West Beirut under Moslem control and East Beirut under Christian control. The 'Green Line' separates the two groups. Car bombings were common in East Beirut until members of the Lebanese Force Command captured the bombers and eliminated them. Syria still hopes to control Lebanon, and after its co-operation with the US during Operation Desert Storm has been able to assert its authority even more.

Acts of terrorism in Lebanon are especially hard to counter, as it is often quite difficult to determine exactly who committed them. Despite tough talk from US politicians, for example, retaliatory action has still to be taken against those responsible for bombing the US Marines barracks in Beirut. Sheik Musewi of the Hezbollah, one of the key planners of the attack on the Marines and the US Embassy, was assassinated in February 1992, but by the Israelis rather than by the US. This led to a retaliatory attack on the Israeli Embassy in Argentina in March of the same year, in which 24 were killed and about 250 injured.

At the behest of Iran, the Hezbollah continued its attempts to undermine Middle East peace talks, while Iran has reportedly purchased three nuclear devices from the former Soviet republic of Kazakhstan. Although Syria has also supported terrorism in the past, Iran seems to remain the greatest threat to security in the Middle East as it continues to attempt to force its fundamentalist views on other Moslem states through the Hezbollah, Islamic Jihad, and other terrorist groups.

Lebanon proved the proverbial quagmire for Israel, France and the US when they became involved. Syria has, of course, committed substantial military assets to Lebanon, but has yet to incorporate it into a greater Syria. For their own reasons, Israel and Iran will continue to oppose Syria's territorial claims to Lebanon. Meanwhile, the Christian and Moslem population of that land will continue to do battle, to some extent because that is all that an entire generation knows.

The potential for military operations to counter terrorism and insurgency is probably greater in the Middle East than anywhere else in the world. The combination of militant Islamic fundamentalism and world dependence upon oil makes the likelihood of counter-insurgencies being fought in the Persian Gulf especially high. The presence of religious and/or ethnic minorities, as well as expatriot Palestinians, in many countries in the area also offers potential for conflict. With Operation Desert Storm, the US and its allies showed a preparedness to become militarily involved in the area, but should they find themselves assisting one of the Gulf states in a counter-insurgency war, as the British did in Oman, high-tech stealth fighters or Abrams tanks will prove much less decisive.

CHAPTER VIII

Strategy and Tactics of Guerrilla Warfare and Terrorist Operations

Although guerrilla warfare and terrorist operations have many similarities, guerrilla warfare normally entails a much broader campaign involving a substantial portion of the population. In fact, terrorism, in many cases, is a highly specialized form of guerrilla warfare waged across the globe rather than within the borders of a country targeted for revolutionary change. Many terrorist movements have arisen from the ranks of those defeated in guerrilla campaigns within their home countries. Therefore, one must first understand the strategy and tactics of the guerrilla in order to understand how the terrorist uses many of the same techniques in his war against society.

GUERRILLA OPERATIONS

Although there will frequently be guerrilla activity in cities, most successful guerrilla movements are based in the countryside. Consequently, an important consideration for any guerrilla movement is the establishment of safe bases in the countryside. One of the first criteria for such bases is that access must be difficult, to prevent security forces from attacking and wiping out the nucleus of the movement before it has reached the strength necessary to enable it to move into full-scale warfare. Mountains, jungles, marshes and other inhospitable areas are therefore best for guerrilla strongholds. Tito's mountain camps, Giap's underground jungle warrens and Lawrence's desert wastelands allowed raiders to return to areas which made pursuit difficult. During the last half-century at least, guerrilla bases have also needed to be shielded from aerial reconnaissance, so jungle canopy, caves or man-made camouflage have become important.

Terrain should be selected which will allow a relatively small number of guerrillas to defend their camps should elements of the security forces reach them, and well-planned withdrawal routes should exist in case a retreat is necessary. One of the guerrillas' great advantages is that they do not need to hold specific ground, though they must remain a force in being. Despite the need for rough, defendable terrain, guerrilla bases still need to be within relatively easy reach

133

of settlements, perhaps one day's travel, to allow the guerrillas to receive food, reinforcements and intelligence. To enable these settlements and the area of operations to be reached, concealed trails are invaluable. Throughout the Vietnam War, VC/NVA infiltration routes were a primary target of US counter-insurgency efforts, and justifiably so. Additionally, routes connecting with other guerrilla controlled areas are highly desirable. A ready source of drinking water is another necessity; this is one reason why mountains and jungles are normally better than deserts for maintaining guerrillas. In addition to villages or settlements, a substantial number of farms near the guerrilla base offers another ready source of food.

With a secure base of operations, the guerrilla band can begin to implement its strategy for victory against government forces. The US Civil War general who said that winning battles consisted of 'gettin' there fustest with the mostest' might well have been summarizing a basic tenet of guerrilla warfare. The guerrilla must attack vulnerable objectives with superior strength, avoiding direct engagements with superior forces. It is important to have bases near operational areas because they enable the guerrillas to assemble rapidly for a mission, then quickly disperse once the operation has been completed. The ability to mix with the population is particularly important, as it allows the guerrilla to return to concealment quickly after an attack. Guerrillas must also maintain the initiative, to keep security forces and the government off balance. As long as government forces are reacting to guerrilla strikes, they will not be able to put a comprehensive counter-guerrilla plan into operation.

Surprise is one of the greatest weapons in the guerrilla arsenal, and it must be exercised using the following:

1. Superior intelligence gathered through sympathizers or by other means
2. Good planning
3. Stealth, especially the use of the night
4. Mobility, through the use of lightly equipped and armed irregulars
5. Speed
6. Determination, through superior belief in a cause.

Other more specific tactics which have proven quite effective for guerrillas against government forces include sniping, delaying tactics against security forces, harassment and deception. Against government installations, stand-off tactics using mortars, rockets, artillery and sniping are most effective.

An especially important tactic for the guerrilla is the ambush, which to be effective should follow certain basic precepts:

1. Launch the ambush at the closest possible range for maximum shock effect
2. Have good intelligence and planning before the ambush
3. Use commanding ground, concealment and camouflage when siting the ambush and positioning the guerrilla forces
4. Remain silent and immobile until the target is in the killing ground
5. Open fire by prearranged signal, and try to immobilize the target within the killing zone
6. Hit hard and fast, inflict maximum casualties and capture all usable equipment and weapons
7. Use good security to cover movement to and from the ambush site
8. Set secondary ambushes to hit reinforcements or escapees
9. Hit and run against superior forces which might regroup and fight back.
10. Have a planned withdrawal route guarded by security detachments
11. Immediately re-merge with the population after the ambush.

Since government forces are often tied to static positions, the raid is another important tactical tool of guerrilla forces, and can be used to destroy fixed installations such as airfields, police stations and harbours. An especially juicy target for a guerrilla raid is a government store or armoury, where arms, equipment and supplies may be captured. A raid may also result in government security personnel being killed or captured, thus helping to demoralize the opposing forces.

Raids are frequently launched after using infiltration to approach the target, often at night. A standard guerrilla raid tactic is to split the force into three elements: the first to eliminate government security personnel; the second to kill or capture personnel and/or capture supplies; and the third to serve as a covering force for the operation.

Another important guerrilla target is the government's lines of communication. Highways, riverways, railways and telephone lines can all be constantly harassed and/or cut to deny government forces ease of movement and communication, and to hurt the economy. It will be virtually impossible for the government to defend all lines of communication; hence, guerrilla efforts can be continually switched to weak points.

Guerrilla movements must exercise as much control of the population as possible. If large segments support the guerrillas through dislike of the government or because of ethnic ties, or as true believers, so much the better; but it is necessary to establish such control in any case. Local leaders who help to make everyone feel part of the struggle are a key element. If possible, the population should be controlled through organization and propaganda, but threats and terrorism will be used as well if necessary.

Since the population must be a source of guerrilla strength, movements are constantly on the watch for spies within the population who would report them to government forces. On the other hand, supporters working for the government make excellent sources of intelligence regarding government plans and operations. Supporters can also help subvert loyal members of the population. Disinformation, such as atrocities carried out while dressed as government troops, may also be used to win segments of the population to the cause.

Terrorism to gain control of the population may include the taking of hostages; often young children who are then trained as guerrillas. Additionally, those who co-operate with the government may be killed, often quite brutally, as an example to others, or have their property destroyed.

As inroads are made into the population, guerrillas can use strikes, demonstrations, riots and other public displays to disrupt government control. Workers at important industrial sites such as power stations can commit sabotage. To be successful, guerrillas must play on the discontent of the population to win support for their campaign against the government.

In implementing their strategy and tactics, guerrilla forces operate from certain points of strength:

1. Their lack of responsibility for providing government services themselves
2. Their highly trained and motivated leaders
3. Their ability to use punishment without due process
4. Their dedication to the cause
5. Their ability to escalate or de-escalate operations at will
6. Their ability to choose the time and place of operations.

TERRORIST STRATEGY AND TACTICS

Many tactics of the guerrilla are also tactics of the terrorist, though acts of intimidation and violence are much more overtly used by the terrorist and are, in fact, often an end in themselves. While the guerrilla will use terrorist tactics to intimidate the population or government forces, the terrorist uses violence to make the population believe that the government is incapable of defending them, and to force the government to take such repressive measures that disillusionment will arise among the population. Terrorist groups can function with far fewer dedicated members than required by guerrilla movements. Many of the most influential terrorist groups have had fewer than 100 active personnel.

While guerrillas may be called the true believers of the revolutionary faith, terrorists are more akin to the monks of revolution, dedicating themselves to creating the climate for revolution through their acts.

Terrorists use very high profile acts, often those which can become media events, such as:

1. Assassination, often in daylight on urban streets, thus asserting their ability to operate at will and the government's inability to protect citizens
2. Bombings, either in public places, such as those acts carried out by the IRA in cinemas, pubs, railway stations, department stores and elsewhere, or directed at selected targets, such as the IRA attack on Lord Mountbatten
3. Kidnappings, for ransom or release of prisoners, but the targets themselves often have symbolic value, such as Aldo Moro or Brig Gen Dozier
4. Hijacking of aircraft, trains, ships, etc. and the use of them, the crews and the passengers as bargaining chips to obtain concessions
5. Robberies of banks and armoured cars to finance continued operations.

Symbolic targets have great appeal to terrorists, because such targets allow them to make a statement through their use of violence. Consequently an important monument, such as the Statue of Liberty or Eiffel Tower, has appeal as a site for a terrorist act. Terrorist acts often have the very practical goal of raising funds through ransoms, or of gaining the freedom of captured comrades. Captured terrorists know that their associates will attempt to gain their freedom, not only as a morale booster, but also because terrorist ranks cannot afford to lose skilled members.

During the era of NATO/Warsaw Pact tensions which spilled over into the less developed countries of the world, there were many safe havens for terrorists, such as Libya, Algeria, Lebanon and Bulgaria. Czechoslovakia was reportedly the centre for plastic surgery to change terrorists' appearances so that they could return to their former haunts. The friendly relationship between the US and Russia, however, has eliminated many of the former terrorist havens, limiting the freedom of operations among terrorist groups. Nonetheless, 'Terrorism International' continues to operate, terrorist groups providing each other with safe houses, weapons, explosives, training facilities and personnel. Thus, the Japanese Red Army carried out operations against Israel for the Palestinians, while Basque separatists and IRA active service units offer each other assistance. As a result, it is very difficult to get an accurate idea of which ethnic or racial group might present a threat, since terrorist groups may trade targets to allow easier infiltration.

Explosive devices have traditionally been 'force multipliers' for terrorist groups. A bomb planted aboard an airliner or in a busy department store or railway station can allow one terrorist to cause a horrendous number of casualties. Recruiting those with the ability to fabricate explosive devices has always been a high priority among terrorist groups. Latterly, however, a more frightening group of potential targets has become available to terrorists. Those in charge of nuclear installations have to plan for the possibility of terrorist attack, since an incident at a nuclear plant would not only offer the potential for an ecological disaster, but could also discredit a government completely. Other potential terrorist targets are the vast computer systems upon which economies and governments now depend. Terrorist groups have frequently recruited among urban intellectuals, so the possibility of them adding skilled hackers to their ranks is very real. Even more frightening is the possibility that terrorist groups might use chemical or biological weapons, which are simple to create and deploy.

Both guerrillas and terrorists share many basic principles in their strategy and tactics. The use of surprise, for example, allows both to exert an influence out of proportion to their numbers. Both also attempt to discredit government forces through their successful attacks on targets of opportunity. Normally, the terrorist will have fewer supporters among the population, but as a result there will be fewer potential traitors to betray him or her. Both have the overthrow of the established government as their goal. However, while the guerrilla uses terror as one tool for accomplishing this end, the terrorist remains locked in the stage of destabilizing a government through acts of terror. The terms used to describe those carrying out unconventional warfare often depend upon point of view. In the US during the Afghan War, for example, one constantly read about the Freedom Fighters, but those same individuals were viewed as terrorists in the Soviet Union. The key point seems to be that guerrillas fight for a cause which remains a clear-cut vision, while terrorists seem to have a nebulous cause which has become subsidiary to the acts of terrorism themselves.

CHAPTER IX

Selecting and Training the Counter-Insurgency or Counter-Terrorist Warrior

COUNTER-GUERRILLA TACTICS

The old cliché of setting a thief to catch a thief is nowhere more appropriate than in countering guerrillas or terrorists. It is not by accident that military units such as the SAS, the Special Forces, or the Selous Scouts, themselves trained to act as unconventional warriors, are frequently the most successful in tracking down and countering unconventional enemies. Asked to give a profile of the perfect counter-insurgency soldier, most experts would probably include many of the following characteristics:

1. Outstanding physical conditioning and stamina, allowing the trooper to push on with little rest for days at a time
2. The ability to survive in rugged terrain, living off the land if necessary, but certainly with food and water carried on the person
3. Highly self-disciplined and motivated, so that he can continue to push on despite hardships and setbacks
4. An expert at stealthy movement and lying in wait, perhaps for days
5. Intelligent and quick-witted, able to stick to a complex plan but also able to improvise if necessary
6. Expert with all types of light infantry weapons
7. Knowledgeable about field medicine
8. The ability to identify with indigenous populations and gain their trust and respect (linguistic ability is a big plus here)
9. Teaching ability for those occasions when the mission is to train local counter-insurgency forces
10. A student of guerrilla warfare; knowing the tactics likely to be used by the enemy and how to counter them
11. Capable of insertion and operations in all types of terrain
12. Expert at field engineering and demolition.

The counter-terrorist warrior needs many of the same skills, though with modification. Much of the training for the counter-insurgency specialist will apply for the counter-terrorist specialist. Counter-terrorist skills include:

1. An especially high degree of expertise with assault/dynamic entry weapons; handguns, sub-machine guns, sniper rifles and shotguns
2. Expertise in specialized explosive devices; stun munitions, CS gas, breaching charges, etc
3. The ability to gain entry to buildings, ships, trains, etc. through rapid and/or covert means including rapelling, scuba, parachute, free climbing, skiing, small boat or other expedient methods
4. Knowledge of terrorist tactics and psychology.
5. The ability to rehearse an assault perhaps hundreds of times, constantly reviewing the operation and attempting to reduce time and risk
6. The ability to absorb very diverse skills (i.e. lock-picking, driving heavy equipment, computer-assisted draughting)
7. The versatility to allow rapid adjustment to diverse missions
8. The ability to function as part of a precision team
9. The ability to function well despite a very high stress level
10. An extremely high state of physical fitness in diverse areas; swimming, running, martial arts, skiing, free-fall parachuting, etc.
11. The ability to merge into urban or rural landscapes during infiltrations before an assault
12. Extreme mission dedication, allowing the counter-terrorist specialist to spend much of his life prepared for possible instant deployment into situations where his actions can save or lose dozens of lives.

The selection process for counter-insurgency and counter-terrorist units is normally multilayered, as the manpower pool from which special operations units are normally selected is often itself the result of a selection process. The SAS, for example, normally selects its recruits from serving members of the British forces who have already displayed a certain degree of military skill. The US Special Forces normally selects from those who have already done at least some military service and who have already been trained as airborne troops. The Rhodesian Selous Scouts, the Soviet Spetsnaz, the South African Reconnaissance Commandos, the Portuguese Commandos, the Bolivian Rangers, the Thai Border Patrol Police and many other such units select from a pool of potential personnel who have already passed through certain selection procedures.

Many counter-terrorist units select their members from an even more refined manpower pool. France's GIGN chooses from among the best of the Gendarmerie Nationale, and Germany's GSG-9 selects from the already élite ranks of the border guards. The SAS rotates the counter-terrorist mission, but whichever squadron has the assignment, the members have been through the SAS's tough selection procedure. The US Special Forces and the Royal Dutch Marines select their counter-terrorist personnel from the ranks of their country's most highly trained special forces units, as do many other countries.

Even with an excellent manpower pool from which to recruit, special assignment units must still develop a selection procedure that yields men capable of performing their missions with a high degree of success. The SAS uses its famous Brecon Beacons selection course to weed applicants, though the process continues during escape and evasion training, team training, and other hurdles faced by all potential members of the regiment. The US Special Forces use their Q (Qualification) Course to weed out unsuitable aspirants, but like the SAS continue to evaluate new members of the groups as they become fully-fledged members of their ODA (Operational Detachment A). The Selous Scouts, whose mission would be to operate as pseudo terrorists and deep-penetration counter-guerrillas, placed great stress on survival in the wild, stamina and land navigation, skills that the SAS, Special Forces and other counter-insurgency forces also stress. Consequently, learning to eat rotten monkey meat was both a selection procedure and a valid learning process for the Selous Scouts. The French Foreign Legion, which has often found itself in the counter-insurgency role, uses the traditional Legion basic training process and harsh Legion discipline as its selection procedure, though the best counter-insurgency troops are normally still those of the 2nd REP, who have been through the additional selection process of the Legion paratroops.

Among counter-terrorist units, selection may be more rigorous or more mission-specific. France's GIGN, for example, has included one-to-one combat with unit hand-to-hand combat instructors or attack dogs in the selection process. It has also used swimming tests with the aspirant bound hand and foot. However, the GIGN also includes the logical prerequisites of shooting ability and fitness in their selection. When formed, Delta Force used a very similar selection course to the SAS's well-tried Brecon Beacons course, while the Navy's SEAL teams can rely on BUDS (Basic Underwater Demolitions School) to weed out the weak or unmotivated from their counter-terrorist or counter-insurgency forces.

The success of the SAS has resulted in many counter-terrorist units adopting similar selection procedures. The Sri Lankan counter-terrorist/counter-insurgency unit has used an even tougher final exercise, requiring a 150-mile march through the jungle in five days or less. All of these selection procedures, however, are primarily designed to assemble the best possible raw material which can be trained for demanding missions. It is the training itself that turns this raw material into highly competent professional light infantry.

Training for counter-insurgency takes two primary forms: individual and team. Generally, good counter-insurgency troops will be trained in a wide variety of applicable skills, but will have one or two real specialities. The US Special Forces, for example, train their members as specialists in intelligence, communications, field medicine, engineering and demolition, or light or heavy weapons. In addition to learning their field thoroughly, they also learn to teach their skills to others, necessary for training guerrillas and counter-guerrillas. Members of the Special Forces will also be cross-trained in at least one other speciality besides their primary one, to allow versatility when members of a team are injured or when a twelve-man ODA is broken into two half-teams.

In line with the use of 'hearts and minds' campaigns, Special Forces demolition experts also learn the engineering skills necessary to build wells, houses, schools, bridges and other public works. In addition to intensive field medical training, Special Forces medics learn to run local clinics and to teach basic sanitation and child care. 'Bush doctors', as the SAS call their medics, are often the most highly trained and invaluable members of a counter-guerrilla force, both for gaining the trust of indigenous populations and for treating their injured comrades.

Members of Special Forces also receive language training applicable to their area of operations. The 7th Special Forces Group (Airborne), which has responsibility for Latin America, will include Spanish speakers, but at least one or two ODAs will include speakers of Portuguese for operations in Brazil. The 10th Special Forces Group (Airborne) is tasked with operations in Europe, and therefore includes those who speak European languages, while the 1st Special Forces Group (Airborne), which operates in Asia, contains those who speak the appropriate languages.

The SAS has fewer primary specialities than the Special Forces, training members of a squadron as demolition specialists, communication specialists, medical specialists or linguists. The SAS normally operates in four-man patrols comprising one specialist in each field. However, most SAS members with some years of service will have served in more than one capacity, and can perform multiple functions. Additionally, the four troops within each SAS squadron each have a speciality – mountain and arctic warfare, scuba and small boat, mobility including desert operations, and HALO. Within each specialist troop there will be four four-man patrols.

The 2nd Foreign Legion Parachute Regiment, which handles many of France's counter-insurgency missions, organizes its specialities by companies within the regiment, similar to the SAS's specialist troops. Specialities include sniping, demolition, mountain and ski, scuba and small boat, HALO, etc. In addition to their specialist skills, individual members of units such as these receive special training in methods of insertion, including parachute or helicopter, land navigation, survival, escape and evasion, and armed and unarmed combat.

All of these individual skills contribute to the skills of the counter-insurgency operational unit. However, certain team skills are also necessary, and must be gained when training as a unit. Patrolling, intelligence gathering, ambush and counter-ambush (including immediate action drills), raiding tactics, tactical reconnaissance, guerrilla philosophy and tactics, scouting, fire discipline, deep penetration of hostile territory, combined operations, organizing and training guerrillas and counter-guerrillas, and many other types of expertise are often acquired while training as part of an operational team.

A good example of specialized teamwork for counter-insurgency is the Drake Shooting method taught to the Selous Scouts, Rhodesian Light Infantry and other Rhodesian counter-insurgency units. As an immediate action drill when ambushed, troops were trained to take under fire any cover or concealment which might hide an attacker. This training eliminated the tendency to freeze when ambushed, and guaranteed rapid return fire to disorient the attacker and possibly cause him to break off the ambush prematurely.

Individual training for counter-terrorism takes many of the same forms as that for counter-insurgency, though many skills will be honed to a much finer level. Weapons usage, for example, must be good for those in counter-insurgency operations, while for those assigned the counter-terrorist mission it must be outstanding. Those assigned to rescue hostages must possess exceptional shooting skills, often gained by expending thousands of rounds of ammunition during initial training, then firing hundreds of rounds per week to keep the skill at the required level. Training in counter-terrorist shooting skills must be highly realistic, and many top units train with live ammunition and using live hostages. This technique is dangerous unless extreme safety is exercised, yet the risk is considered acceptable to develop counter-terrorist commandos who can burst into a darkened room, rapidly identify hostile targets and immediately neutralize them with head shots from a sub-machine gun or pistol. Obviously, counter-terrorist shooting skills must not only emphasize accuracy, but also speed and rapid decision-making regarding when to shoot and when not to shoot.

The counter-terrorist warrior needs an array of other individual skills. One is ability at hand-to-hand combat. The possibility of infiltrating an airliner or other restricted environment held by terrorists, or of being at such close quarters that a weapon cannot be used, requires that members of counter-terrorist units are extremely competent at unarmed combat. Once again, constant training is necessary to keep such skills at their highest possible level.

Team training for counter-terrorist units places special emphasis on the rapid entry and clearing of a building or form of transport such as a bus or ship. During entry, each member of a team must perform his assigned role in conjunction with other team members, whether it be observing, preparing to take a long-range killing shot as the team penetrates a terrorist site, blowing a door just before the team goes through it, or acting as 'tail gunner' to provide rear security for the team. Even during stealth entries, when silence is most important, teamwork is just as vital. The point man must recce corners and other blind spots during an approach, while other members of the team remain constantly alert to their own arcs of vision. During entries through windows, one or more team members will often boost others up and through. All of these skills require constant training so that the drills are performed automatically, even under stress.

This is especially true when a hostage rescue unit has to clear a building with numerous rooms. Two men will normally be assigned to carry out the room entry, neutralizing any threats, while additional team members follow them in and move on towards the next room. Training and constant communication allow complex clearing operations of this type to be carried out successfully. Members of entrance teams must be able to rely on each other very greatly, as one man must trust his partner to cover the arc of fire in his area of responsibility, or trust the man behind him to cover his rear. Only constant team training and operational practice can build the high level of confidence necessary to create a competent hostage rescue and crisis entry team.

For counter-terrorist units, too, team training proves its worth if members of the unit are assigned to executive protection. Their four- or five-man foot escort formations, vehicle loading and unloading drills, attack on principal drills and advance planning for a VIP visit all reflect the actions of a highly trained and highly drilled team.

Because the level of training and mission readiness required of those in counter-insurgency and counter-terrorism is so high, members of such units frequently rotate to other assignments within a few years. This offers various advantages. Burn-out is avoided, and a steady flow of new personnel to be integrated into a unit tempers experience with new ideas and initiative. In addition, expertise is spread throughout an army or national police force as those with specialist training move to assignments which are less demanding, but in which knowledge of the techniques of countering terrorists or guerrillas is invaluable.

Both the counter-insurgency and the counter-terrorist warrior must be willing to undergo constant retraining, as the enemy will often change his tactics in response to government force successes. Training scenarios must be varied and interesting, to keep the edge that special operations troops need when called upon. Although physical skills must be kept at an extremely high level, intellectual skills must not be neglected either. Knowledge of the enemy – his psychology, philosophy, history, strategy, tactics, leaders, successes and failures – greatly increases the counter-terrorist or counter-guerrilla team's chances of defeating him. To be successful, such specialist teams must be the most highly trained in a nation's military and police establishment.

CHAPTER X

Tactics Against Insurgents and Terrorists

Although many of the tactics used to deny insurgents their support also apply to denying support to terrorist groups (which are often, in fact, offshoots of guerrilla bands), some tactics are distinct. The two will therefore be considered independently.

INSURGENTS

Guerrilla warfare may be waged on its own, as in Malaya, Rhodesia or Oman, or it may be waged in support of a more conventional war, as in the Soviet Union in World War Two, Vietnam, and, to some extent, Borneo. When guerrillas are fighting in support of conventional forces it may be necessary to defeat those forces first, to dishearten the irregulars and eliminate their source of supply, before they can be defeated. Support by at least a relatively large segment of the population is of extreme importance to guerrilla movements. Bad governments drive the population into the guerrilla fold, and make this aspect of insurgency easier for the guerrillas.

To help remove the support of the population from the guerrillas and gain it for the government, counter-insurgency forces normally need to use a combination of tactics aimed at winning the 'hearts and minds' of the population, especially those of minorities who have often felt disenfranchised. Political activity, including the replacement of officials and the passing of fair laws, is frequently a first step. Vietnam and other counter-insurgency campaigns have shown that good local officials, free from corruption and honestly concerned about the local population, are an excellent counter to guerrilla propaganda and blandishments. Guerrillas realize this, and popular local officials are often the targets for assassination. When implemented correctly, protected village plans which consolidate the population for both administration and protection are a very effective political tool as well.

Economic action to improve a population's standard of living is normally another excellent tool to help dry up the 'sea' in which the guerrilla must swim, according to Mao. Often going hand-in-hand with economic action are civic action programmes. Such programmes help the locals improve their education, public works, health, sanitation, agriculture and other basic aspects of their lives. Better agriculture normally means an improved standard of living. The SAS in Oman, the US Special Forces in Vietnam, and other skilled counter-insurgency forces have given high priority to helping tribesmen grow more crops or breed healthier livestock, and this has paid enormous dividends in gaining support from the population. Education, of course, enables a population to improve its economic condition, but it can be a two-edged sword. If the government is not sincerely trying to improve their lot, a better educated population may spot corruption more readily. On the other hand, education helps them to recognize guerrilla propaganda for what it is.

Civic action and other such projects help psychological action projects aimed at getting diverse groups, especially minorities liable to fall prey to guerrilla blandishments, pulling towards the same national objectives. More subtle psy ops may be designed to remove popular support for the guerrillas. Programmes which encourage defection from guerrilla ranks often serve several purposes. Those coming over offer a source of intelligence, show the population that life among the guerrillas is quite harsh, and cause discord in the guerrilla ranks, as security measures are often made harsher and distrust is sown through the fear that comrades are about to defect.

As long as guerrilla forces are in the field taking military action, government forces must also continue to take military action against them in support of the various political, civic and psychological actions. With troops well trained in counter-insurgency, military action can complement the hearts-and-minds campaign. The great danger is that government forces will take draconian action against the population, thus driving them into the guerrilla camp. The primary military objective in countering guerrilla forces is to find, fix and destroy them. To accomplish this, the counter-insurgency forces must have access to good intelligence about them, and this frequently comes from the population. As a result, military forces often become involved in psy ops, civic action projects and population security, to show that they are fighting a common enemy. Another primary military objective is to control population and resources, to deny the guerrillas access to sources of supply.

Police forces and indigenous irregulars can both be highly effective components of counter-guerrilla operations. Naval and air forces are also key components, as they can help exercise border control to prevent guerrillas being resupplied across the border, or to stop them using a neighbouring country for sanctuary. Specially trained quick-reaction forces, preferably airmobile or, in wet environments, small-boat-borne, must be on call to help exploit any contact with guerrilla forces instantly. It is also important to have élite light infantry which can operate on long-range patrols into guerrilla sanctuaries to deny the insurgents any safe territory. Military operations should be geared to the geography of the area in which they are taking place. In a single-resource country (i.e., one highly dependent on oil or mining) the military might need to exercise resource control on the principal industry. To allow certain areas to become free-fire zones, where any movement will be attributed to guerrillas, it may be necessary to concentrate the population into protected villages. Finally, police and military personnel should be schooled in counter-insurgency warfare techniques, should understand diverse social, ethnic, and religious groups, and should speak the language of their area of operations. In countries with minority population, it is very important to incorporate members of those minorities into the security forces to help win the trust of the people.

Counter-insurgency forces need to realize that guerrilla movements normally labour under certain disadvantages which should be exploited at every opportunity. The clandestine life-style of guerrilla fighters frequently causes them to suffer severely from mental and physical stress. Being on the run, and often being the target of government searches, usually enhances the guerrilla's sense of insecurity. This is one reason why programmes allowing guerrillas to turn themselves in without punishment are often one of the most successful counter-insurgency tactics. The lack of access to quality medical care, combined with food shortages, can also cause a deterioration in the guerrilla's physical condition. Even hardened warriors will find that sleeping in jungles or mountains will take its toll as well, particularly in movements which include many fighters who grew up in urban areas.

Guerrillas frequently live in fear of violence to themselves and their families. Although this violence might come from government forces, there is often a fear of attack by rival guerrilla groups or in retaliation for a perceived betrayal of the 'movement' for which the fighter is actually risking his life and liberty.

When the government can array formidable counter-insurgency forces, guerrillas often suffer from a sense of numerical inferiority, a feeling of facing insurmountable odds. This may well be combined with a fear not only that they cannot win, but that they will probably be treated as common criminals if captured, rather than heroic freedom fighters or even prisoners of war. In many countries this means that guerrillas face harsh incarceration, possibly with torture, and even execution. Likewise, sophisticated, technologically superior forces ranged against guerrillas can sometimes undermine morale, though this is not always the case. In Vietnam, the US often tried to substitute technology for good light infantrymen, but without success. When used properly, however, technology can give counter-insurgency forces an advantage.

Security is such a problem for guerrilla forces that they are often devoured by paranoia. Effective unit members might be killed as suspected spies, and a stable life-style is impossible owing to the constant need to move bases of operations. This need to be constantly on the run makes it very difficult, too, for guerrilla forces to establish training bases, unless there is access to a friendly border. Each time the government's deep penetration forces locate a hidden base and attack it, therefore, the dividends are multiplied, since in addition to any destruction which is wrought, the sense of insecurity among the insurgents is increased dramatically, adding to their morale problems.

In some guerrilla movements (in Malaya, for example) the insurgents have attempted to grow their own food, but they usually depend on the local population for food, intelligence, manpower and other needs. Therefore, if government forces can isolate the population from the guerrillas they will greatly hinder the insurgents' ability to carry out operations.

To destroy or severely weaken a guerrilla army, decisive action must be taken whenever a guerrilla force is located. Intelligence about the location of the guerrillas must be positive, whether obtained from informants, local observers, long-range reconnaissance patrols, by electronic or airborne surveillance, or by other means. Intelligence information should also be studied to ensure that the guerrillas are not attempting to lure security forces into an ambush. Once the guerrilla location is known, an operation must be planned quickly, details being revealed on a need-to-know basis to keep the operation secure. Rapid deployment forces, often airmobile or airborne, should be sent in with sufficient support to seal off the area and encircle the guerrillas. Guerrilla units are often quite adept at moving in darkness, so in that circumstance plans must be made to contain them and troops skilled at night operations must be deployed. Once in position, the security forces should hit the guerrillas hard, sealing off escape routes or turning them into additional killing zones to eliminate escaping insurgents.

The cliché that the best defence is a good offence applies especially to guerrilla warfare, as constant harassment of the guerrilla forces keeps them from organizing major operations. Harassing operations also help prevent guerrilla infiltration into critical areas. Various methods may be used in combination to keep the pressure on the guerrilla forces. Reconnaissance patrols and raids can inflict damage and locate guerrillas, as well as destroying some of their limited supplies. When patrols locate guerrillas, airmobile reaction forces can be called in along with air, artillery or naval gunfire support. Guerrillas often have relatively unsophisticated communication methods which can be monitored and intercepted. In Rhodesia, for example, they frequently used letters. Aerial surveillance can not only locate guerrilla bases, but also force the guerrillas even deeper into mountains or jungles. Checkpoints can limit guerrilla operations and keep sympathizers from resupplying them. Chemical and biological agents such as defoliants may be used, though they proved a double-edged sword in Vietnam.

The most useful counter-guerrilla forces are often small, highly mobile units such as those used by the US Special Forces, British SAS, Rhodesian Selous Scouts and Russian Spetsnaz. Stay-behind forces who hide and set ambushes can be used very effectively, as they were by the US during the Vietnam War. Other useful 'force multipliers' in counter-insurgency are well-trained scout dogs and their handlers, snipers willing to hide and wait for their shots, and communications intercept personnel.

Another important counter-guerrilla strategy is population and resource control. One of the most effective uses of military personnel in counter-insurgency operations is to limit guerrilla access to the population and to resources needed to survive and fight. Among the most effective techniques is the use of checkpoints, though in urban areas, especially, they can slow movement and traffic dramatically and alienate the population from the government. Checkpoints should therefore be used with discretion and kept as efficient as possible. In conjunction with checkpoints, search operations will often allow an area to be swept for insurgents. For this to be effective, however, blocking forces must be deployed in sufficient numbers to prevent escape from the cordon. Another, lower-profile approach is the surveillance of known sympathizers to determine when a surgical raid might result in the removal of important guerrilla leaders. One of the sought-after results of any of these tactics is the apprehension of guerrilla sympathizers. As well as removing support, such apprehensions send messages to sections of the population wavering between the government and guerrillas.

The next group of measures used in population control has overtones of what developed countries would call police state tactics, and can be counter-productive if kept in place for too long and handled harshly. Such measures include the registration of civilians, followed

150

by the frequent examination of identity documents. Public and private transport and communications may also be restricted, and all of these measures may be combined with a curfew. Round-ups or sweeps may then be conducted and any people without proper documentation may be detained. Obviously, however, such a degree of interference in citizens' lives is not going to endear the government to them.

Control of resources can also deprive guerrillas of items needed to enable them to continue the fight. Controlling the production, storage and distribution of food, for example, can either push the guerrilla to starvation or at least focus his energies on obtaining sustenance, rather than on blowing up police stations. When food controls have been implemented, the amount of food which may be purchased at one time is often set, to prevent sympathizers from passing food to guerrillas. Alternatively, the population might be required to buy ready-prepared food which will spoil if not eaten quickly. Again, the inconvenience caused to the population by such measures will often undermine faith in the government if they continue for too long. The control of arms, explosives, medicine and money may also hinder guerrilla operations, though control of arms can also inhibit the ability of the people to protect themselves and make them easy prey for the guerrillas.

Finally, certain areas may be totally evacuated and left as buffer zones or free-fire areas, where anyone moving is assumed to be a guerrilla. There are great advantages to this system, though segments of the population will react strongly to being removed from ancestral homes. In a small country, too, it may be impossible to waste limited land resources. Most importantly, those removed from their homes must be accommodated at least as well as they were previously for their 'hearts and minds' to be won over to the government. Too often, populations are evacuated to what are virtually concentration camps, creating a whole new group of guerrilla sympathizers and potential recruits.

Control of the borders, especially if a neighbouring country is assisting and harbouring guerrillas (as was the case with Indochina and Vietnam, and Rhodesia and South Africa), is another very important aspect of counter-guerrilla tactics. A key prerequisite for this type of operation is good intelligence, to learn how the guerrillas deliver personnel, supplies, equipment and communications. Entry and exit routes, frequency of crossing, and volume of traffic must be determined, as well as the type of transportation in use. Terrain along borders and possible sanctuaries on both sides must be evaluated before border denial operations begin. When they start, the development of a restricted zone along the border will normally be the first step in preventing infiltration and exfiltration. To allow crossing attempts to be determined, censors may be sown, mines placed and observation posts established. Friendly members of the population may be established in border villages to act as buffers and to provide intelligence and mutual protection.

Patrols may be mounted along the border, as they were in Borneo, and in certain situations cross-border strikes may be launched into guerrilla strongholds in another country. Such strikes are often great morale boosters for the country launching them, and they send a pointed message to the country whose territory is violated. Guerrilla morale may be very adversely affected, as they will feel that there is no safe area. On the other hand, world opinion in the United Nations will often be mobilized against such strikes.

For these counter-guerrilla tactics to be effective, they must be carried out in combination. The government must show exceptional will to defeat the insurgency, and must be willing to make the political and economic reforms necessary to win over a substantial part of the population. Members of the security forces must be trained to take effective action without driving friendly or uncommitted sections of the population into the guerrilla fold. Some civil liberties will have to be infringed at least temporarily, and care will have to be taken to ensure that measures introduced to protect the population do not become part of an institutionalized police state.

COUNTER-TERRORIST TACTICS

Many of the tactics used against guerrillas may also be used against terrorist groups, especially those designed to remove terrorists from sources of support. In general, terrorists will have less broad-based support and will rely upon a few loyal supporters of the movement for supply and sanctuary. Intelligence is especially important, both in identifying these supporters and in attempting to determine potential targets. The better the intelligence agency, the better the counter-terrorist effort.

In terrorist incidents involving hostages, the first tactic is usually to isolate the site of the incident to limit the casualties the terrorists can inflict, and also to prevent their contact with outside accomplices. Power and other utilities will be cut off, and telephone lines or other methods of communication will almost certainly be cut. Once the terrorists and their hostages have been isolated, some form of communication link will be established to enable trained hostage negotiators to begin discussions with the terrorists. Negotiators will normally have a multi-purpose agenda which will include attempting to gain the freedom of the hostages; gathering intelligence about the terrorists, their demands and their intent; and analyzing the likelihood that the terrorists will soon begin harming the hostages.

There are different philosophies of negotiation, all of which are valid in certain situations. Some negotiators are expert at establishing empathy between themselves and the terrorist leader, thus lessening the danger to the hostages. Good negotiators will be able to persuade the terrorists to release hostages in return for food, or because of medical conditions. In addition to reducing the number of potential victims, this tactic allows security forces to interrogate those released to gain information about the terrorists.

Another negotiation tactic is to wear the hostage takers down with trivia. If they ask for food, go through an entire menu with them, having them choose what they want. If they want a bus, go into detail about what type, where they want it parked and who will drive it. Hundreds of such small decisions can distract the terrorists from killing hostages, and can also erode their revolutionary zeal. It is currently believed, incidentally, that food should be supplied unprepared, so that terrorists and hostages have to work together to prepare it. It is thought that this will help to establish a bond between them, making it harder for the terrorists to start killing the hostages.

Still another negotiation philosophy is that the job of the negotiator is to keep the terrorists occupied until the assault team can go in and kill them. In effect, the negotiator is a distraction, used to draw at least one terrorist to the telephone or window for a sniper to shoot, or for the assault team to neutralize.

As soon as the members of a counter-terrorist unit arrive on the scene of an incident, their first step is to form a 'go plan', a simple method of assaulting the site, based on the intelligence available at the time. It is necessary to have such a plan in readiness, in case the terrorists start killing hostages and immediate action is required. The 'go plan' can be constantly revised as more information is gained about the terrorists, their armament, the location and the hostages.

As more sophisticated plans develop, various types of entry must be considered. A stealthy approach and entry is most desirable, as the terrorists will not know an assault is imminent and will not start killing the hostages. Most assaults to rescue hostages begin as stealth assaults, but they will usually become dynamic at some point, when speed takes precedence over stealth. Once a dynamic assault begins, those carrying out the rescue must clear areas as quickly as possible, so that follow-up teams can move into additional rooms or areas until the safety of all hostages is secured.

An alternative type of dynamic entry is explosive entry, in which a breach is blown to allow the rescue team to enter from an unexpected direction. Explosive entries themselves often act as a distraction to keep the terrorists from taking hostile action. Other devices are used for the same purpose, the best known being the 'flash, bang' stun grenade developed by the SAS. Stun grenades, it is hoped, will cause the terrorists to freeze momentarily in surprise, giving the rescuers an edge. However, some terrorist groups are now familiar with the use of stun grenades, and have developed methods of countering them which it would be inappropriate to discuss here.

When carrying out dynamic entries, assault teams will normally be armed with pistols and sub-machine guns. They will shoot until the opponent is stopped, even if it takes an entire magazine from the weapon, as in the controversial SAS shootings on Gibraltar. Body armour will be worn by assault teams, and in some cases the first troops through the door will use a body bunker, though such a device is costly in time when rapid entry to save hostages is necessary. Members of assault forces are trained to shoot in low light conditions, so if power to the incident site has not already been cut, it may be cut just before the assault to give the entry team another advantage.

Distraction is also an important element of an assault, whether it be a jackhammer and other construction equipment to cover the noise of an assault, as in the Dozier rescue, or a low-flying jet, as in the DePunt train operation. Such distractions should cover the final approach of the assault forces and also draw the terrorists' attention in the wrong direction. Another form of distraction may be the disguising of the assault forces as something else, perhaps the maintenance crew of a hijacked airliner or the crew of a garbage truck collecting trash in the rear of the incident site. Another important entry tactic is simultaneous breaching in more than one place, and an entry at one point can be used as a distraction for a primary entry nearer the hostages.

Snipers are another key tactical element in the counter-terrorist operation. They should be placed so that they can serve as intelligence sources as well as shooters, offering a tactical option. On counter-terrorist operations, snipers must be given a 'green light' to take a shot whenever they feel that the hostages are threatened or, in certain circumstances, whenever they have a terrorist in their sights. Normally, more than one sniper, preferably at least three, should be assigned to each target. Snipers will often take their shot in conjunction with an assault entry, taking out the closest threat or threats to the hostages or to the assault team.

Counter-terrorist tactics must take into consideration, too, the possibility of hostages falling prey to the 'Stockholm Syndrome' and beginning to sympathize with the terrorists. At Princes Gate, for example, one terrorist was shielded from the SAS by hostages. The possibility of a terrorist hiding amidst the hostages must also be considered; tactics include controlling the hostages until they can be cleared once the site is secure.

Assaults on airliners, buses, trains, automobiles, oil rigs and other special targets involve special tactics. In some cases aboard transport, for example, snipers using highly penetrative special ammunition may be able to kill the terrorists through the skin of the vehicle, train or aircraft. At least one rescue unit tackles a terrorist with a hostage in an automobile by running on to the top of the vehicle and shooting the terrorist through the roof. In assaults on linear targets such as trains, aeroplanes or buses, teams must obviously avoid approaching from opposite sides, to prevent members getting hit in a crossfire. Special tactics for clearing the seats of trains, buses or aeroplanes row by row must also be devised and rehearsed. For any type of assault, in fact, the teams try to find a vehicle or building as similar as possible to the one occupied by terrorists with which to rehearse.

Many other tactical options are available to the counter-terrorist team, but they cannot be discussed here if they are to remain in the counter-terrorist repertoire. Suffice it to say that national counter-terrorist teams have both high-tech devices and superbly trained personnel which allow them to carry out operations which might stretch credibility if included in works of fiction.

CHAPTER XI

Future Threats

In June 1993 the US was rocked by FBI arrests of Islamic fundamentalist terrorists who planned to bomb the United Nations and other targets in New York City, and assassinate prominent American statesmen along with President Mubarak of Egypt. Almost simultaneously, the US launched a strike against Iraqi Intelligence headquarters in retaliation for an attempt on the life of former President George Bush. Europe was not exempt, either, as 29 Turkish targets throughout Western Europe were struck by Kurdish terrorists to draw attention to the plight of their people. Militant fundamentalist Islam appears very likely to breed even more terrorism in the 1990s than in the 1980s.

Although the FBI has been quite successful in preventing acts of terrorism, the World Trade Center bombing on 26 February, which resulted in six deaths and more than a thousand injuries, showed that the US, which has allowed numerous militant Islamic groups to operate within its borders owing to lax immigration laws, is highly vulnerable to attack. The eight Moslem fundamentalists arrested in June 1993 were plotting to blow up the UN building, the New York Federal building and two Hudson River tunnels, and to assassinate Senator Alfonse D'Amato and others. Known as the 'Beta Cell' to the FBI, this group included two conspirators also implicated in the World Trade Center bombing. At the time of the FBI raid they were mixing fertilizer and diesel fuel to create a bomb of the type used at the World Trade Center. The World Trade Center bombers and the Beta Cell members were closely affiliated with Sheik Omar Abdel Rahman, a fundamentalist mullah advocating the overthrow of the Egyptian government who is also believed to have influenced the assassins of Anwar Sadat.

Traditionally, terrorist acts have not been committed in the US because most groups wanted to keep the country as a sanctuary. Additionally, the FBI has a very good reputation, and the chance of being caught and jailed or deported remains high. Nevertheless, the terrorist infrastructure in the US runs quite deep, particularly in large urban areas and near university campuses. It appears that, in the future, both in the US and abroad, religious terrorism, particularly that supported by Iran, will predominate more than more traditional political or ethnic terrorism such as that of the PLO.

The US and Western Europe may be especially vulnerable, as the number of terrorist acts in 1992 was down to 362 from a peak of 650-700 per year in the 1980s, the lowest for 17 years. This may lead some security agencies to relax, believing that they have the problem under control. In the US, for example, many of the counter-terrorism experts assembled in the 1980s have been moved to other jobs. The removal of safe havens in Eastern Europe and the Soviet Union has made it harder for some terrorist groups to operate, but Iran, Iraq, Libya, Syria, North Korea, Cuba, Sudan and Pakistan still support terrorist groups. The US is being targeted not just because it supports Israel, but also for its alignment with the secular Arab governments. Many of the most militant young Moslems have fled to the US after crackdowns in Arab states, and lax US immigration laws originally designed to protect political refugees allow them to remain.

The latest arrests seem to link the terrorists in New York directly with Sudan, two intelligence officers of that country reportedly having planned to place the bombs in the UN Building. Funding came from Iran, and was funnelled through Sudan. Sudan, in fact, has become Iran's surrogate for spreading Islamic revolution, much as Cuba was formerly the Soviet Union's primary evangelist of Communist revolution. Not only is funding being funnelled to the US from Iran for attacks against the US, but money is being siphoned through the US to fund Hamas, a radical Islamic organization with a large following among young Palestinians. Israel's crackdown on the organization, however, has forced Hamas to move many of its operations to the US. The bombing and attempted bombing in New York may, however, have repercussions as US citizens call for measures to be taken against militant Islamic organizations in their country.

Beta Cell members have also been linked to the 1990 slaying of Rabbi Meir Kahane, the founder of the Jewish Defense League, and one of the assassination targets was New York Assemblyman Dov Hikind, who had called for harsh penalties in the Kahane murder. Senator D'Amato became a target by calling for the deportation of Sheik Rahman, while Hosni Mubarak and UN Secretary General Boutros Boutras-Ghali, an Egyptian Coptic Christian, were targeted because of their tough stand against Islamic fundamentalism.

One likely result of the World Trade Center bombing and the close call with Beta Cell is that many of the tough anti-bombing measures in effect in Israel and London will be instituted in New York City. Americans, notoriously antagonistic to being inconvenienced, will not take kindly to draconian measures designed to frustrate bombers. On the other hand, the US has traditionally been a sleeping giant which it is dangerous to awaken, and the bomb threats in New York and the attempted assassination of former President Bush have increased pressure on US lawmakers and leaders to act. Military strikes against Sudan are one possible reaction, but military action against Iran, though likely to happen as the result of a coalition among many countries, is not probable at the time if writing.

Acts by Kurdish groups have already been mentioned, and the fact that the Kurds have been played off against Iran and Iraq by the US and Western Europe in the past may well result in another embittered displaced minority which, like the Palestinians, turns to terrorism as the only way to draw attention to their plight. Bosnia and Kurdistan are excellent examples of what some experts see as potential sources of future 'mass terrorism', in the form of 'ethnic cleansing' campaigns. Bosnia is especially dangerous, because the Moslem population has been virtually crushed between the Croat and Serb nutcracker. The latest 'peace' plan would allow 50 per cent of Bosnia to remain in Serb hands, 30 per cent in Croat hands and 20 per cent, in two land-locked pockets, in Moslem hands. This compromise is highly unfair to the Moslem population, but appears to be supported by the EEC in an attempt to make the problem go away. Bosnian Moslems, however, are already receiving support from militant Islamic groups, and appear likely to be politicized by the atrocities committed against them. Consequently, the emergence of new terrorist groups drawn from those who have seen the horror in Bosnia seems probable. Although the Serbs and Croats would be their most likely targets, the combination of Serbian and Croatian willingness to take draconian action and the view among Bosnian Moslems that the US and Western Europe have left them to their fate may cause them to look further afield for targets.

Perhaps the greatest terrorist threat for the future is that posed by techno-terrorism. The bombing of two heavily used tunnels serving New York City, as part of the June 1993 plot foiled by the FBI, would have been a prime example of terrorist acts aimed at the infrastructure of large urban areas. Such terrorist acts would allow terrorist groups to hold entire cities or societies hostage by threatening to destroy or disrupt critical services. The tunnel linking France and Great Britain will offer an inviting target for the IRA or other groups, just as dams, bridges, power stations and other critical structures may prove attractive, particularly in societies which, hitherto, have not found it necessary to guard such facilities.

Of course, the greatest threat of techno-terrorism concerns nuclear devices. The US has really only faced one such attempt in the past, when the FBI foiled a 1980 plan to hijack the nuclear submarine USS *Trepang* and fire a nuclear missile at the east coast of the US. However, other incidents have illustrated the potential danger. In 1979, 150lb of enriched uranium was stolen from a General Electric fuel processing plant by an employee who then attempted to extort $100,000. He was caught, but had he contacted the Libyans or Iranians, he might have been far more successful. It is an open secret that the Israelis managed to appropriate an entire shipment of uranium, and over the years thousands of pounds more have disappeared from processing facilities around the world. Who knows where it has ended up?

The threat of a nuclear device being created is real, since the technology is available and the materials are accessible. College students have assembled a nuclear device as a class project, and instructions have appeared in print and on television. Nevertheless, the construction of a device remains extremely difficult, because massive resources are required to process nuclear fuel into weapons-grade plutonium. There is also a strong possibility that an attempt to create a nuclear device could result in premature detonation, killing those fabricating it, though even this would create great danger for anyone nearby. Tom Clancy's recent novel, *The Sum of All Fears*, effectively enumerates many of the problems to be encountered.

Most experts believe that terrorist groups are more likely to steal or purchase a small nuclear device, rather than fabricate one. The break-up of the Soviet Union has, of course, caused a great deal of concern about the fate of the thousands of nuclear devices, and rumours persist in the intelligence community that Iran has purchased two devices from Kazakhastan. To prevent the theft of nuclear devices in the US, special Safe Secure Trailers (SSTs) are used to transport nuclear weapons and other nuclear materials. These trailers have bullet proof glass, armour plating and special axles which lock at the touch of a button, rendering the vehicle immobile. Additionally, each trailer travels with numerous armed guards. Finally, no nuclear weapons are complete as transported. To deal with the possibility of a stolen nuclear device, or one brought into the US, the Nuclear Emergency Search Team (NEST) exists, with the technology to track down a nuclear device rapidly. With palletized equipment stored at critical locations throughout the US, NEST can respond very rapidly to find a nuclear device. On practice call-outs NEST has always located devices very quickly, and was successful on the one actual incident to which it responded. There have been dozens of call-outs which turned out to be false alarms. NEST is an excellent counter-nuclear-terrorism force; one which the EEC and Russia would be well advised to emulate.

The sabotage of a nuclear power plant has been considered an even greater threat, and in the US has resulted in each plant being required to train a reaction team to a high level of skill. Additionally, nuclear power plants are equipped with various security systems which allow emergency shutdown and isolate critical areas from intruders. Various federal assault teams have also trained on worse-case scenarios involving nuclear installations, and have developed tactics for countering the occupation of a site.

In some ways, the threat of biological or chemical terrorism is even greater, because of the ease with which such materials can be created and then dispensed in urban areas in the air, water or even from vehicles. Most advanced biology or chemistry students could produce some type of dangerous agent. Additionally, because they are more widely disseminated, chemical or biological weapons are more easily obtained through theft. This threat has materialized in the US on more than one occasion. In 1976, corporations were threatened with germ attacks if a ransom was not paid, and biological materials were actually placed in New York City's water supply, though no harm was caused. At present, no equivalent to NEST exists to deal with the threat of biological or chemical warfare, which could be even more deadly than a nuclear device.

As the June 1993 planned attacks against New York City illustrated, disruption of services remains another fearsome terrorist threat. Four major viaducts bring water to Los Angeles. Electrical networks, gas and oil pipelines, and tunnels and bridges offer other inviting targets. Today, the disruption of telecommunications and/or computer networks is another threat which must be taken very seriously. So dependent has modern business and government become on such networks, that a hacker-terrorist could cause the loss of billions of dollars simply by creating one megavirus. Although most important computers are equipped with security systems, such systems have been broken into before. Many experts view the telecommunications/computer links around the world as the area most vulnerable to techno-terrorists.

The loss of the Soviet Union as the primary backer of Marxist insurgencies may have made it harder to finance and arm insurgents, and may have removed the Cold War surrogacy aspect of guerrilla warfare as practised by those fighting wars of liberation against Western democracies and by those fighting the same types of wars against Communist governments. However, as long as there are dispossessed minorities and/or repressive governments, it is likely that guerrilla wars will be raging somewhere in the world. The emergence of new states in the wake of the break-up of the Soviet empire will certainly offer fertile ground for insurgency, while the spread of militant Islamic fundamentalism will cause the search for an oasis from which revolution can be spread throughout the Middle East and Africa.

At the time of writing, UN and US actions in Somalia have really done little to stabilize the country. Unless a powerful central government can be formed which has the acceptance of most of the clans, warlords will continue to fight while most of the population starves. If a government was imposed on the Somalis, it is likely that some clans, at least, would carry out guerrilla warfare against that government. The British Army remains in Northern Ireland fighting what is, in truth, a counter-insurgency war; one of the most successful of all time, in fact, when one considers how many active members of the Provisional IRA there are at any given time. Many experts believe that merging the North with Eire is the best solution, although it is not particularly palatable to most Ulster Protestants. Protestants living in the South have certainly not found the government of Eire intolerant. However, since the IRA has stated that it wants a Marxist government for all of Ireland, and since it is unlikely that Protestant terrorist groups such as the UVF would gladly accede to this, merging the North with the South in Ireland might get the British out of the counter-insurgency/counter-terrorist campaign, but it would leave the government of Eire to deal with it.

Likewise, no solution acceptable to both the Israelis and the Palestinians seems in the offing, and Israel will therefore have to continue a counter-insurgency/counter-terrorist campaign, particularly in the occupied territories. As fundamentalist Islamic groups work upon young Palestinians, it is likely that this conflict could become even more bitter.

Other areas where insurgencies are likely to continue are Bosnia and Kurdistan, though, as previously discussed, wide-ranging acts of terrorism are also probable offshoots of fighting in these areas. With counter-insurgency no longer an aspect of the Cold War, the US and other Western democracies will probably be less likely to become involved in counter-insurgency warfare unless their national interests are severely threatened. The invasion of Kuwait by Iraq, for example, threatened the flow of oil to the West and, hence, led to military action. It is equally likely that, should Islamic fundamentalism lead to an insurgency in Saudi Arabia which threatens the flow of oil, the US and its allies would become involved. Less obviously critical to US strategic interests, but of prime importance, is the mineral wealth of some African countries. Once again, it is conceivable that, if a revolutionary movement liable to be hostile to the West struck Zaire or some other mineral-rich countries, the US would send counter-insurgency

161

assistance. The 3rd Special Forces Group (Airborne), for example, is specially trained for operations in Africa.

As the threat of a war with the Soviet Union has receded, the US and the other members of NATO have begun to restructure their armed forces. The US is eliminating some of its Army divisions, some air wings and at least one or two aircraft carrier groups. With 'small wars' more likely to occupy the US and the EEC countries, there has been some stress on creating quickly deployable units. The Falklands conflict showed Britain's Ministry of Defence that light forces such as the Commandos and Parachute Regiment, as well as the special operations forces, were invaluable elements in projecting power over long distances. Likewise, in Desert Storm it was the US 82nd Airborne Division and 101st Air Assault Division which arrived quickly and demonstrated the will to defend Saudi Arabia until the heavy armoured divisions could arrive. Such quickly deployable Army units, along with the Marine Amphibious forces, allow the US to react quickly if its interests or citizens are threatened. Although it is much more concerned with internal affairs these days, Russia maintains many of her airborne divisions to allow flexible, rapid action internally or externally.

In dealing with counter-insurgencies and counter-terrorism, special operations forces remain the West's most quickly deployable and combat-ready response element. The US now has all of its special forces organized under Special Operations Command. This joint command controls the Army's Rangers, Special Forces, Psychological Warfare, Civil Affairs, and special operations aviation forces; the Navy's SEAL Teams, SEAL Delivery Vehicle Teams, and special boat units; and the Air Force's special operations forces. Great Britain can deploy the SAS or the Special Boat Squadron for special operations. Other highly competent units within NATO include France's 2nd Foreign Legion Parachute Regiment, Belgium's Para Commandos, Italy's Incursori, Holland's Marines and various other commando and parachute units.

As the EEC moves towards ever closer ties, and as the UN takes on the responsibility for more concerted military action, as in Operation Desert Storm, there seems to be a sound argument for creating combined counter-terrorist/counter-insurgency forces. The problem, of course, remains that one man's terrorist is another man's freedom fighter, but assuming that this semantic problem can be resolved, at least in the case of countering terrorism, what would be the chances of forming a successful joint counter-terrorist unit?

The EEC appears to have the best chance of creating a joint force with the authority to act anywhere within the EEC. There is already a precedent, as there are executive protection teams for EEC officials which have authority across national frontiers. Such an EEC counter-terrorist force could draw on the fact that there is already substantial specialized expertise within member countries. For dealing with threats to oil rigs or shipping, for example, a joint force based on the British Special Boat Squadron and the Italian Incursori, with additional members from other countries' combat swimmer/marine units would seem to be highly viable. For operations in Alpine areas or in Norway or Sweden, specially trained personnel from France's GIGN, Italy's Carabinieri and Alpini, Germany's Jaeger, the SAS's Mountain Troop, and the Royal Marines Mountain and Arctic Warfare cadre, combined with specialized mountain/ski troops from other countries, could operate anywhere their special skills were required. Finally, for urban counter-terrorist operations, skyjackings and other traditional counter-terrorist operations, the SAS, GIGN, GSG-9, the Royal Dutch Marines and the Carabinieri could form the basis for a force able to operate anywhere in Europe. Logically, the combat swimmer/small boat elements could be maintained in 50- to 100-man units positioned in the Mediterranean and along the Atlantic coast ready for instant deployment. Similar-sized Alpine elements could be positioned in the Alps and Scandinavia, while the urban assault/counter-skyjack units could also be positioned throughout Europe in 50/100-man elements.

There is little doubt that the members of these units could work well together. Most train extensively together in any case, and share weapons and tactics. The question would be whether or not the political leaders could create a workable joint command that would allow quick reaction and would show the will to commit counter-terrorist forces as needed. This is normally the greatest problem facing counter-terrorist forces serving one country. It would probably be magnified when serving a multinational coalition.

The creation of a UN counter-terrorist force would face even greater problems. The argument in favour of such a force is that many of the problems of carrying out rescues across national borders could, theoretically, be solved if a UN force was dealing with the government of the country where the hostages were being held, rather than another national government. A good example of the problems encountered in the past were those faced by the Egyptian Lightning Unit when it carried out an assault on a hijacked airliner on Malta. It appeared that the Egyptian assault force might have to fight the Maltese police in addition to combatting the hijackers. Likewise, when the US Delta Force was following a hijacked TWA airliner around the Middle East, one problem was co-operation of the various governments.

It would be naive to assume that countries would be willing to concede the right to deal with internal hostage situations. It would also be unrealistic to assume that powerful nations such as the US,

China or Russia would completely cede all right to carry out unilateral operations to rescue their citizens in other countries. Neither would Israel be likely to give up the right to save Jews, bearing in mind the world's past record of leaving Jews to their fates. However, should a truly viable UN counter-terrorist force be formed, one which had the authority to act and the backing of the Security Council, many other nations which now maintain at least some counter-terrorist capability would realize that their ability to carry out external rescues was severely limited, and that their citizens might stand a better chance of being rescued by a UN force. There could therefore be substantial support for such a unit. Aircraft and ship hijackings would probably occupy this force the most, though other terrorist incidents across national boundaries might call for their deployment.

Logically, a UN counter-terrorist force would need to be drawn from all, or certainly most, member countries. This in itself could cause problems if force members were recruited from Libya, Iran or other countries with records of supporting terrorism, as missions or tactics could be compromised. Thus loyalty to the unit would be one of the most critical factors in the success of a multinational counter-terrorist force. Language, weapons and tactics would be other problems to overcome. Each member of a UN counter-terrorist unit would have to be capable of speaking at least two, preferably three languages. Logically, English would probably be the most universal language and, therefore, the *lingua franca* for the unit. Depending on regional assignment, the second language could be Spanish, Arabic, Swahili, Chinese, French, Russian, etc. Such a force would have to be organized so that personnel could work with members from anywhere in the world, so a standard training programme would have to be developed to ensure that shooting techniques, repelling techniques, explosive-entry tactics and other such skills were standardized. Weapons standardization would also be important, both from a logistical standpoint and also to ensure that personnel sent to operate with different sub-units would be safe and skilful with any weapons used. Certain weapons have achieved a high degree of standardization among counter-terrorist units (i.e. the Heckler & Koch MP5 sub-machine gun), so the selection of standard weapons should not prove a great difficulty.

To allow for training and leave time and yet still have 'go teams' positioned for immediate deployment at key locations around the world, perhaps 1,000 personnel would be required. It would probably be easier to form teams for operations in some areas than in others. A North American team, for example, drawn primarily from citizens of the USA, Canada and Mexico, would offer fewer problems than a Middle Eastern team, which would theoretically have to combine Israelis with personnel from various Arab nations. Even on the North American team, though, there might be fears among the Canadian and Mexican personnel that they would be submerged by their more powerful neighbour. Forming an Asian component with the interests of China, Japan, Vietnam, Thailand, Malaysia, Indonesia and others fully represented might also prove difficult.

Nevertheless, traditionally, élite military and police units build esprit de corps and unit pride which often overcomes ethnic or religious differences. Should the formation of a UN counter-terrorist force ever prove viable, it must be hoped that unit esprit de corps and perception of a true humanitarian mission would go a long way to overcome national differences among personnel. The fact that UN Secretary-General Boutros-Ghali recently called for standby arrangements for member states to provide specially trained peacekeeping units seems to indicate that units earmarked for UN service are today considered desirable. Hence, the possibility of a UN counter-terrorist force is certainly not out of the question.

As the recent plot in New York and the plot to assassinate former President Bush in Kuwait graphically illustrate, political assassination will probably continue to be a terrorist and insurgent tactic. The last two decades have seen the assassination of leaders such as South Korea's President Park, Egypt's President Sadat, President Zia of Pakistan, Indian Prime Ministers Indira Gandhi and Rajiv Gandhi, and Prime Minister Palme of Sweden among others. Political assassinations not only destabilize countries by undermining the democratic process, but they also undermine the faith of populations in their governments' ability to protect them. In countries such as Colombia, where the assassination of judicial and political leaders has become especially widespread, both willingness to serve the country and willingness to take decisive action if serving are undermined by a climate of fear.

No political leader who appears publicly can be made invulnerable to assassination. The US Secret Service is as good as any bodyguard force in the world, yet US Presidents have proven frighteningly vulnerable. The freer the society, in fact, the more vulnerable its leaders usually are. The best close protection teams can only make their principal a harder target. Of course, the protective team must itself remain loyal. Indira Gandhi ordered an assault on the Golden Temple, the most sacred of Sikh shrines, and this undermined the loyalty of her Sikh bodyguards, one of whom assassinated her. On the other hand, the loyalty of Mikhail Gorbachev's KGB protective team during the attempted coup in the Soviet Union probably saved his life. When foreign powers become involved in assassination attempts, as Iraq did in the attempt on former President Bush, or as North Korea did in the assassination of South Korea's President Park, harsh military action, or possibly an attempt on the guilty country's leader, would seem to be the only response likely to curb such behaviour. Such actions, which are beyond the pale of normal relations between countries, are hard to punish in any international forum.

Whether carried out by multinational forces or by government troops operating internally, the three primary types of 'dirty war' likely to be encountered in the next decade will remain counter-insurgency, counter-terrorism and counter-assassination. In each case, certain basic precepts will continue to apply.

COUNTER-INSURGENCY

In countering guerrilla movements, probably the most basic requirement is that the government being defended is a viable one. The South Vietnamese government, the puppet Afghan Government and the white minority government in Rhodesia were all incapable of defence for one reason or another, thus undermining very effective military actions. In Oman, on the other hand, the replacement of the old Sultan by his son, Qaboos, allowed much-needed reforms to be implemented, preparing the way for an effective counter-insurgency campaign.

If the government is sound, or if a sound government is installed, the next step is to wrest the population from guerrilla control. Political, economic and religious reforms will often be the first step, though an information campaign to counter guerrilla propaganda will need to be implemented as well. Such information must be demonstratively true. The encouragement of economic stability and removal of the motivation to be a guerrilla will go a long way towards broadening government support. Although in some cases it is the middle class which supports insurgencies, more often it is the peasant class. Ensuring the availability of educational opportunities and medical facilities, and granting freedom of religion, will generally weigh heavily among the peasants. Providing honest and fair local government and police, and allowing a reasonable standard of living, are also basic first steps in drying up support for the guerrilla cause.

Assuming the government is viable, a counter-insurgency strategy should not be put into effect until political and military goals have been clearly established under a strong leader who has the authority to ensure that the goals are compatible. One of the most important jobs of the leader is to ensure that various agencies such as the police, the military and the intelligence and civil affairs agencies are working together to accomplish the established goals. During the early stages of the campaign, while the war for the hearts and minds of the people is being waged, the police and the military will have to contain the guerrilla threat and begin reoccupying territory which has come under guerrilla control. Since it is often hard to separate the guerrilla from the population at this stage, it is very important that the police and military avoid committing atrocities which can drive the population even more into the guerrilla camp. Not only will this ensure that the people remain neutral, but in many cases they will become active suppliers of intelligence about the guerrillas.

As early as possible, the government must take decisive action to remove the initiative from the guerrillas. For this reason it may be necessary, at a fairly early stage, to grant the government special legal powers, though checks and balances must be maintained to prevent civil rights violations. If such special powers are implemented fairly, and the population truly believes that they are emergency powers which will be rescinded when the emergency is over, then the population will usually be supportive. One measure which has often proved counter-productive, however, is restriction of firearm ownership, which renders the population defenceless while allowing the guerrillas to be armed. By doing so, the government becomes the oppressor. Security forces must keep in mind that the purpose of emergency powers is to separate the guerrillas from the population, and to protect the population while identifying guerrillas and making it difficult for them to operate. Normally, only a small percentage of a country's population will be active supporters of a guerrilla movement, but, likewise, only a small percentage will be active supporters of the government. Most just want to get on with their lives. However, they may be frightened or waiting to see what happens before they make a commitment to either side. These are really the ones who must be won over if a counter-insurgency campaign is to be successful. The ability of security personnel to understand the language spoken by these people, their political aspirations, and their medical and civic needs, will play a large part in determining whether or not they are won over.

While trying to make the lives of the population better, security forces want to make life harder for the guerrillas. The more difficult it becomes for them to find food or a place to sleep, the less time they have to plan attacks or to recruit. As a result, population and food denial are important counter-guerrilla tactics. In implementing population controls, government forces must, however, be very careful that those relocated find themselves in better circumstances, or at least in equal circumstances to those they have left, rather than in an environment that resembles a concentration camp. Food denial programmes should also be implemented so that farmers do not lose a market for their crops. The best systems are usually those in which the government purchases the crops and then sets up a distribution system which prevents food reaching the guerrillas.

Frequently, the perception among the population and security forces that the guerrillas are winning can be as detrimental as if they really are doing so. Consequently, sustaining morale is another key element of fighting a successful counter-insurgency. The will to continue the effort is also important, and is directly related to morale. Many guerrilla wars have been won because the guerrillas showed more will than their opponents; those in Indochina, Vietnam, Rhodesia and Afghanistan are examples.

This will becomes manifest when security forces take the iniative away from the guerrillas. The sooner the guerrilla is put on the defensive, the better. One way to do this is by denying him any safe areas, and the use of highly mobile élite light infantry such as the US Special Forces, the Soviet Spetsnaz or the British SAS, which can operate in small units, staying in the field for long periods to stalk their prey, is an excellent beginning. Such units must be able to survive and fight in desert, jungle or mountain; whatever the terrain which shields the guerrilla. Technology is no substitute for well-trained light infantry, though air support, intrusion detection systems and other modern weapons can provide support for the light infantryman. Nevertheless, it is the light infantrymen who will respond to the intrusion detection systems or harry the guerrilla to the point where air power or artillery can be used against him. Light infantry used for counter-insurgency missions must be capable of operating at night, when the guerrilla usually feels most confident, and should be expert at ambush and counter-ambush to better the guerrilla at this tactic. Most of all, counter-insurgency infantry must patrol constantly, particularly in areas where guerrillas normally infiltrate.

To allow counter-insurgency forces to be effective, good recent intelligence is vital. Aerial surveillance, long-range reconnaissance patrols and turncoats can all alert patrols to guerrilla locations. Since it is always possible that the guerrillas will have sympathizers either in local security forces or among those living around bases, care must be taken not to telegraph operations. Once guerrilla bases are located, they can be raided, and ambushes or booby traps can be set along infiltration routes. Another effective tactic used by the SAS and US Special Forces, among others, has been to booby trap guerrilla supply caches. Doctoring weapons and ammunition, for example, not only causes guerrilla casualties, but strongly undermines their morale and confidence in their weapons. One of the most effective techniques in

Vietnam was to convert grenades found in caches so that they had instantaneous fuses.

An excellent tactic in winning over the local population is to encourage them to form their own local self-defence force. By arming and training local militias, the government shows that it trusts the population. This also frees military and police personnel from static village defence chores. By helping to build village defences, schools, wells, etc., military engineers contribute to winning the population over, as well as preparing for local defence. Local militiamen are often particularly effective if used as strike forces in their own area, as they know the trails as well or better than the guerrillas. Local knowledge is very valuable in counter-insurgency operations.

With the security forces taking effective action and the population being won over, the next effective tactic is to encourage guerrillas to rally to the government cause. As food becomes scarcer and the guerrilla life becomes more dangerous, the knowledge that guerrillas can turn themselves in with little fear of harsh treatment will often deplete their ranks even more than the security forces could. Guerrillas who turn themselves in are excellent sources of intelligence, and often make highly effective and surprisingly loyal government scouts. Rhodesia's Selous Scouts recruited heavily among turned terrorists, and few proved unreliable. The tactic of using pseudo-guerrillas such as the Selous Scouts has proven effective again and again, both as an offensive and as a psy ops tactic, because the presence of pseudos makes guerrillas unsure of any other guerrilla groups that are strange to them, and undermines confidence. So paranoid did the guerrillas in Rhodesia become owing to the Selous Scouts, that it was not uncommon for fire-fights to break out among guerrilla bands who distrusted each other.

Graphical and political considerations can be highly important in determining the outcome of counter-insurgency campaigns. One of the most important is whether or not the guerrillas have the support of a bordering country, which would provide safe havens and permit the flow of supplies. Normally diplomatic pressure will have to be brought to bear, and perhaps cross-border raids will have to be launched to 'persuade' the country to cease its support. However, if the country is a staunch supporter of the guerrillas, it is unlikely that even these tactics will have any effect. The presence of disaffected ethnic, racial or religious minority groups within a country normally creates fertile ground for an insurgency, while a homogeneous population is very unlikely to be a good basis for insurgency. The country's geography is also highly important, as terrain suitable for guerrilla strongholds is normally necessary to support an effective insurgency. Mountains or jungles are usually best for guerrilla bases. Long coastlines are also useful to the guerrillas, as they allow clandestine infiltration of supplies and weapons, as well as personnel.

Finally, it must be borne in mind that fighting a counter-insurgency campaign can be very costly, and the government must be prepared to face that fact. The cost will not only be incurred in actual cash outlay, but in lost agriculture, mineral or manufacturing wealth. The sultans of Brunei and Oman both had the advantage of immense oil wealth in to finance their respective counter-insurgency campaigns. France, on the other hand, found that the immense cost of World War Two had virtually bankrupted the country, making the costs of two long counter-insurgency campaigns in Indochina and Algeria unbearable. Sometimes even scarcer than financial resources in fighting a counter-insurgency campaign are the will to win and the intelligence to implement a campaign which takes harsh measures against guerrillas without committing atrocities against the population as a whole. It should be remembered, too, that though insurgencies are usually politically based, they have been used by Communist guerrillas against democracies and by democratic guerrillas against Communist oligarchies. In either case, the basic precepts of guerrilla warfare and counter-guerrilla warfare remain the same, though democracies or enlightened monarchies have normally been able to implement reforms more readily when attempting to counter an insurgency.

COUNTER-TERRORISM

In countering terrorism, some precepts carry over from counter-insurgency, particularly that of being careful in implementing laws which may affect the civil rights of the population. Since terrorist groups will normally have far fewer members than guerrilla organizations, one of the first steps to counter them is to gather intelligence about the group's membership. Infiltration of the group is one excellent method for identifying members, as the FBI's successful counter-terrorist effort in New York City during June 1993 graphically illustrated. Paranoia and tension among members of terrorist groups frequently grows as they are forced to spend time couped up together in hide-outs, so captured terrorists may prove to be excellent sources of intelligence. The fact that many terrorists are drawn from middle-class, educated families frequently means that, once they are identified, photographs will not be that difficult to find. However, Carlos, 'The Jackal', normally made it a point not to be photographed. An important part of counter-terrorist operations, therefore, is to study the principal terrorists and tactics which a counter-terrorist force is likely to encounter.

Normally, specially trained counter-terrorist units carry out much better operations than *ad hoc* units. Most military units trained to assault a site will burst in using maximum firepower, while a hostage rescue unit will strike surgically, applying maximum force to the hostage takers but avoiding injury to the hostages if at all possible. Purpose-assigned counter-terrorist forces will also train more specifically in the skills necessary for their missions (i.e. precision sniping, explosive entry and clandestine surveillance). Each of these skills may well be within the training of standard military or police special operations units, but unless these units are trained specifically for hostage rescue their mindset will be different. Rapid response to terrorist incidents, especially those involving hostages, is very important, so in addition to assigning specific personnel to counter-terrorist duties, there must be enough of them to allow instant deployment.

Terrorist bombers demand entirely different skills. In addition to the availability of well-trained bomb disposal personnel, a strong educational effort is necessary to alert the public and the security forces to what they should look for, so that possible explosive devices are rapidly identified. Counter-terrorist personnel assigned to prevent or counter bombings may make use of offensive as well as defensive measures. The British, for example, made excellent use of scanners to explode remotely triggered IRA bombs prematurely, not only blowing up some bombers, but making the IRA look inept. The SAS shooting of three IRA bombers in Gibraltar was also a good example of offensive tactics against bombers, hitting them before they could place their explosive device. Mechanical Semtex 'sniffers' at airports, and trained dogs, are also sound anti-bombing measures.

In general, however, counter-terrorist units as normally constituted have a primary mission to rescue hostages. Once hostages are taken, the first step is to attempt to make the situation static. In the case of an airliner, this means getting it on the ground and keeping it there if possible. Trains, buses, ships or any other type of transport should be stopped. Ironically, in certain barricade situations, if the hostage takers ask for a bus or vehicle it may be advisable to give them one, since there might be a chance for a sniper to shoot them as they move with the hostages towards the vehicle.

Assuming that the hostage takers are static in a building or stationary form of transport, the next step is to contain the area by establishing a security perimeter to prevent the terrorists from receiving reinforcements or information from the outside. Control of their methods of communication is also important for the latter reason. Snipers should be positioned as soon as the counter-terrorist unit is on the scene. These will give the unit commander the option of eliminating the terrorists with long shots, and will provide an added source of intelligence, because the snipers will usually be on high ground and using enhanced optical sights. Through controlled communications, trained hostage negotiators should attempt to open a dialogue with the hostage takers, while the entry team prepares an immediate 'go plan' to be implemented should the terrorists start killing the hostages. This plan will be quite simple at first, but as intelligence is gained about the hostages, the terrorists and the location in which they are being held, the plan will become more sophisticated.

The negotiator or negotiators will attempt to achieve the release of the hostages and the surrender of the terrorists, but failing this, will play for time, attempting to establish a rapport with the terrorists. In the process of talking with the terrorists, the negotiator will attempt to gain information and also to wear the terrorists down with small decisions, such as lengthy discussions about what type of food they would like sent in, or which brand of cigarettes. The negotiator must also be prepared, at some point, to inform the team leader that the incident is not going to be resolved through negotiations, and that other actions may be called for. Throughout the process, as well, the team commander will have been gathering additional intelligence from released hostages, video and audio surveillance, sniper reports, hostages' families, those who know the terrorists, and other sources.

As a result, when negotiations break down, the team commander should have developed a plan for a rescue operation. While the negotiator has bought time and attempted to talk the terrorists out, the rescue team will have found a structure as close in design as possible to that occupied by the terrorists, and will have practised the rescue plan intensively. As each situation will vary, so will each plan, but most hostage rescues will have certain basic elements in common. The plan will normally be based on the use of stealth and distraction to gain a few extra seconds. If possible, multiple entries as close as possible to the hostages will be made. Once the entry is made, the rescue teams will move quickly to clear rooms. The assumption will have to be made that the terrorists have placed explosive devices and, hence, any terrorists not instantly surrendering and showing themselves harmless will have to be killed. Hostages must be treated with suspicion because of the possibility that an unknown terrorist might be among them, or that the Stockholm Syndrome has taken effect, and one of the hostages may have become sympathetic to the terrorists during the ordeal. As a result, even the hostages will be temporarily restrained after they have been rapidly evacuated from the site where they have been held. Simultaneously with the assault, the snipers will normally have been given the green light to shoot any terrorists they have in their sights. During the entry itself, distraction devices such as stun grenades may be employed, though some terrorist groups now train for the possibility of having to face stun grenades. Each second which passes without all of the terrorists being put out of action increases the likelihood of hostage or rescue party deaths, so the rescue teams will have to move very quickly, though they must not become careless.

Once the rescue is complete, members of the hostage rescue team should be removed from the scene as soon as possible, so that their identities, equipment and methods remain as much an enigma as possible. Members of counter-terrorist units should do as much cross-training with similar units in other countries as possible, to sharpen skills and learn new methods and to study terrorist groups operating elsewhere.

Because of the high level of readiness required of those assigned to hostage rescue units, as well as the stress entailed in the mission, personnel should remain with the unit long enough to become effective, but should be rotated before staleness or burn-out sets in. This rotation into other military or police units is extremely useful, as it also disseminates counter-terrorist expertise more widely among a country's security forces. The SAS system of rotating a squadron on to counter-terrorist duties (Counter-revolutionary Warfare duties in SAS terminology) for one year, and then rotating them on to other duties, ensures that wherever SAS personnel are assigned there will almost certainly be some with relatively recent counter-terrorist experience and, thus, the ability to carry out a rescue if necessary.

To help prevent staleness and enhance preparedness, counter-terrorist personnel should engage in the most realistic training scenarios possible. Many countries also use their national counter-terrorist units for prison riots, raids on very dangerous criminals, VIP security and other missions where their expertise is valuable. Members of counter-terrorist units may spend some time flying as air marshals, or providing embassy security in high-threat countries. Both of these assignments have the added benefit of aquainting members of the national hostage rescue unit with the procedures and equipment/buildings of likely terrorist targets. As part of their training, members of counter-terrorist units should also carry out surveys of as many potential sites of terrorist assault as possible. The SAS and SBS, for example, have trained at Buckingham Palace, the Houses of Parliament, on North Sea oil rigs, and aboard the *Queen Elizabeth II*.

No matter how good the counter-terrorist forces of a country may be, they must be backed by a sound intelligence network to supply them with information about their targets, and a government with the will to take a stand against terrorism and commit the counter-terrorist units despite the likelihood of complaints in the press and in international arenas such as the UN when draconian action is taken. Such action is often called for. Dead terrorists cease being a threat; imprisioned live terrorists are a stimulus to further terrorist incidents in attempts to free them.

Counter-assassination

Good intelligence is the first step in countering political assassination, as it frequently allows pre-emptive action at an early stage of a plot. Within the intelligence community, the rumour has persisted for years that the approachment between Egypt and Israel came about because the Mossad warned Egypt's Mouk-habarat of an impending assassination attempt on Anwar Sadat. Those charged with protecting world leaders must assume, however, that not every assassin will be caught through intelligence gathering. As with those on counter-terrorist units, members of executive protection teams also study photographs of known assassins so that they might recognize them in crowds. Those in executive protection also study previous assassinations and their perpetrators to learn about assassins and their *modus operandi*. Agents of the US Secret Service spend time during training at mental hospitals, observing aberrant behaviour to help them recognize threats in a crowd.

In protecting their principal, members of protective teams try to limit access as much as possible, but those in the political limelight frequently want to remain approachable by their constituents or subjects and, hence, will venture into crowds or at least attend receptions. To limit the availability of weapons to those approaching the principal, magnetometers are now frequently set up at social functions attended by those in the political limelight. In Washington, DC, in fact, it has now become a status symbol to attend functions where the guests must pass through metal detectors. Protective teams plan carefully when their principal will appear in public, choosing speaking positions which are not conducive to sniper attacks; checking for explosives, then sealing the area; positioning the principal behind a bullet proof podium; positioning 'bullet catchers' (lesser VIPs or hangers-on) around the VIP as a shield; and planning emergency evacuation procedures. When the VIP is important enough, in the US at least, the Secret Service counter-sniper team is positioned to watch likely locations for a sniper. Trained to shoot incredibly accurately and very rapidly, the counter-sniper team is both a deterrent and a valid offensive tactic against potential snipers.

Another key preventive tactic is the denial of prior knowledge to potential attackers. A VIP's schedule should be kept as secret as possible, though with political leaders this is very difficult. Routine should be avoided at all cost, as any routine allows assassins to plan an attack. Routes should be varied, and alternative routes should always be available in case plans have to be changed at the last minute. VIP drivers should know how to carry out offensive and defensive driving tactics, including J-turns, bootlegger turns and rams. Drivers should also know the fastest routes to secure medical facilities and secure areas such as national police facilities, military installations, etc.

Before a VIP visit, an advance team should have visited the city and checked potential routes, looking for possible trouble spots from traffic jams to buildings likely to house snipers. Additionally, when a VIP is moving from location to location an advance team should move ahead, remaining in radio contact with the close protection team to alert them of any potential threats which might cause them to abort the visit or alter plans.

VIP protection teams must be trained intensively in skills such as foot and vehicle escort techniques, counter-ambush tactics, hand-to-hand combat, marksmanship, explosive ordnance reconnaissance, emergency medical techniques and body shielding. The last of these is important, as members of protection teams are trained to interpose their bodies between the threat and their principal. Although they have to be capable of close-quarters combat with weapons or hands and feet, they must understand that their first priority is to remove their principal from danger. Consequently, when a team is under attack, normally only one or two members closest to the attack will stand and fight, while the remainder get the principal away. Two precepts are important here. Those standing and fighting are buying time for their principal, and must continue to shield with their bodies even as they engage attackers. Additionally, those evacuating the principal must bear in mind the possibility that the attack in progress may be a feint, and that there are additional assassins still to come.

Even the best protection teams, such as those from the US Secret Service, the Russian KGB, the French GSPR and the British SAS or the Special Branch of Scotland Yard, realize that if the principal goes out in public, he or she is vulnerable. All that the team can do is make an assassination attempt very difficult and hope that the potential assassin will be deterred or will choose a 'softer' target elsewhere. That is what countering dirty wars is really about – making one's country a hard target, one that is so costly to attack that no guerrilla, terrorist or assassin is willing to face the consequences.

CHAPTER XII

Guide to World Counter-Insurgency and Counter-Terrorist Forces

Argentina

For counter-insurgency duties, the Army's airborne brigade, three mountain brigades and a jungle brigade have special training which is most applicable. Counter-terrorist duties are handled primarily by CEPOC of the federal police and a special counter-terrorist squad of the air force. Formerly, a special unit known as 'Halcon 8' was formed for the World Cup in 1978.

Australia

The principal Australian unit for both counter-insurgency and counter-terrorism is the Australian Special Air Service. Those assigned to the counter-terrorism mission are known as the TAG unit. Members of this unit also handle counter-terrorist tasks assigned to combat swimmer units in some countries, such as assaults on oil rigs or hijacked ships. Federal and state police in Australia also deploy special operations groups, equivalent to American SWAT teams, which can handle certain incidents. The Commando Regiment is also trained in special warfare and counter-insurgency operations, and can be deployed to supplement the SAS if needed.

Austria

Austria has a relatively small but well-trained group of what would be termed airborne rangers in the US, who could be deployed on counter-insurgency missions if needed. For counter-terrorist duties, the 'Cobra' unit or GEK of the Gendarmerie has responsibility throughout the country.

Bahrain

Trained for counter-terrorism and probably for counter-insurgency is U Group of the Public Security Force. This 60-man unit was trained by the British SAS, and is considered quite competent. Its officers are primarily former members of the SAS, and the NCOs are primarily former members of the Pakistani SSG. There is another unit of about 100 men within the Bahraini Defence Force with some specialized training applicable to CI and CT operations.

Belgium
For counter-insurgency duties, Belgium's Para-Commando Regiment receives the most applicable training, and has been deployed in the past, especially to the former Congo colonies. The ESI of the Gendarmerie Royale handles counter-terrorist duties for the Belgians.

Bolivia
Ever since US-trained Bolivian Rangers hunted down Che Guevara, this country's special operations forces have had a sound reputation for counter-insurgency operations. The paratroop battalion, three Andean regiments, two Ranger regiments, and six horse cavalry regiments all have some counter-insurgency skills. The 2nd Ranger Regiment, however, has received special forces training and should be most current on CI tactics. For counter-terrorism, the Army's 'Polivalente' unit receives special training.

Brazil
Specialized counter-insurgency training is given to the two paratroop brigades and the five jungle infantry battalions, the latter being especially well-trained in CI. Brazilian marines, especially the special operations battalion, also receive some CI training. Counter-terrorist duties are handled by the army's 'Project Talon' and the Commando Company of the 1st Special Forces Battalion, though the Federal Police may also deploy their TOC unit in certain scenarios.

Brunei
The Sultan of Brunei has traditionally footed the bill for one Gurkha battalion to remain in Brunei as a counter-insurgency force. There is, however, a small Special Operations Section of the Royal Brunei Police trained as a counter-terrorist unit.

Canada
Although the Royal Canadian Mounted Police SERT handled the counter-terrorist mission previously for Canada, that mission has now been passed to the Canadian Special Service Force, which would also handle the counter-insurgency mission.

Chile
There are eleven special Andean regiments which have some counter-insurgency capability, but the primary CI units are the army special

forces battalion, the naval marine detachments and field units of the Carabineros, the national police. Counter-terrorist missions may be carried out by the army's 'Cobras', the navy's combat swimmers, or the combined Carabinero/army UAT. The air force's FACH has a counter-terrorism role, presumably against air piracy.

China
The People's Republic of China has three airborne divisions which are trained in guerrilla warfare tactics and could function in the counter-insurgency role if necessary. Counter-terrorist capability rests with a special police brigade.

Colombia
The Colombian Ranger battalion and paratroop battalion are the primary counter-insurgency forces, though the Lancero School, located in Colombia, trains all Colombian officers in what would be considered ranger skills in the USA, and thus diffuses counter-insurgency training throughout the army. Additionally, there are marine forces available for certain counter-insurgency duties. Much of Colombia's counter-insurgency efforts have been directed against the drug cartels and guerrillas working in conjunction with them. Colombia has quite an array of counter-terrorist forces, including GOES, a special operations group of the Policia Nacional, GASDA of the air force, GCA of the navy/marines, special anti-extortion and anti-kidnapping groups of the army, and various other police and military units. The very number of units with this mission indicate how widespread terrorism is in Colombia.

Czechoslovakia
Members of the Czech airborne brigade, and also of the reconnaissance battalions, who were trained for assignment to Czech divisions in the days of the Warsaw Pact would be available for counter-insurgency duties if needed. Primary counter-terrorist responsibility reportedly exists with one of the parachute battalions which has a marked special forces mission.

Denmark
Should Denmark need a unit for counter-insurgency duties, the most likely to be assigned would be the army's Jaegerkorpset or rangers, which also have at least some counter-terrorist assignments. Other Danish CT units include the navy's Fromandskorpset, which are trained for maritime rescue operations, and some special police units.

Ecuador
For counter-insurgency, Ecuador has two special forces groups and two jungle brigades, while the armed forces have a PUMA unit to carry out the counter-terrorist mission.

Egypt
For counter-insurgency, the two parachute brigades and 26 commando battalions of the Egyptian Army would have the primary mission, though there are also marines, including combat swimmers who could be used on specialized CI missions. Egypt's primary counter-terrorist unit is Force 777, which is considered part of the army's Commando Command.

El Salvador
Having been engaged in counter-insurgency fighting for more than a decade, the Salvadoran armed forces have developed their airborne troops and special light counter-insurgency infantry units for this mission. Two special forces groups also operate on extended CI missions. For counter-terrorist operations, a unit known as CEAT exists.

Finland
Should Finland need counter-insurgency forces, it is likely that most of its ski-trained infantry units could function in the role, though the specially trained parachute reconnaissance personnel would be even more highly suited. Counter-terrorist duties rest with the Bear Unit of Helsinki's Mobile Police. This 40-man unit has countrywide responsibilities, including hijackings of aircraft or ships.

France
France has numerous troops which have received at least some counter-insurgency training, a substantial number of which have been deployed operationally to former colonies. Foremost, of course, are the troops of the French Foreign Legion, the 2nd Parachute Regiment being considered the élite of the élite. The RPIMa's, which are the parachute regiments which can be deployed overseas, also have a counter-insurgency role, as do some naval infantry units and combat swimmers. Anti-terrorist responsibility rests with the GIGN of the Gendarmerie Nationale and RAIDs of the Policia Nationale.

Guatemala
This country has coped with guerrilla movements for quite some time. The Guatemalan armed forces are organized with the CI mission as a primary one. There is, in fact, one specifically designated counter-

insurgency battalion group, though most would call the unit special forces. The Guatemalan Special Forces are very well trained in counter-insurgency; some say they are the best in Latin America. There is also a paratroop battalion which has received CI training. The fourteen mobile detachments of the National Police are also trained in counter-insurgency, and are used for that task. The BROE, the Guatemalan counter-terrorist unit, is also drawn from the National Police.

Germany
Perhaps the best-trained counter-insurgency forces within the current German Army would be the Jaegers or rangers, though most of these are spread amongst the Fernspah (LRRPs) or the battalions of the 1st Airborne Division. Border guards of the Bundesgrenzchutz could also be deployed on counter-insurgency duties if needed. Germany's counter-terrorist unit, GSG-9, is also drawn from the border guards, and ranks as one of the most effective in the world.

Greece
Probably the most highly trained counter-insurgency force is the Special Raiding Battalion or special forces battalion of the Greek Parachute-Commando forces, though any of these élite troops could function well in the CI role. Counter-terrorist responsibility lies with the Special Mission Platoon of the Athens City Police, though there are also two anti-hijack units stationed at Athens and Thessaloniki airports.

Honduras
The primary CI unit is the special forces group, but there is also an airborne battalion which has been deployed on this mission. The primary counter-terrorist unit, the COE, is drawn from the army's Special Forces Command, and comprises about 60 personnel. A Cobra unit of the Public Security Forces or national police has also had CT duties.

Hong Kong
Should the need arise while Hong Kong is still a Crown colony, the Gurkhas stationed there would handle CI duties. Counter-terrorist assignments fall to the Police Special Duties Unit, which has been trained to quite a high standard by the SAS.

Hungary
Since the break-up of the Warsaw Pact, Hungary has one parachute battalion which would probably be the unit tasked with both CI and CT missions.

India
Members of the parachute brigade would assume counter-insurgency duties as needed. Counter-terrorist capability lies with a unit known as the 'Black Cats', drawn from the Para-Commandos.

Indonesia
Perhaps because of the diverse nature of Indonesia's Islands, this country fields a wide array of counter-insurgency and counter-terrorist forces, some of whom carry out both missions. The leading CI unit would probably be the KOPASSANDHA, or Special Forces Command. The Mobile Brigade of the National Police (PELOPOR) is another unit with CI training and missions, as is the air force's KOPASGAT, or Airborne Fast Reaction Force. Other units from the Marines/Combat Swimmers have received CI training as well. For counter-terrorist missions there is almost as much diversity. Detachment 81, drawn from the army's Special Forces, has some claim to being the principal unit, though SATGAS GEGANA of the National Police has been in existence longer. The air force also has a unit, known as SATGAS ATBARA, which is an anti-skyjacking force. Units within the marines and navy have training in assaulting oil rigs and ships. They include the KESATUAN GURITA and the JALA MENGKARA, the latter being marines trained to retake oil rigs.

Ireland
Currently, the Irish Republic has seen little need for counter-insurgency forces, though the Irish Rangers are quite well trained and could handle this mission as well as others, including counter-terrorism. Within Eire, however, primary responsibility for counter-terrorism falls to the Special Task Force of the Garda Siochana's Special Branch, a 40-man unit which has received training from GSG-9, the RCMP and other such formations.

Israel
In some respects the Israeli armed forces have been fighting a limited counter-insurgency against infiltrating or resident Palestinian guerrillas for decades and are therefore organised with this mission in mind. Once again, however, certain units by nature of their training are better suited for the counter-insurgency mission, particularly the airborne troops, the Golani Infantry Brigade, Sayaret Matkal (the General Staff Reconnaissance Unit), and the Naval Commandos. The Border Police are also deployed on counter-insurgency/counter-terrorist duties. The Border Police have a unit trained specifically to carry out hostage rescues, and Sayaret Matkal has also had a hostage rescue capability.

Italy

Italy can draw specialized personnel from many units. Should a CI mission arise, the Alpini mountain troops, the Folgore Airborne Brigade, the San Marco Marines, the Incursori (combat swimmers), and the Carabinieri (the national police) all have applicable training. At times, the Carabinieri have been engaged in what is virtually a counter-insurgency war against the Mafia on Sicily. For counter-terrorist operations, the principal units are the Incursori for seaborne acts and the GIS of the Carabinieri for other operations. Another unit, the NOCS, drawn from the civil police, carried out the rescue of kidnapped American Brig Gen Dozier.

Japan

The post-war Japanese Self Defence Forces have been structured on the basis of Japan's neutrality, and have not foreseen the need for extensive counter-insurgency training. The army's airborne rangers seem to have the most applicable skills, however. Counter-terrorist duties fall to various police Special Action Units or, on Okinawa, the Special Intervention Unit.

Jordan

One of the best special operations units in the Middle East, particularly when its size is considered, is Jordan's Special Forces Brigade. The three battalions of this unit could be used readily for counter-insurgency operations, while the 101st Special Forces Battalion is trained particularly for the counter-terrorist mission.

Kenya

Although the Kenyan Army has had a parachute company, the Police General Services Unit (GSU) has a paramilitary function and was specifically trained and formed for counter-insurgency operations. The Reconnaissance company of the GSU also functions as Kenya's counter-terrorist unit, and has an excellent reputation.

South Korea

The ROK special forces brigades, of which there are seven, are quite similar to US Special Forces Groups and are trained for various special warfare missions, including counter-insurgency, though counter-infiltration from the North has often been their assignment. Special Forces personnel were also used in 1980 to put down a student revolt in Kwanju. There are other special operations personnel, including combat swimmers and marine reconnaissance units, who could be used readily on counter-insurgency operations. In fact, probably the entire

ROK Marine Corps, which is trained along US lines, could be deployed on CI missions. For counter-terrorist duties, the 707th Special Mission Battalion of the Special Forces has received intensive training, particularly in preparing for the Seoul Olympics. Additional police units were trained to a high level in preparation for the Olympics as well. ROK special operations personnel have high standards and are highly respected for their abilities.

Malaysia
Because various areas which are now part of Malaysia have experienced guerrilla wars in the past, the Malaysian Special Services Regiment and the two Para Kommando regiments receive substantial training in counter-insurgency. Members of other Malaysian infantry units receive at least some CI training. There is also a Police Field Force which can operate in the CI role. For counter-terrorist operations, the Malaysian Navy has a unit designated 'Delta', while the Royal Malaysian Police have a Special Action Unit trained for hostage rescue.

Mexico
The Mexican army fields almost 70 infantry battalions, many of which could function in the CI role, though the two paratroop battalions and the special forces battalion are the units trained especially in counter-insurgency. Additionally, the Federales and Rurales could be used for counter-insurgency, and have been. The army has a Counter-terrorist Intervention Group for counter-terrorist missions.

Morocco
The closest thing to a counter-guerrilla force is the army's Para-Commando Brigade, though other units are specially trained for Saharan operations. The counter-terrorist unit, trained by the French, is named GIGN like the French unit, and is drawn from the Gendarmerie.

Netherlands
In the Netherlands, as in many Western European countries, counter-insurgency has not had a high priority in the training of troops, but the members of the Dutch Commando Companies or their 104th Long Range Reconnaissance Company troops could function in this role. Perhaps the most likely troops to be used on CI, should the need arise, would be the highly trained Dutch Marines. The BBE of the Royal Dutch Marines also functions as the country's principal counter-terrorist unit, though the BSB of the police also has a counter-terrorist mission.

New Zealand
Both the counter-insurgency and counter-terrorist missions fall to the New Zealand Special Air Service.

Norway
Once again, counter-insurgency has not ranked high on the list of skills for the Scandinavian countries, but the Jaeger, which are the equivalent of rangers or commandos, could handle this assignment. Counter-terrorism would be handled either by a counter-terrorist platoon drawn from the Jaeger or by the Readiness Troop of the National Police.

Oman
The Sultan's Special Force is the most highly trained unit in the Omani armed forces, but after the Dhofar War most infantry units received at least some civil action and counter-insurgency training. The Sultan's Special Force is also the primary counter-terrorist unit, though there is also a Special Task Force of the police with some responsibility for CT.

Pakistan
The Special Service Group of the army has three very well trained para-commando battalions which have counter-insurgency skills. A 175-man counter-terrorist unit is also drawn from the SSG, though there is also an SCU unit in the Islamabad Police.

Paraguay
Parachute troops assigned to the air force, marines (who function as riverine troops), horse cavalry units and the National Police can all function in the counter-insurgency role, as can certain infantry battalions. The counter-terrorist unit is the FOPE of the police.

Peru
Owing to the extended campaign against the Shining Path, Peru has organized her police and armed forces with counter-insurgency as a high priority. The airborne battalion and the commando battalions probably function best in the hunter/killer counter-guerrilla role, but the troops of the jungle division and some of the mountain infantry units also have counter-insurgency training. The Police Republican Guard and Civil Guard both also function in the counter-insurgency role, though by strict definition they are police. The Sinchi Battalion of the Civil Guard has an anti-terrorist role.

Philippines

Guerrillas have probably been operating somewhere in the Philippines ever since the end of World War Two. As a result, counter-insurgency training has always been considered important for the Philippine armed forces. Probably the most highly trained CI forces are those of the Special Forces and the Inshore Boat Company of the marines. Various units have counter-terrorist assignments, including PAFSECOM of the air force, which has the counter-skyjack mission, the Light Reaction Force (LRF) of the constabulary, the INPFF of the National Police, and the army's SSATF from the Special Forces.

Poland

The 6th Pomorska Air Assault Brigade includes most of Poland's special operations personnel, and would be the unit used on counter-insurgency, if needed. The 4101st Paratroop Battalion also has a counter-terrorist mission.

Portugal

During the counter-insurgency wars in Mozambique and Angola, Portugal maintained several specialized commando units trained in CI, but after the colonial pullback about 5,000 airborne troops remain, as well as some marines who could handle counter-insurgency operations if needed. For counter-terrorism, the GOE of the Public Security Police are assigned.

Russia

During the war in Afghanistan, the Soviets (as they were at that time) used their Spetsnaz airborne, airmobile and mountain troops for counter-insurgency missions. Experienced personnel will remain in all these units, which could be used again for counter-insurgency operations. For counter-terrorist operations various units exist, including the Spetsnaz, Naval Infantry Spetsnaz, OMON of the MVD, and a team from the KGB Border Guards.

Saudi Arabia

Members of the Saudi National Guard, as well as army para-commandos, could be used on CI operations, especially to protect the oilfields and the holy monuments in Mecca and elsewhere. The fundamentalist assault on the Great Mosque at Mecca stimulated the formation of a strong counter-terrorist capability in Saudi Arabia, and today that mission is assigned to members of the 3,500-strong Special Security Forces. Some members of the National Guard have also received CT training.

Senegal

In the past, France has undertaken counter-insurgency operations in Senegal, but the country now has its own parachute and commando companies which could be deployed. It also has a French-trained GIGN counter-terrorist unit.

Singapore

This small country has a group of well-trained para-commandos trained in counter-insurgency operations, as well as counter-terrorist operations in the case of the 1st Commando Battalion. The Police Tactical Team, initially trained by GSG-9, also has the counter-terrorist mission.

South Africa

In addition to the Reconnaissance Commandos, South Africa has had various specially trained counter-insurgency units, including one formed of Bushmen. A substantial number of Rhodesians joined the South African Army after the fall of Rhodesia, bringing CI experience with them. Counter-terrorist duties fall to the South African Police Special Task Force and, for certain situations, the Rail and Harbour Police.

Spain

The Spanish Foreign Legion has specialized in counter-insurgency operations for many years, as have the Spanish Special Forces. Additionally, Spain has well-trained airborne and marine troops who can function in this role. Counter-terrorism falls to two excellent units, GEO and UEI.

Sri Lanka

Counter-insurgency operations against the Tamils have been described elsewhere, but these operations have forced Sri Lanka to address the problem using various light infantry and police units. The most highly trained in both counter-insurgency and counter-terrorism is the Army Commando Squadron, which received its instruction from the SAS. The air force also has a commando unit, and the police have two counter-terrorist units, the SOU and STF, both of which function in the CI and CT roles.

Sweden

As with the rest of Scandinavia, Sweden does not take the threat of counter-insurgency seriously, and therefore does not train specialized troops in this mission. However, Sweden does train airborne reconnaissance and guerrilla troops who could function quite well in the CI role if needed. Counter-terrorist duties fall to a special unit of the Stockholm police.

Switzerland
The Swiss Army receives extensive training in functioning as a guerrilla force should the country be invaded, and could switch over to the CI role very well. The reserve system, which allows virtually every home to keep military weapons, would prove highly effective at dealing with an insurgency. Counter-terrorist duties fall to the 'Stern' units of each canton.

Taiwan
Much of the training of Taiwan's special operations forces has focused on acting as guerrillas on the Chinese mainland against the PRC, so guerrilla and counter-guerrilla warfare skills are well-honed among the Amphibious Reconnaissance Commandos and the Special Forces. Other army and marine elements could function well in this role, too. Counter-terrorist duties are handled by Thunder Squad of the police.

Thailand
Counter-insurgency operations have been carried out by the Thais for many decades with the Special Forces, Border Patrol Police, army ranger and reconnaissance personnel, marine reconnaissance personnel and other airborne special operations troops assigned to various missions. Counter-terrorist duties are split among the 4th Battalion of the 1st Army Division, the Air Force Commando Company with counter-hijack duties, and units of the Border Patrol Police and Royal Thai Police.

Tunisia
The only specialist unit in the Tunisian army has been a para-commando battalion which has had counter-insurgency training. The USGN of the Garde Nationale is the principal counter-terrorist unit, though it has also undertaken what could be considered counter-insurgency operations.

Turkey
Turkey fields special operations troops specially trained in guerrilla warfare and able to switch easily to the CI role. Additionally, Turkish commandos are well trained élite light infantry also able to carry out this mission. Counter-terrorist duties are handled by the 'Suicide Commandos' and elements of the National Police.

United Kingdom

In addition to the SAS, which has specialized in counter-insurgency, the Parachute Regiment, the Brigade of Gurkhas and the Royal Marine Commandos have all received specialized CI training. Also, deployments to Northern Ireland and Belize, among other places, have given most units of the British regular army experience in counter-insurgency operations. Counter-terrorist operations fall primarily to the SAS, though the Special Boat Squadron also has some duties, and Commachio Company of the Royal Marines has responsibility for the North Sea oil rigs.

United States of America

The Special Forces, Marine Corps and Navy SEALs perhaps receive the most counter-insurgency training, but other light infantry units, including the 82nd Airborne Division and 101st Air Assault Division, could be readily deployed on CI missions. Counter-terrorism falls to various units, including the Army's Delta Forces, the Navy's SEAL Team Six, Marine Corps Fleet Anti-Terrorism Security Teams and the FBI's HRT. All of these are quite well trained and very competent.

Venezuela

The army's parachute brigade receives the most training in counter-insurgency, though marine personnel also receive some CI training. The 20,000-strong National Guard also has personnel trained in counter-insurgency methods. Counter-terrorism is handled by the Special Intervention Brigade, which was originally formed as a counter-insurgency unit and can still function in this role as well as CT.

Index

189